THE RAF ASSOCIATION
PUZZLE BOOK

Also by Dr Gareth Moore

The Mindfulness Puzzle Book
The Mindfulness Puzzle Book 2
The Mindfulness Puzzle Book 3
The Mindfulness Puzzle Book for Kindle
The Mammoth Book of Logical Brain Games
The Mammoth Book of Brain Games
The Mammoth Book of New Sudoku
The Mammoth Book of Fun Brain Training
The Mammoth Book of Brain Workouts
The World Puzzle Championship Challenge
The Beautiful Flower Dot-to-dot Book

About the Author

Dr Gareth Moore is the author of over 100 puzzle and brain-training books for both children and adults, including *The Mindfulness Puzzle Book, The Mammoth Book of New Sudoku* and *The Ordnance Survey Puzzle Book.*

He is also the creator of the daily brain-training website BrainedUp.com, and runs popular puzzle site PuzzleMix.com.

Find him online at DrGarethMoore.com

DO YOU HAVE WHAT IT TAKES TO FLY WITH THE BEST?

THE RAF ASSOCIATION **PUZZLE BOOK**

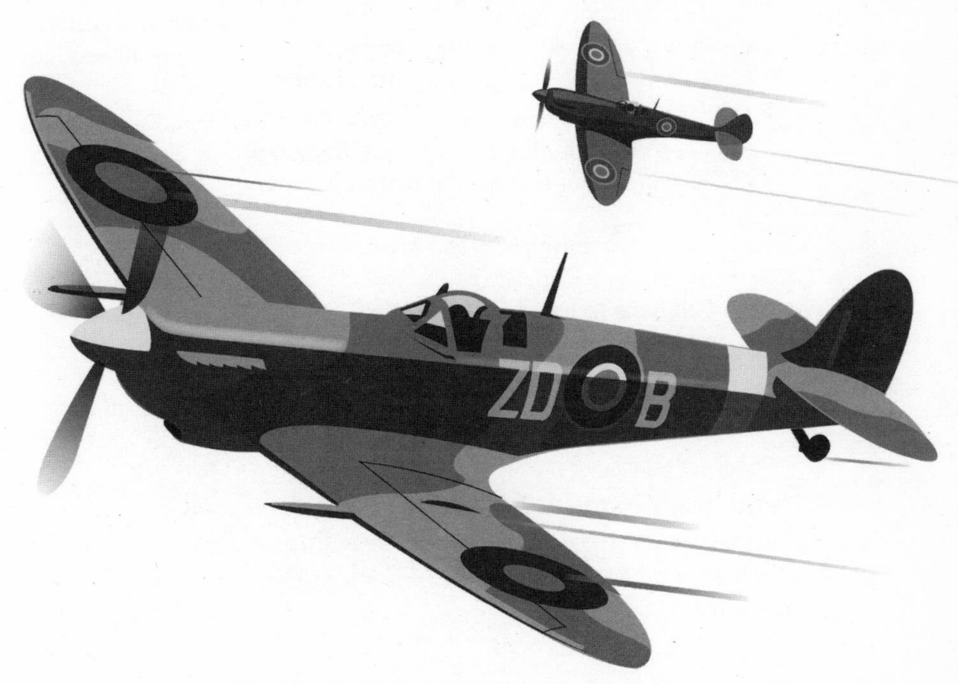

DR GARETH MOORE

ROBINSON

ROBINSON

First published in Great Britain in 2020 by Robinson

1 3 5 7 9 10 8 6 4 2

For image credits, see page 253

A CIP catalogue record for this book
is available from the British Library.

ISBN: 978-1-47214-532-1

Typeset in Gill Sans MT and Palatino Linotype by Dr Gareth Moore
Printed and bound in Great Britain by Clays Ltd, Elcograf S.p.A.

Papers used by Robinson are from well-managed forests and other responsible sources.

Robinson
An imprint of
Little, Brown Book Group
Carmelite House
50 Victoria Embankment
London EC4Y 0DZ

An Hachette UK Company
www.hachette.co.uk

www.littlebrown.co.uk

A minimum of £1,000 from the proceeds of this book will be paid to the Royal Air Forces Association, a registered charity with charity number 226686 [England and Wales] SC037673 [Scotland].

CONTENTS

ROYAL AIR FORCES Association

The charity that supports the RAF family

The RAF Association is one of the leading providers of welfare assistance to the RAF community, giving support to serving and veteran RAF personnel and their families. Our charity provides a wide variety of services to support all members of the RAF community who require assistance to improve their physical or mental wellbeing.

As its President, I am proud that the RAF Association never rests on its laurels. Over recent years, it has transformed itself beyond recognition to make sure it meets the constantly changing needs of those it supports. This underpins our ambition to support a resilient, empowered RAF community across all generations.

Indeed, the Association supports many thousands of individuals of all ages each year, transforming lives as a result. The Association prides itself on empowering people by giving them the expert advice and practical support they need to stay strong in challenging times.

This work is simply not possible without the support of the public. By purchasing this puzzle book, you are directly helping those in the RAF community to get support in their hour of need.

Thank you.

Air Marshal Sir Baz North, President – RAF Association

To find out more about the vital work the RAF Association carries out, please visit: www.rafa.org.uk

Introduction

Welcome to *The RAF Association Puzzle Book*, packed from cover to cover with a huge range of flight-based puzzles, challenges and quizzes.

Pilots require a great range of skills in order to safely fly aircraft, and similarly throughout this book you'll be tested on a wide variety of challenges. These range from pure logic puzzles that require no existing knowledge, through to other tasks that may benefit from at least a passing familiarity with related flight-related topics, such as the world's airlines, airports, and historic knowledge of aeroplanes. Extremely specialist knowledge is never required, however.

The first chapter consists purely of cognitive challenges. In this section you'll pit your brain against a series of logical reasoning puzzles, with four of each type of puzzle – and the puzzles are arranged within each set in order of increasing difficulty.

The second chapter is all about survival skills, with challenges covering a wide range of areas, from codebreaking through to word and calculation skills.

In chapter three you'll be tested on your visual abilities, including following directions given in various formats, while chapter four will assess your memory skills with a range of timed exercises.

Finally, the fifth chapters will call upon your knowledge with a wide mix of puzzles, covering everything from air force roundels to parts of an aircraft, and from flight pioneers to aircraft silhouettes. With a range of formats, most puzzles can be tackled by using common sense, even if you don't immediately know the answers to the questions.

Full solutions are at the back, along with puzzle explanations where relevant.

CHAPTER 1

COGNITIVE CHALLENGES

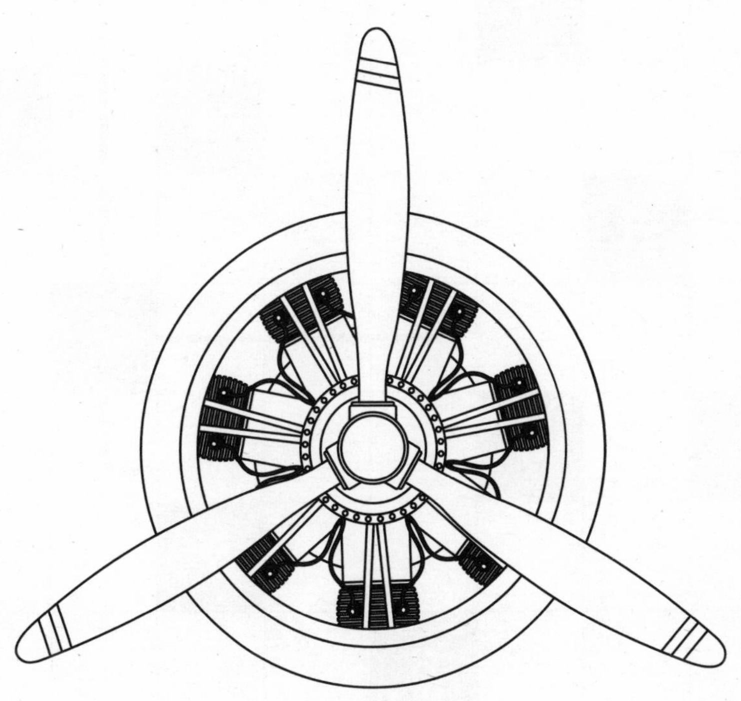

Signal Strength 1

Mission 1: Identify the areas covered by each beacon

Briefing:

Find the area covered by the signal broadcast from each of the shaded beacons. Each beacon transmits horizontally and/or vertically in the same row and/or column to the given number of squares. No more than one beacon can broadcast to a single square. One clue is solved already, to show how it works.

				6			
		1					
					4		6
	8						
						7	
5		4					
					7		
			6				

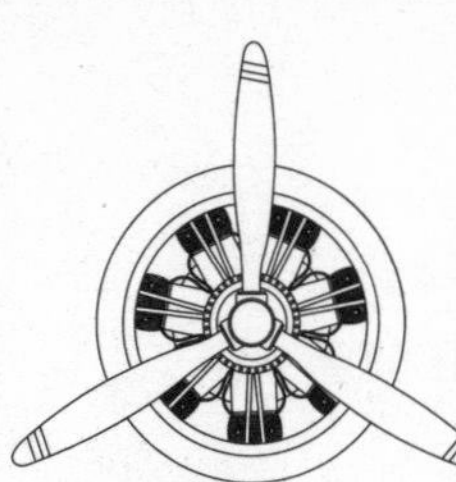

Signal Strength 2

Mission 2: Identify the areas covered by each beacon

Briefing:

Find the area covered by the signal broadcast from each of the shaded beacons. Each beacon transmits horizontally and/or vertically in the same row and/or column to the given number of squares. No more than one beacon can broadcast to a single square.

<table>
<tr><td></td><td></td><td></td><td></td><td></td><td>7</td><td></td><td></td></tr>
<tr><td></td><td></td><td></td><td>8</td><td></td><td></td><td></td><td></td></tr>
<tr><td></td><td>1</td><td></td><td></td><td>3</td><td></td><td></td><td></td></tr>
<tr><td></td><td></td><td></td><td></td><td></td><td></td><td></td><td>9</td></tr>
<tr><td>9</td><td></td><td></td><td></td><td></td><td></td><td></td><td></td></tr>
<tr><td></td><td></td><td></td><td>2</td><td></td><td></td><td>1</td><td></td></tr>
<tr><td></td><td></td><td></td><td></td><td>7</td><td></td><td></td><td></td></tr>
<tr><td></td><td></td><td>7</td><td></td><td></td><td></td><td></td><td></td></tr>
</table>

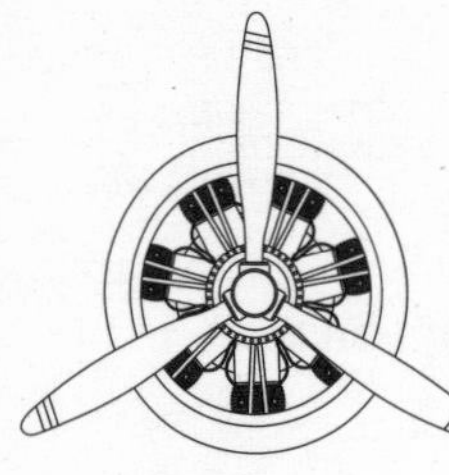

Signal Strength 3

Mission 3: Identify the areas covered by each beacon

Briefing:

Find the area covered by the signal broadcast from each of the shaded beacons. Each beacon transmits horizontally and/or vertically in the same row and/or column to the given number of squares. No more than one beacon can broadcast to a single square.

	5						1	
				6		3		
			2				5	
9								
				5				
								9
	4				2			
		3		6				
	1						5	

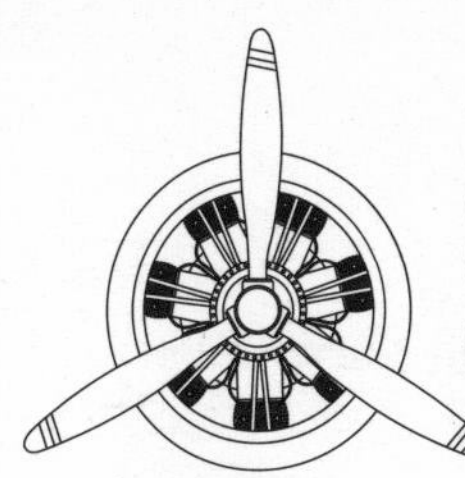

Signal Strength 4

Mission 4: Identify the areas covered by each beacon

Briefing:

Find the area covered by the signal broadcast from each of the shaded beacons. Each beacon transmits horizontally and/or vertically in the same row and/or column to the given number of squares. No more than one beacon can broadcast to a single square.

		5				3			
								9	
					5				2
				6					
8							4		
		3							7
					9				
3				4					
	8								
			3				5		

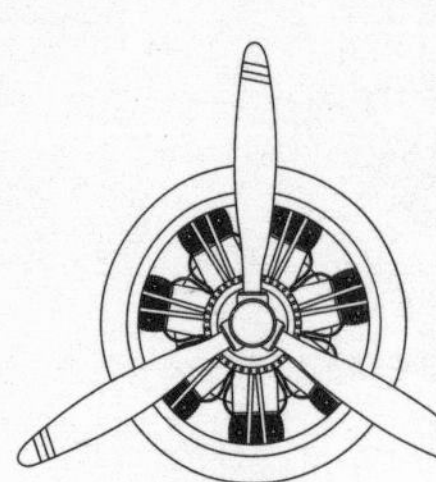

Clouds 1

Mission 5: Find the cloud locations based on the clues

Briefing:

Reveal some clouds hiding in the grid. Each cloud is a rectangle or square of shaded grid squares, at least two grid squares wide by at least two grid squares tall. Clouds cannot touch – not even diagonally. Number clues specify the number of shaded grid squares in each row and column.

						5
						5
						0
						5
						5
						5
3	5	2	5	5	5	

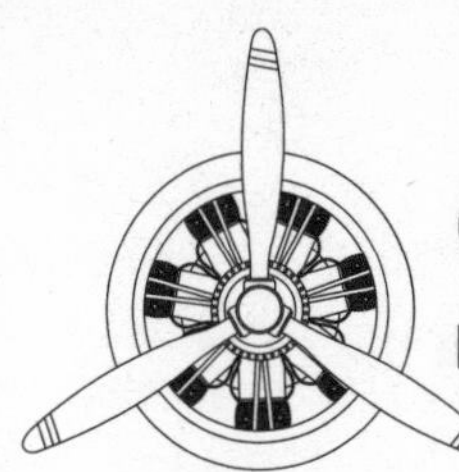

Clouds 2

Mission 6: Find the cloud locations based on the clues

Briefing:

Reveal some clouds hiding in the grid. Each cloud is a rectangle or square of shaded grid squares, at least two grid squares wide by at least two grid squares tall. Clouds cannot touch – not even diagonally. Number clues specify the number of shaded grid squares in each row and column.

							2
							5
							5
							0
							2
							4
							4
3	3	3	3	2	4	4	

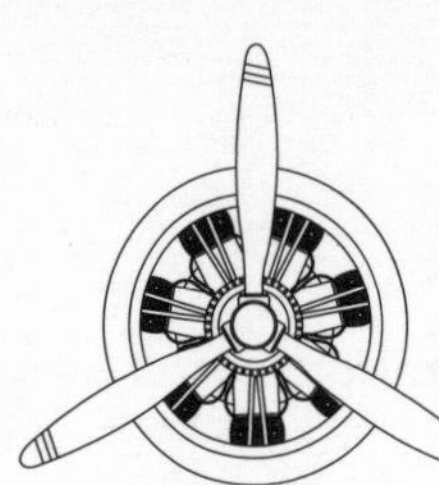

Clouds 3

Mission 7: Find the cloud locations based on the clues

Briefing:

Reveal some clouds hiding in the grid. Each cloud is a rectangle or square of shaded grid squares, at least two grid squares wide by at least two grid squares tall. Clouds cannot touch – not even diagonally. Number clues specify the number of shaded grid squares in each row and column.

<table>
<tr><td></td><td></td><td></td><td></td><td></td><td></td><td></td><td></td><td>2</td></tr>
<tr><td></td><td></td><td></td><td></td><td></td><td></td><td></td><td></td><td>4</td></tr>
<tr><td></td><td></td><td></td><td></td><td></td><td></td><td></td><td></td><td>6</td></tr>
<tr><td></td><td></td><td></td><td></td><td></td><td></td><td></td><td></td><td>2</td></tr>
<tr><td></td><td></td><td></td><td></td><td></td><td></td><td></td><td></td><td>3</td></tr>
<tr><td></td><td></td><td></td><td></td><td></td><td></td><td></td><td></td><td>5</td></tr>
<tr><td></td><td></td><td></td><td></td><td></td><td></td><td></td><td></td><td>2</td></tr>
<tr><td></td><td></td><td></td><td></td><td></td><td></td><td></td><td></td><td>2</td></tr>
<tr><td>5</td><td>5</td><td>0</td><td>3</td><td>5</td><td>2</td><td>4</td><td>2</td><td></td></tr>
</table>

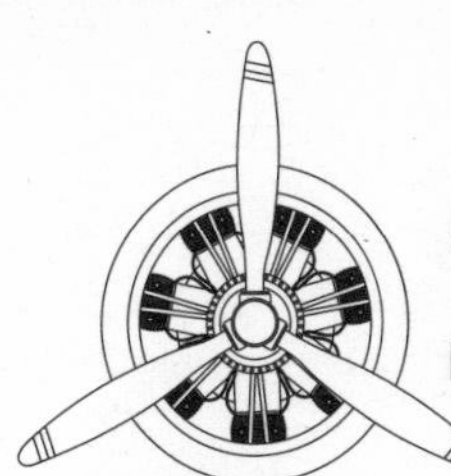

Clouds 4

Mission 8: Find the cloud locations based on the clues

Briefing:

Reveal some clouds hiding in the grid. Each cloud is a rectangle or square of shaded grid squares, at least two grid squares wide by at least two grid squares tall. Clouds cannot touch – not even diagonally. Number clues specify the number of shaded grid squares in each row and column.

									3
									3
									2
									6
									4
									4
									3
									5
									2
2	4	4	0	4	7	5	3	3	

Fences I

Mission 9: Draw a loop that visits every dot

Briefing:

Join every dot to form a single loop, using only horizontal and vertical lines. Each dot must therefore have exactly two lines connected to it. Some lines are already given.

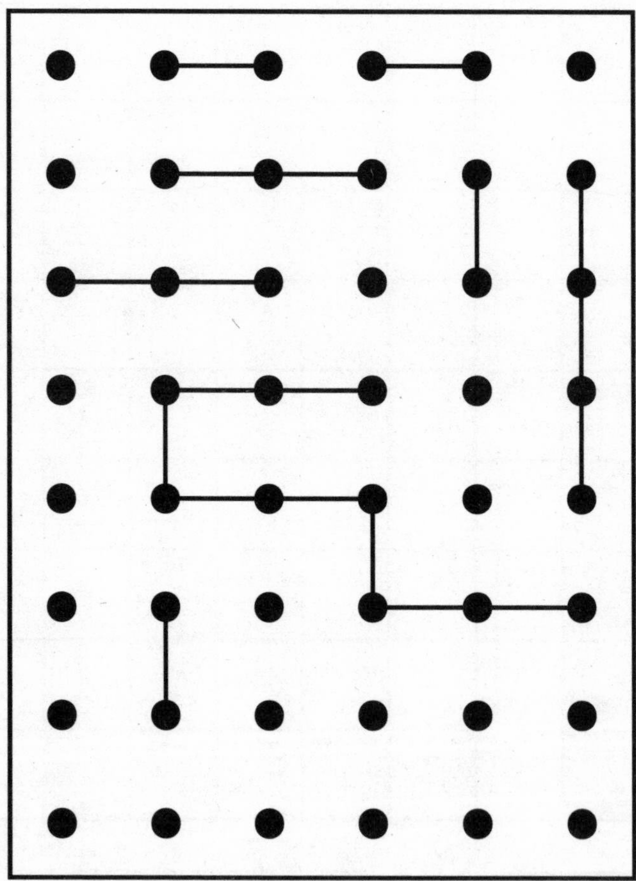

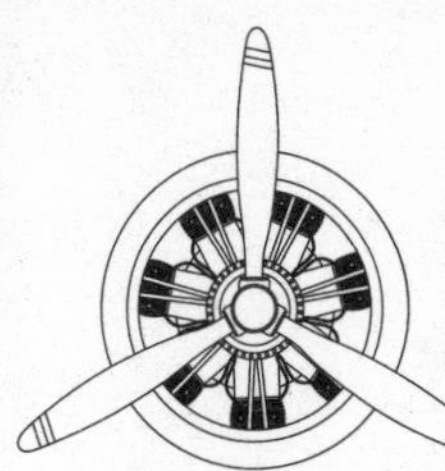

Fences 2

Mission 10: Draw a loop that visits every dot

Briefing:

Join every dot to form a single loop, using only horizontal and vertical lines. Each dot must therefore have exactly two lines connected to it. Some lines are already given.

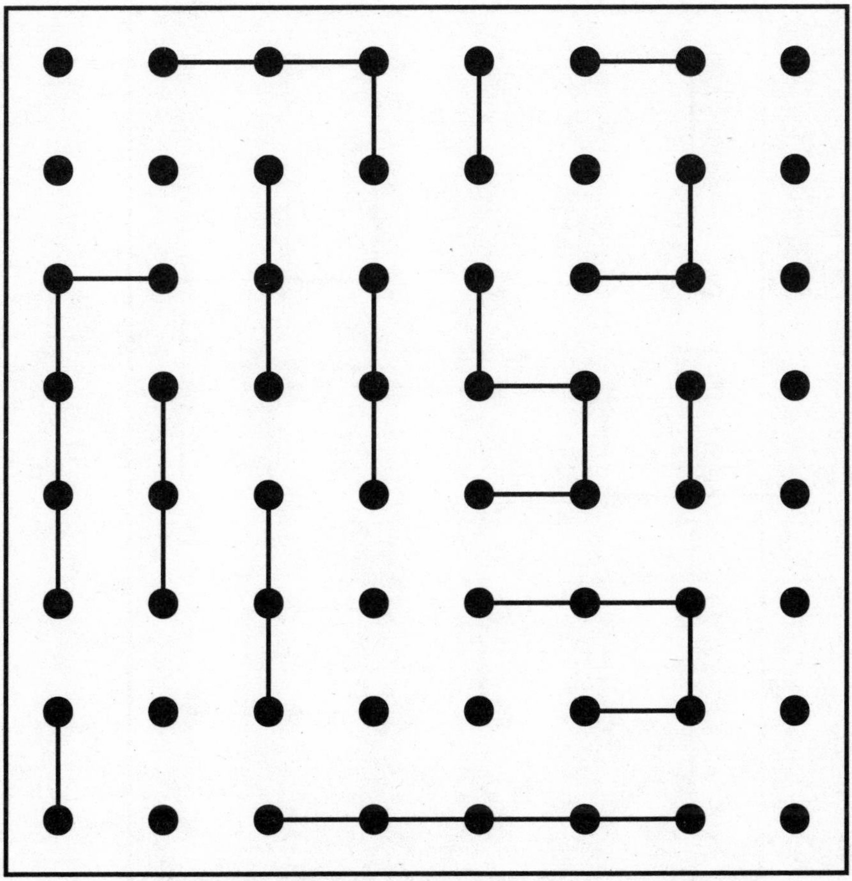

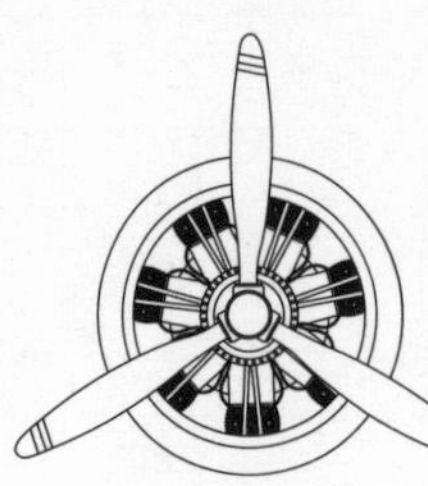

Fences 3

Mission 11: Draw a loop that visits every dot

Briefing:

Join every dot to form a single loop, using only horizontal and vertical lines. Each dot must therefore have exactly two lines connected to it. Some lines are already given.

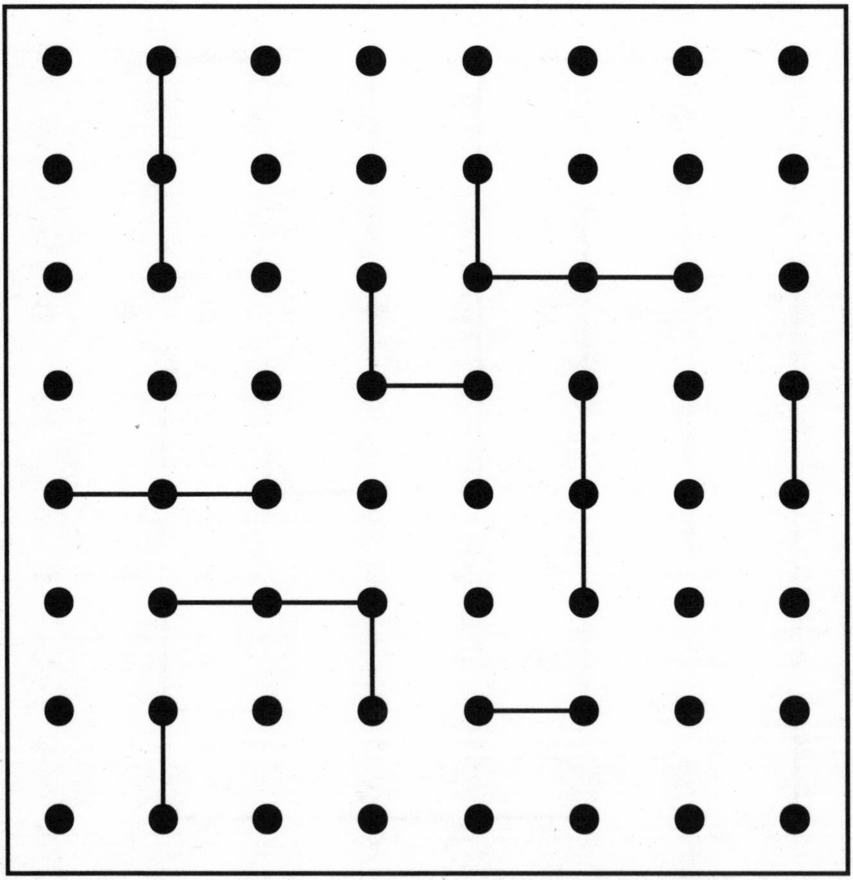

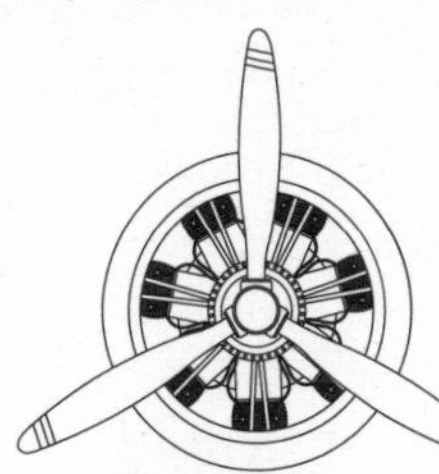

Fences 4

Mission 12: Draw a loop that visits every dot

Briefing:

Join every dot to form a single loop, using only horizontal and vertical lines. Each dot must therefore have exactly two lines connected to it. Some lines are already given.

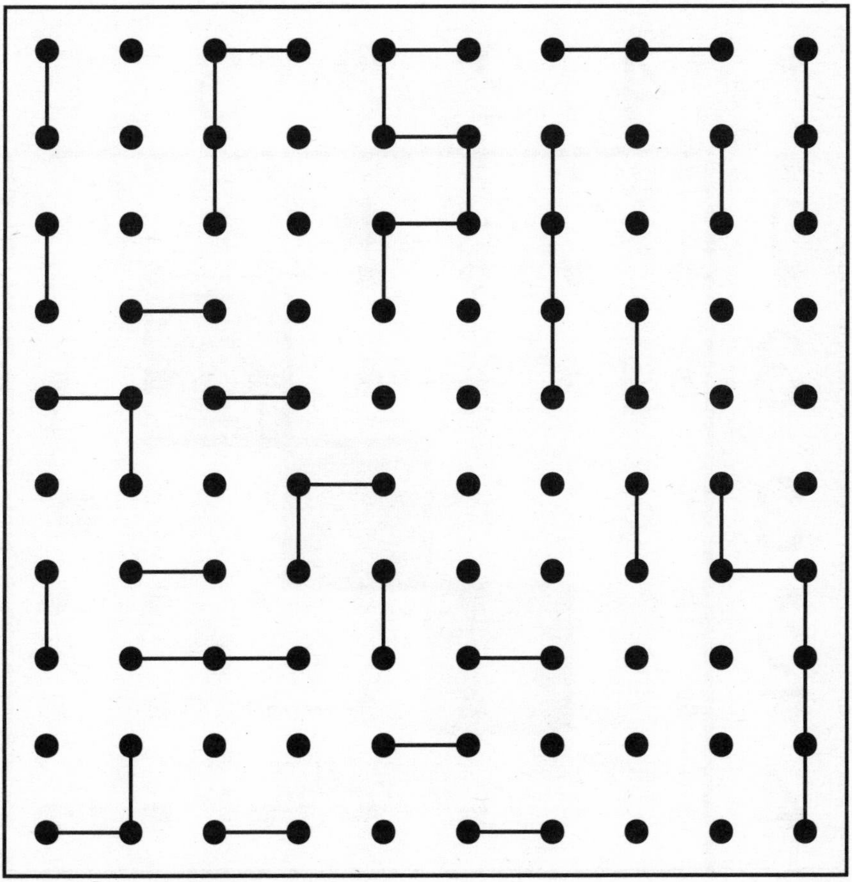

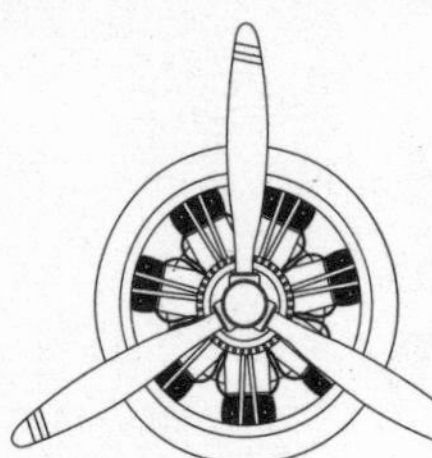

Flight Path 1

Mission 13: Plot the correct flight path

Briefing:

Draw a path that joins the two black dots, travelling horizontally or vertically from dot to dot. The path cannot visit a dot more than once, or cross over a shaded square. Digits outside the grid reveal the total number of dots visited by the path in each row and column.

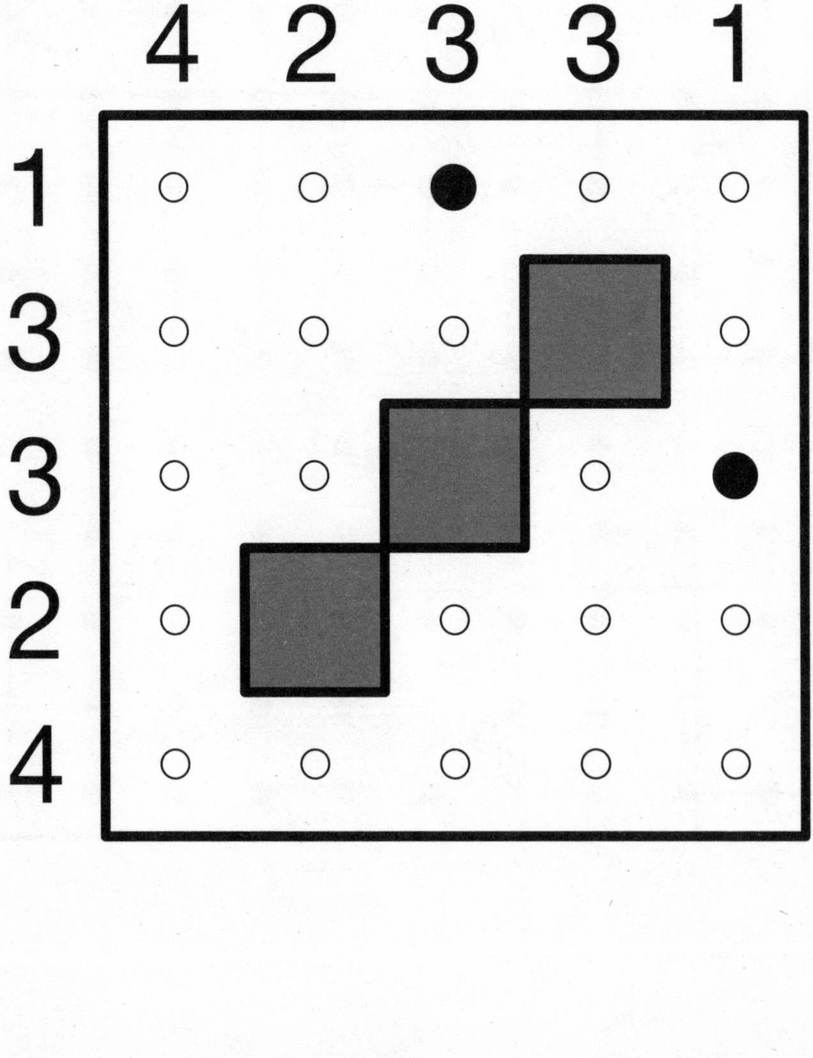

	4	2	3	3	1
1	○	○	●	○	○
3	○	○	○	■	○
3	○	○	■	○	●
2	○	■	○	○	○
4	○	○	○	○	○

Flight Path 2

Mission 14: Plot the correct flight path

Briefing:

Draw a path that joins the two black dots, travelling horizontally or vertically from dot to dot. The path cannot visit a dot more than once, or cross over a shaded square. Digits outside the grid reveal the total number of dots visited by the path in each row and column.

	5	5	4	2	1	2
3	○	○	●	○	○	○
1	○	○	○	○	○	○
2	○	○	■	■	○	○
3	■	○	○	○	○	○
6	○	○	○	○	○	○
4	○	○	○	○	○	●

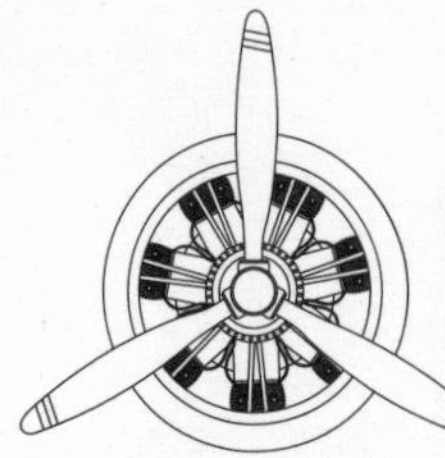

Flight Path 3

Mission 15: Plot the correct flight path

Briefing:

Draw a path that joins the two black dots, travelling horizontally or vertically from dot to dot. The path cannot visit a dot more than once, or cross over a shaded square. Digits outside the grid reveal the total number of dots visited by the path in certain rows and columns. Those without a number may have any number of dots visited.

			1			
2	●	○	○	○	○	■
2	○	○	○	○	○	○
	○	○	○	○	○	●
2	■	○	○	○	○	○
	○	○	○	○	■	○
5	○	○	○	○	○	○

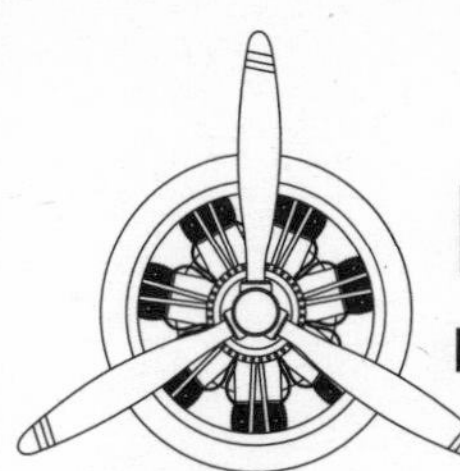

Flight Path 4

Mission 16: Plot the correct flight path

Briefing:

Draw a path that joins the two black dots, travelling horizontally or vertically from dot to dot. The path cannot visit a dot more than once, or cross over a shaded square. Digits outside the grid reveal the total number of dots visited by the path in certain rows and columns. Those without a number may have any number of dots visited.

		2	5			
	○	○	○	○	○	○
4	○	○	○	○	●	○
	○	○	○	○	○	■
5	○	○	○	○	○	■
5	○	○	○	○	○	○
2	○	○	○	■	○	●

Futoshiki 1

Mission 17: Place digits while obeying inequalities

Briefing:

Place a digit from 1 to 5 in each empty square so that no number repeats in any row or column. Also, each inequality sign must be obeyed so that each arrow points to the smaller of certain pairs of digits.

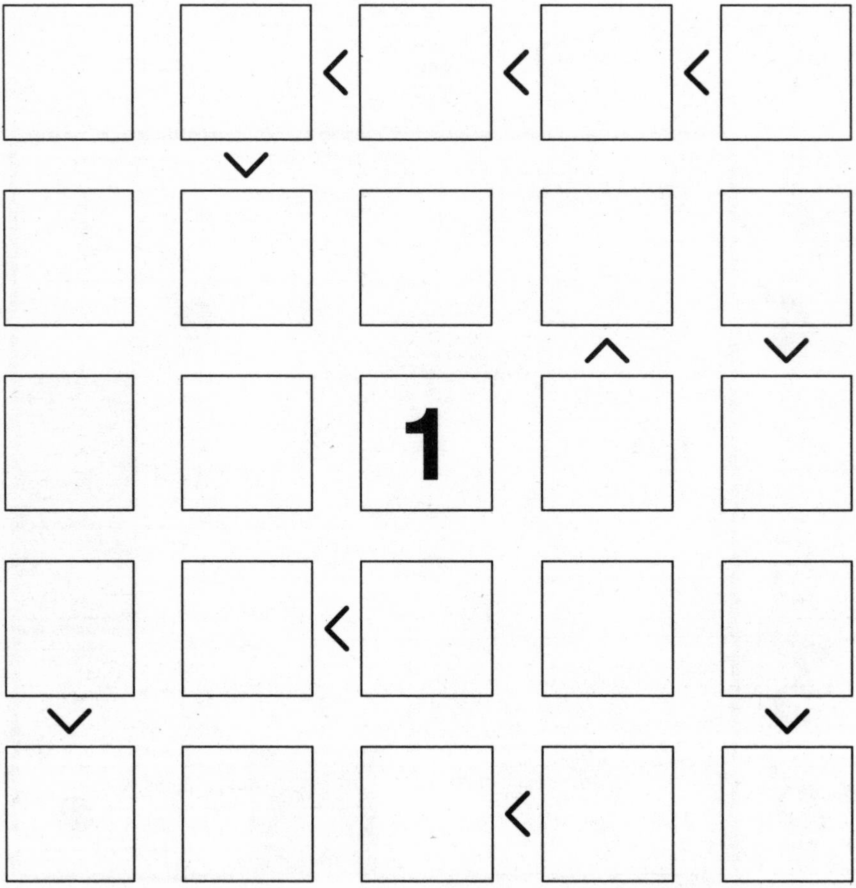

			<		<		<	
		∨						
						∧		∨
				1				
			<					
∨								∨
					<			

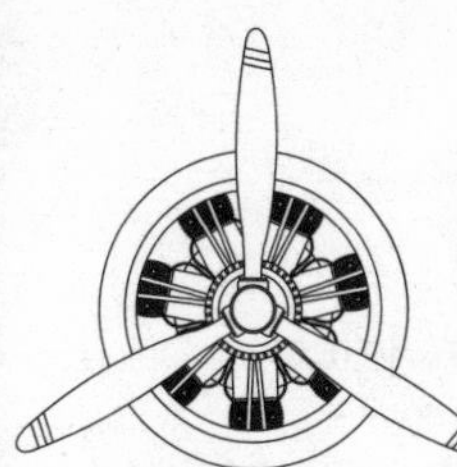

Futoshiki 2

Mission 18: Place digits while obeying inequalities

Briefing:

Place a digit from 1 to 6 in each empty square so that no number repeats in any row or column. Also, each inequality sign must be obeyed so that each arrow points to the smaller of certain pairs of digits.

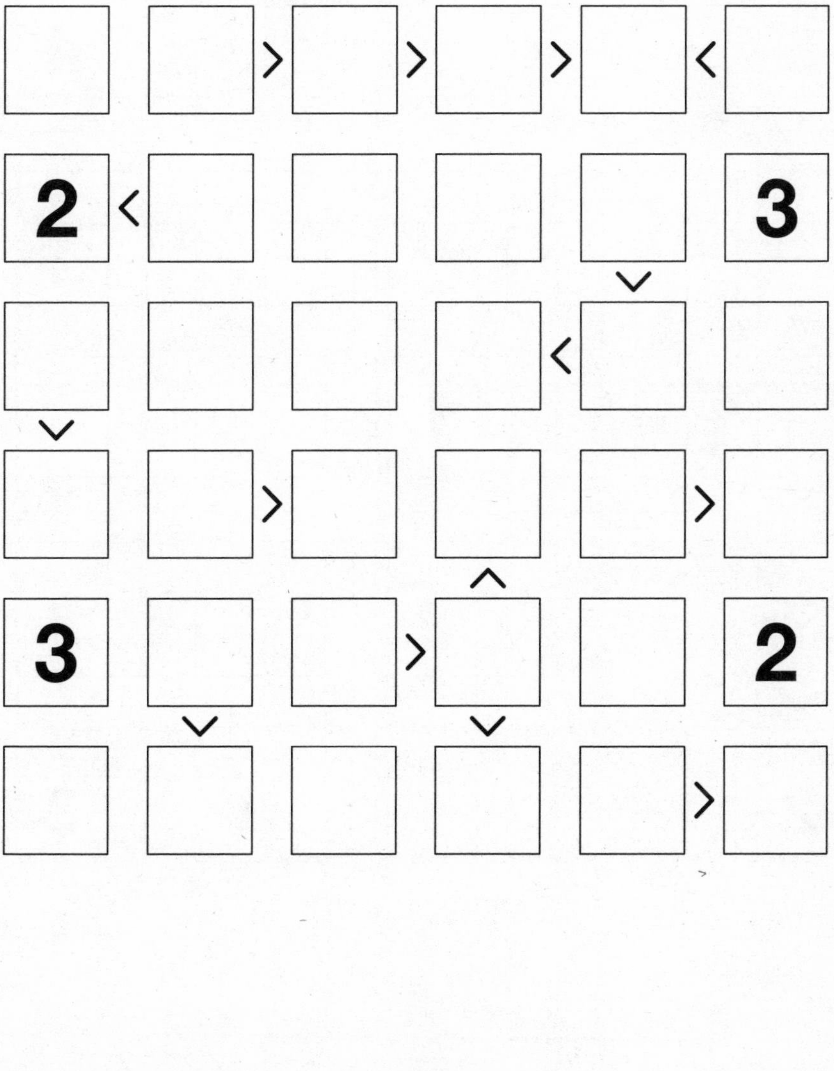

			>		>		>		<	
2	<									3
								∨		
							<			
∨										
			>						>	
						∧				
3					>					2
		∨				∨				
									>	

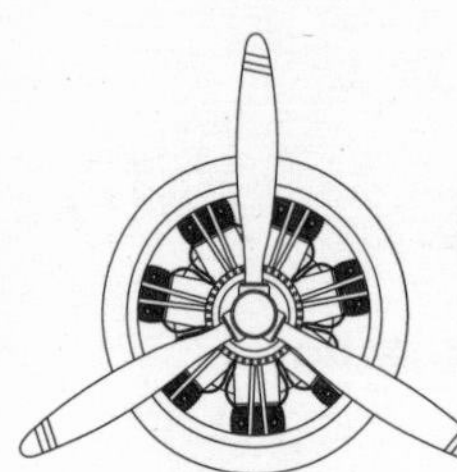

Futoshiki 3

Mission 19: Place digits while obeying inequalities

Briefing:

Place a digit from 1 to 7 in each empty square so that no number repeats in any row or column. Also, each inequality sign must be obeyed so that each arrow points to the smaller of certain pairs of digits.

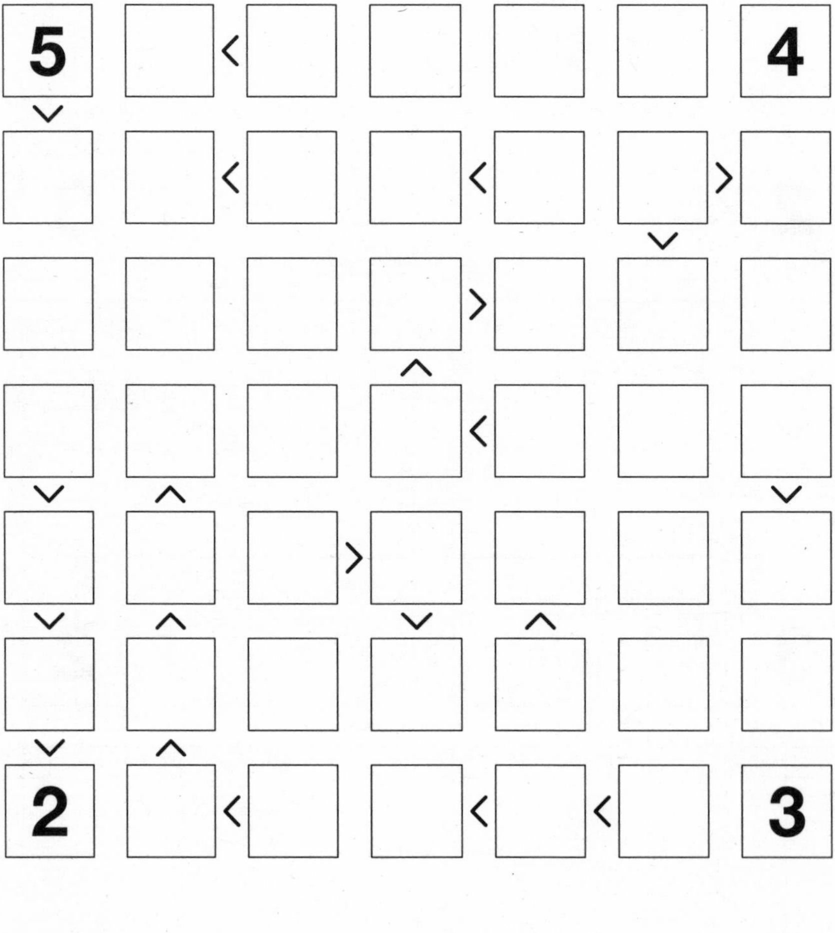

5			<									4
∨												
			<				<				>	
										∨		
							>					
						∧						
							<					
∨		∧										∨
					>							
∨		∧				∨		∧				
∨		∧										
2			<				<		<			3

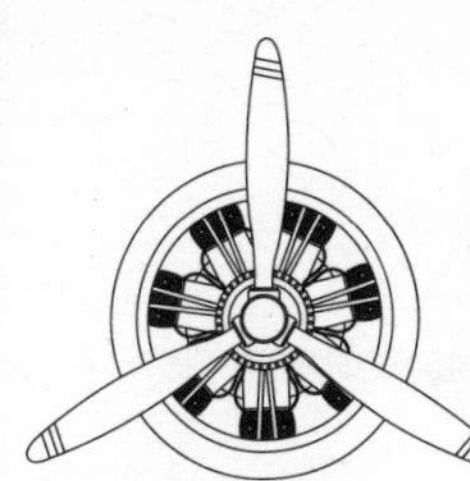

Futoshiki 4

Mission 20: Place digits while obeying inequalities

Briefing:

Place a digit from 1 to 8 in each empty square so that no number repeats in any row or column. Also, each inequality sign must be obeyed so that each arrow points to the smaller of certain pairs of digits.

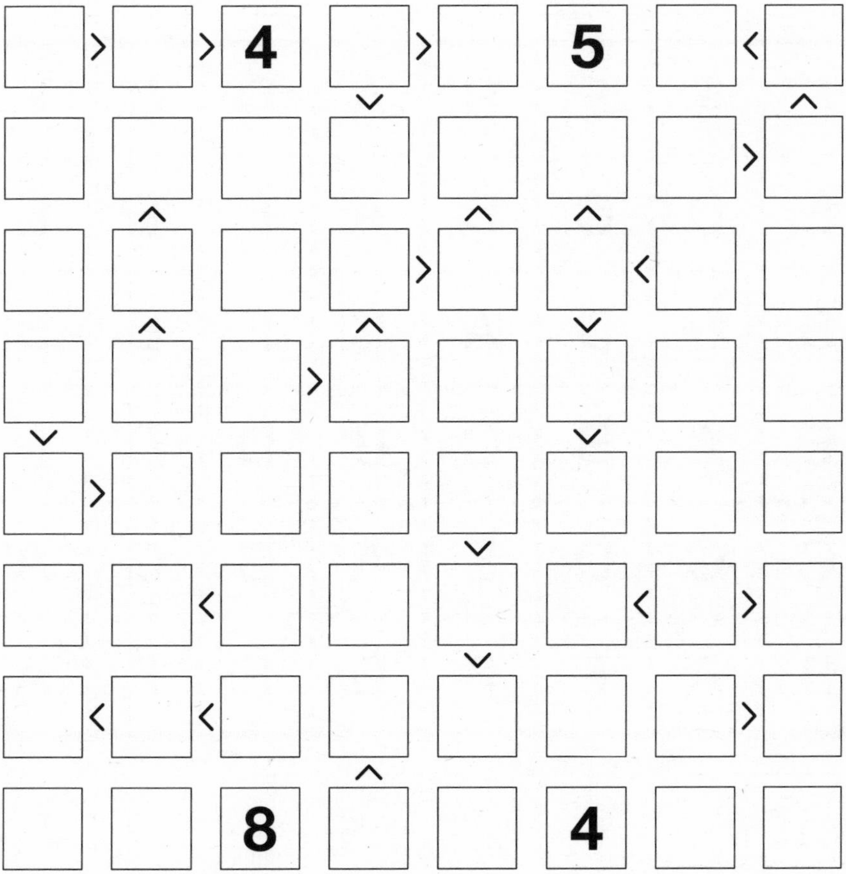

	>		>	4			>			5			<	
						∨								∧
													>	
		∧						∧		∧				
							>				<			
		∧				∧				∨				
					>									
∨										∨				
	>													
								∨						
			<								<		>	
								∨						
	<		<										>	
						∧								
				8						4				

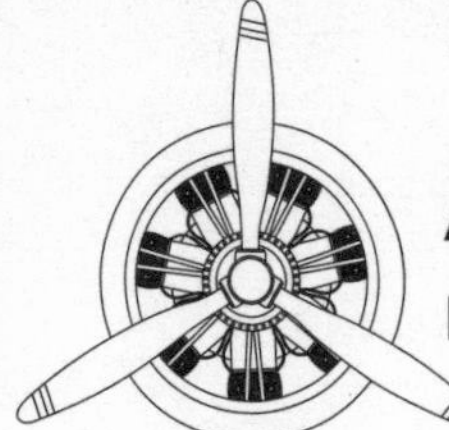

Area Division 1

Mission 21: Draw dividing walls to create separate areas

Briefing:

Draw along some of the dashed lines to divide the grid into a set of areas, each containing one of every letter from A to F.

F	E	E	B	A	D	C	F
E	D	C	B	A	F	E	E
B	D	D	A	C	F	B	B
E	A	B	C	B	D	D	F
C	C	D	E	A	C	C	A
B	A	F	F	D	E	F	A

Area Division 2

Mission 22: Draw dividing walls to create separate areas

Briefing:

Draw along some of the dashed lines to divide the grid into a set of areas, each containing one of every letter from A to D.

B	D	D	A	D	A	D	B
D	C	C	B	A	C	D	C
C	A	D	A	C	B	C	A
B	D	A	A	B	C	A	B
A	B	C	D	C	B	D	A
C	B	A	D	B	C	D	B

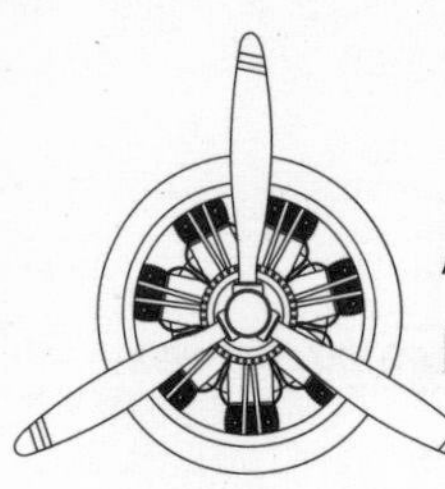

Area Division 3

Mission 23: Draw dividing walls to create separate areas

Briefing:

Draw along some of the dashed lines to divide the grid into a set of areas, each containing one of every letter from A to G.

B	A	E	C	A	G	B
C	D	G	F	D	C	E
A	E	E	G	F	F	A
D	F	B	C	D	B	D
G	B	G	C	B	C	A
A	E	F	G	D	E	E
B	F	A	C	G	D	F

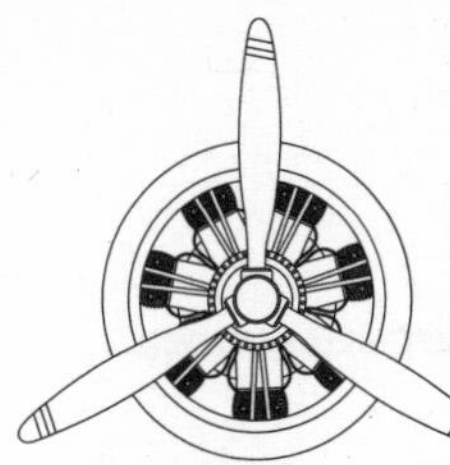

Area Division 4

Mission 24: Draw dividing walls to create separate areas

Briefing:

Draw along some of the dashed lines to divide the grid into a set of areas, each containing one of every letter from A to D.

D	B	C	D	B	D	A	D
B	D	A	A	C	D	B	C
C	B	C	A	B	B	C	A
D	C	A	C	D	C	A	B
A	D	C	B	A	D	B	A
C	C	D	A	A	D	D	C
A	B	A	B	C	C	B	C
D	B	B	D	A	A	D	B

Line Sweeper 1

Mission 25: Find a loop that obeys the given constraints

Briefing:

Draw a loop that passes through some of the empty grid squares, using only horizontal and vertical lines, and without visiting any square more than once. The loop must visit the given number of squares neighbouring each number, including diagonally neighbouring squares.

							3
4	7						
					7		
			6				
				7		7	4
	8						

Line Sweeper 2

Mission 26: Find a loop that obeys the given constraints

Briefing:

Draw a loop that passes through some of the empty grid squares, using only horizontal and vertical lines, and without visiting any square more than once. The loop must visit the given number of squares neighbouring each number, including diagonally neighbouring squares.

3				2			3
	8					7	
4			5				
						5	
		4		3	4		

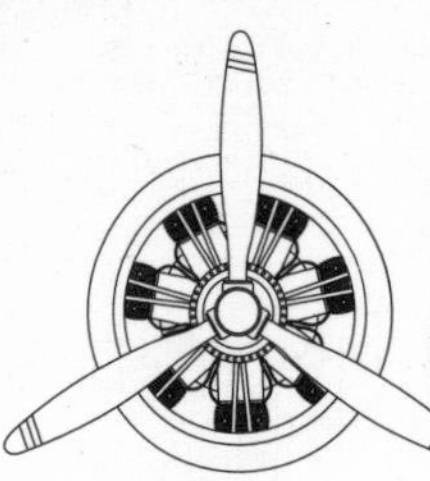

Line Sweeper 3

Mission 27: Find a loop that obeys the given constraints

Briefing:

Draw a loop that passes through some of the empty grid squares, using only horizontal and vertical lines, and without visiting any square more than once. The loop must visit the given number of squares neighbouring each number, including diagonally neighbouring squares.

						7		
	3	4			6			5
	2		6		5			
			8					5
4					8			
							8	
			5					

Line Sweeper 4

Mission 28: Find a loop that obeys the given constraints

Briefing:

Draw a loop that passes through some of the empty grid squares, using only horizontal and vertical lines, and without visiting any square more than once. The loop must visit the given number of squares neighbouring each number, including diagonally neighbouring squares.

						5			
		5						7	
			6						
					7				5
			7			7			
4									
									5
4			7			6	7		
		7							
				5					3

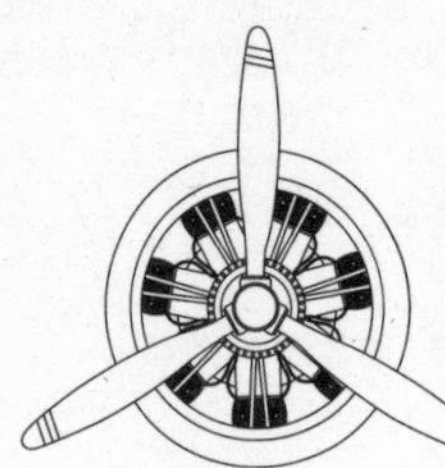

Meadows I

Mission 29: Divide the grid into squares

Briefing:

Draw along the dashed lines to divide the grid into squares measuring 1×1 units or larger, with no unused areas left over. Every square must contain exactly one circle.

○				○		○
			○	○		
○			○			
	○	○				○
					○	○

Meadows 2

Mission 30: Divide the grid into squares

Briefing:

Draw along the dashed lines to divide the grid into squares measuring 1×1 units or larger, with no unused areas left over. Every square must contain exactly one circle.

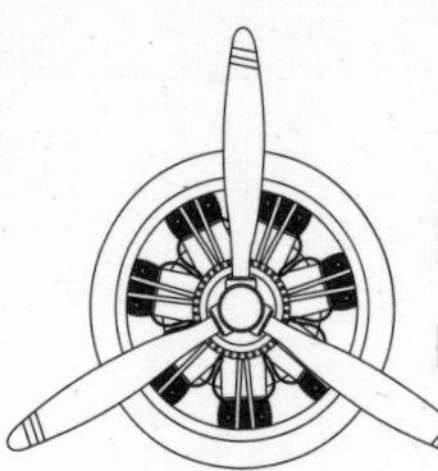

Meadows 3

Mission 31: Divide the grid into squares

Briefing:

Draw along the dashed lines to divide the grid into squares measuring 1×1 units or larger, with no unused areas left over. Every square must contain exactly one circle.

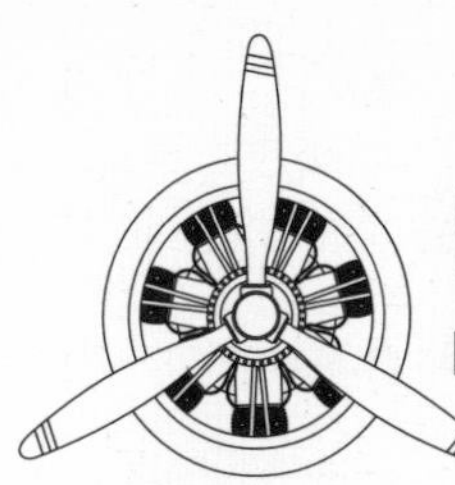

Meadows 4

Mission 32: Divide the grid into squares

Briefing:

Draw along the dashed lines to divide the grid into squares measuring 1×1 units or larger, with no unused areas left over. Every square must contain exactly one circle.

<table>
<tr><td>○</td><td>○</td><td></td><td></td><td></td><td></td><td></td><td></td><td>○</td><td></td><td></td><td></td><td></td></tr>
<tr><td></td><td></td><td>○</td><td></td><td></td><td></td><td></td><td></td><td></td><td></td><td></td><td>○</td><td></td></tr>
<tr><td>○</td><td></td><td></td><td></td><td></td><td></td><td></td><td></td><td></td><td></td><td></td><td></td><td></td></tr>
<tr><td></td><td></td><td></td><td></td><td>○</td><td></td><td></td><td></td><td></td><td></td><td></td><td></td><td></td></tr>
<tr><td>○</td><td></td><td></td><td></td><td></td><td></td><td></td><td></td><td></td><td>○</td><td></td><td></td><td></td></tr>
<tr><td></td><td>○</td><td></td><td></td><td></td><td></td><td>○</td><td></td><td>○</td><td></td><td></td><td></td><td></td></tr>
<tr><td></td><td></td><td></td><td></td><td></td><td></td><td></td><td></td><td></td><td></td><td></td><td></td><td></td></tr>
<tr><td></td><td></td><td></td><td>○</td><td></td><td></td><td></td><td></td><td>○</td><td></td><td></td><td></td><td></td></tr>
<tr><td>○</td><td></td><td></td><td></td><td></td><td></td><td></td><td></td><td></td><td></td><td></td><td></td><td>○</td></tr>
<tr><td></td><td></td><td></td><td></td><td>○</td><td></td><td></td><td></td><td></td><td>○</td><td></td><td></td><td></td></tr>
<tr><td></td><td></td><td></td><td></td><td></td><td></td><td>○</td><td></td><td></td><td></td><td>○</td><td></td><td></td></tr>
<tr><td></td><td></td><td></td><td></td><td></td><td></td><td></td><td></td><td></td><td></td><td></td><td></td><td></td></tr>
<tr><td></td><td>○</td><td></td><td></td><td></td><td></td><td></td><td>○</td><td></td><td></td><td></td><td></td><td></td></tr>
</table>

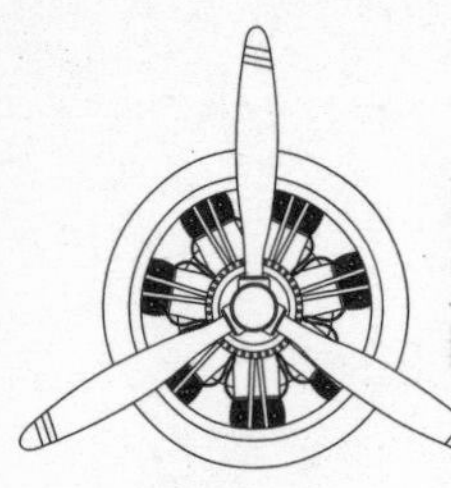

Number Search I

Mission 33: Locate the numbers as quickly as possible

Briefing:

Can you find all of the listed numbers in the grid? They may be written in any direction, either forward or backward, including diagonally.

2	6	3	9	1	2	9	6	1	5	4	1
7	3	1	7	9	7	1	5	8	1	7	7
6	7	5	0	6	6	9	0	0	6	2	9
9	2	7	1	3	1	2	2	2	2	4	6
0	3	5	5	6	1	6	3	6	7	2	9
4	1	4	5	6	9	3	3	9	4	5	6
5	1	4	5	0	1	4	4	9	9	5	1
4	1	6	4	2	5	8	4	7	5	8	4
2	9	0	0	3	7	3	8	6	1	4	4
1	4	8	6	1	9	9	4	0	5	2	1
4	2	2	8	6	7	4	6	9	2	9	6
9	0	4	8	2	0	1	0	5	7	3	1

23516	44169	57201	75191
24540	46591	58177	92713
28674	50102	61639	94871
39654	54629	73009	9789

Number Search 2

Mission 34: Locate the numbers as quickly as possible

Briefing:

Can you find all of the listed numbers in the grid? They may be written in any direction, either forward or backward, including diagonally.

4	5	1	9	2	2	0	0	6	9	2	8	4	4
0	5	8	7	7	2	5	0	5	5	2	7	7	2
8	2	4	6	8	8	9	6	3	1	4	3	5	0
6	6	4	8	8	5	6	8	5	0	8	5	3	0
8	6	0	1	3	1	7	3	4	8	5	0	3	6
8	7	2	1	3	7	2	8	5	8	3	8	6	6
5	6	2	5	2	5	8	4	6	6	4	2	8	0
3	3	6	7	3	6	6	8	5	7	1	4	4	1
6	2	0	6	4	1	4	9	3	4	6	6	8	7
0	9	3	3	3	6	7	3	8	6	3	3	7	2
3	6	1	6	4	6	4	5	4	2	8	8	2	3
4	2	8	7	8	2	9	0	2	2	0	0	8	3
7	3	6	8	0	5	2	7	8	6	4	5	6	4
1	9	3	5	3	5	4	4	8	6	6	0	2	1

23685 37616 51806 73668 86012
2430 4200 56166 74924 87274
31435 43884 66253 78578 92200
34240 48448 68124 78635 98205

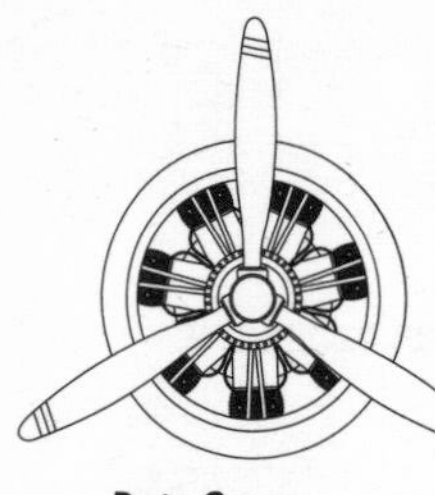

Number Search 3

Mission 35: Locate the numbers as quickly as possible

Briefing:

Can you find all of the listed numbers in the grid? They may be written in any direction, either forward or backward, including diagonally.

0	4	3	9	1	8	8	8	0	0	4	6	0	4	5	8
2	8	1	2	0	0	4	0	6	8	9	2	2	8	1	5
2	2	0	6	2	0	0	9	0	0	0	2	2	0	6	9
0	5	7	9	1	3	3	3	2	5	5	3	8	5	8	9
4	0	9	2	3	9	3	5	2	8	6	1	4	4	2	7
3	1	5	5	7	8	6	8	8	5	0	5	8	3	2	1
1	0	2	4	4	5	0	5	8	5	6	9	0	1	7	7
3	8	6	0	0	8	0	0	4	8	8	3	0	0	2	1
1	0	5	4	0	5	8	7	5	6	8	0	7	1	2	2
0	0	3	5	7	1	2	2	8	9	9	8	8	6	2	6
2	5	8	3	3	1	3	3	9	3	7	1	6	8	0	5
9	3	2	2	9	0	0	1	9	5	9	2	4	4	2	8
6	1	6	8	6	6	9	8	6	8	0	5	6	1	6	3
0	8	1	8	3	3	1	0	1	0	5	8	2	5	2	0
1	8	3	2	0	2	4	6	8	2	4	2	8	3	2	7
4	5	6	1	5	0	6	8	0	5	4	0	8	4	2	2

134508	374007	492809	824286	972652
135008	385621	511063	833223	997171
218939	410692	51682	835625	
285010	450180	605165	880046	
325637	480450	823540	888646	

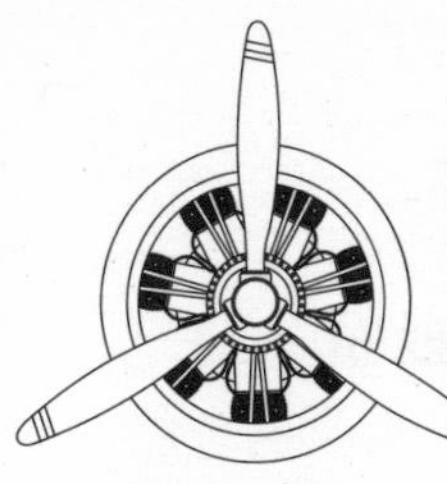

Number Search 4

Mission 36: Locate the numbers as quickly as possible

Briefing:

Can you find all of the listed numbers in the grid? They may be written in any direction, either forward or backward, including diagonally.

3	0	0	9	4	0	4	1	7	4	2	2	6	1	1	5	1	0
3	3	5	0	4	9	6	1	9	0	2	5	9	5	1	4	6	7
3	0	0	6	4	9	9	4	4	6	6	8	7	8	3	8	4	8
5	6	4	9	0	8	6	4	7	7	9	0	1	9	6	9	3	2
6	3	5	8	4	5	8	4	8	0	0	8	8	4	1	3	5	9
1	9	4	5	3	9	2	3	0	0	6	5	7	7	6	7	4	9
5	1	9	5	9	9	0	9	4	4	3	5	8	9	7	7	5	5
3	9	2	8	4	7	1	1	2	9	4	4	5	4	1	9	2	9
0	4	3	8	5	5	0	8	8	1	8	4	5	4	2	2	2	8
3	8	8	9	0	4	0	0	9	8	4	0	3	9	0	2	6	4
7	3	0	4	4	3	1	8	8	8	8	9	8	6	8	5	0	0
5	3	2	8	9	2	2	1	0	3	8	9	1	8	9	4	7	4
2	6	3	1	5	9	5	1	8	0	9	0	4	5	4	3	2	0
9	8	9	2	2	6	0	1	6	0	2	8	9	9	4	0	1	3
0	0	7	0	0	9	8	7	5	3	9	3	5	5	5	9	9	6
6	0	2	8	6	7	4	0	9	4	5	2	7	3	5	9	1	8
0	4	8	5	9	3	4	9	8	8	0	9	4	9	5	1	8	3
4	4	1	8	0	4	4	4	7	8	7	7	6	4	7	9	5	2

111709	294540	445580	558960	898086
144439	30351	445963	592988	940417
156901	369316	478776	783899	954308
229823	401400	47952	819537	995553
287894	428146	522607	864280	

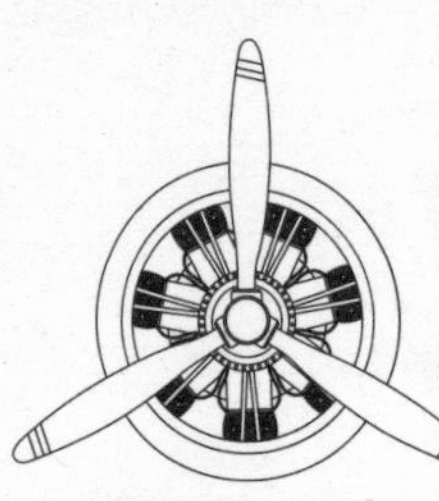

Spiral Galaxies 1

Mission 37: Draw rotationally symmetric regions

Briefing:

Draw along some of the grid lines in order to divide the grid up into a set of regions, so that every square is in exactly one region. Every region must contain exactly one circle, and the region must be symmetrical in such a way that if rotated 180 degrees around the circle it would look exactly the same. One is marked already, to show how it works.

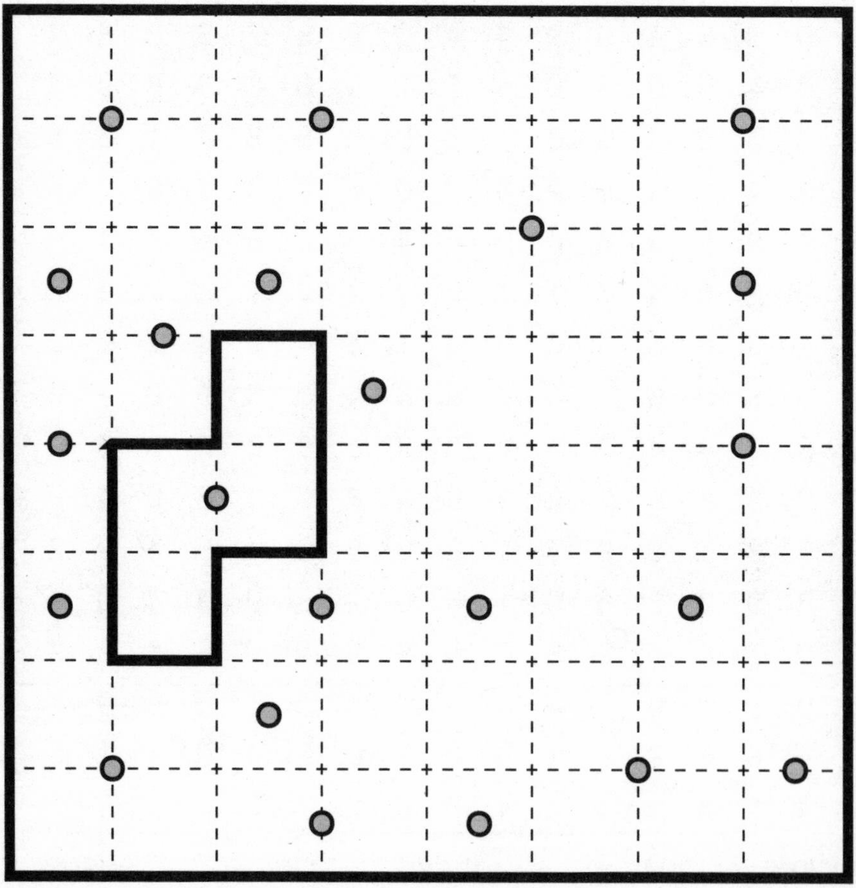

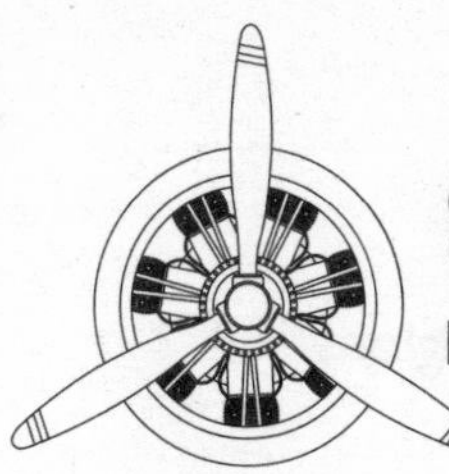

Spiral Galaxies 2

Mission 38: Draw rotationally symmetric regions

Briefing:

Draw along some of the grid lines in order to divide the grid up into a set of regions, so that every square is in exactly one region. Every region must contain exactly one circle, and the region must be symmetrical in such a way that if rotated 180 degrees around the circle it would look exactly the same.

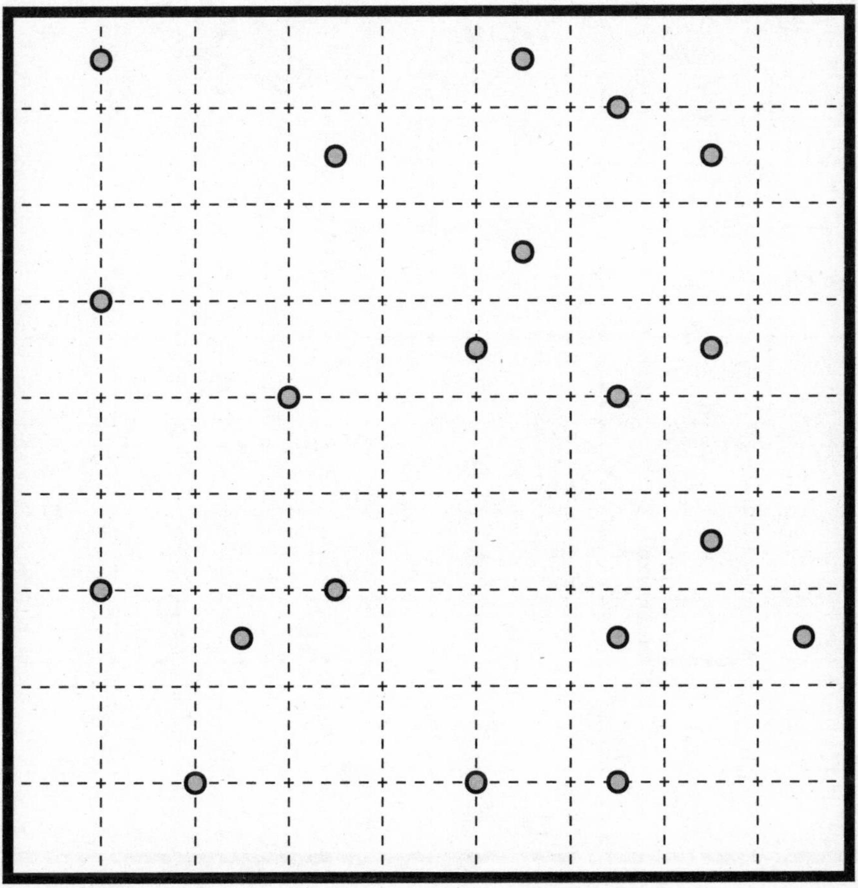

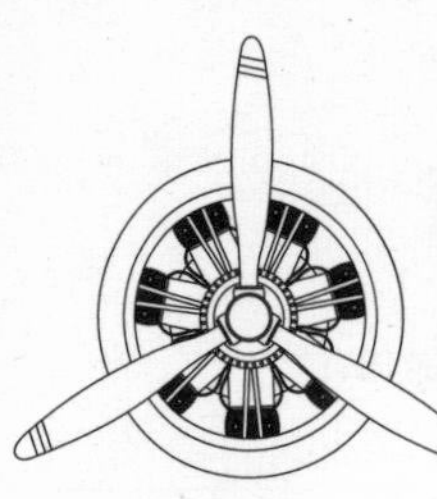

Spiral Galaxies 3

Mission 39: Draw rotationally symmetric regions

Briefing:

Draw along some of the grid lines in order to divide the grid up into a set of regions, so that every square is in exactly one region. Every region must contain exactly one circle, and the region must be symmetrical in such a way that if rotated 180 degrees around the circle it would look exactly the same.

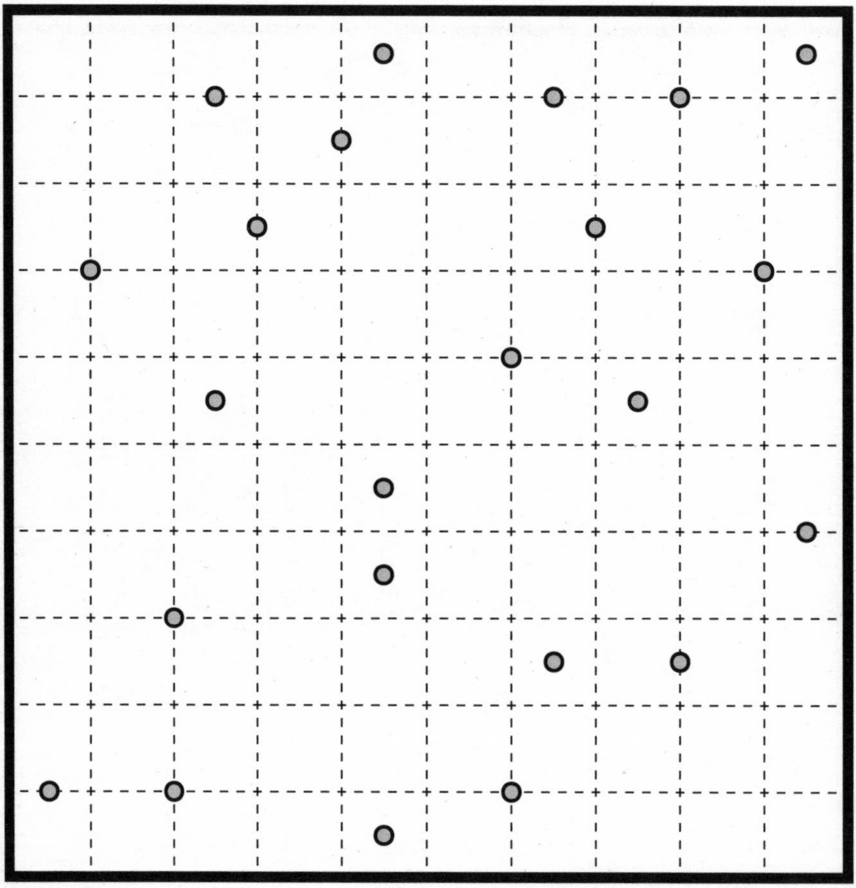

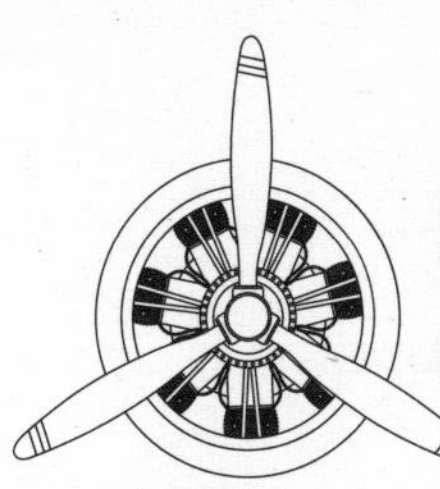

Spiral Galaxies 4

Mission 40: Draw rotationally symmetric regions

Briefing:

Draw along some of the grid lines in order to divide the grid up into a set of regions, so that every square is in exactly one region. Every region must contain exactly one circle, and the region must be symmetrical in such a way that if rotated 180 degrees around the circle it would look exactly the same.

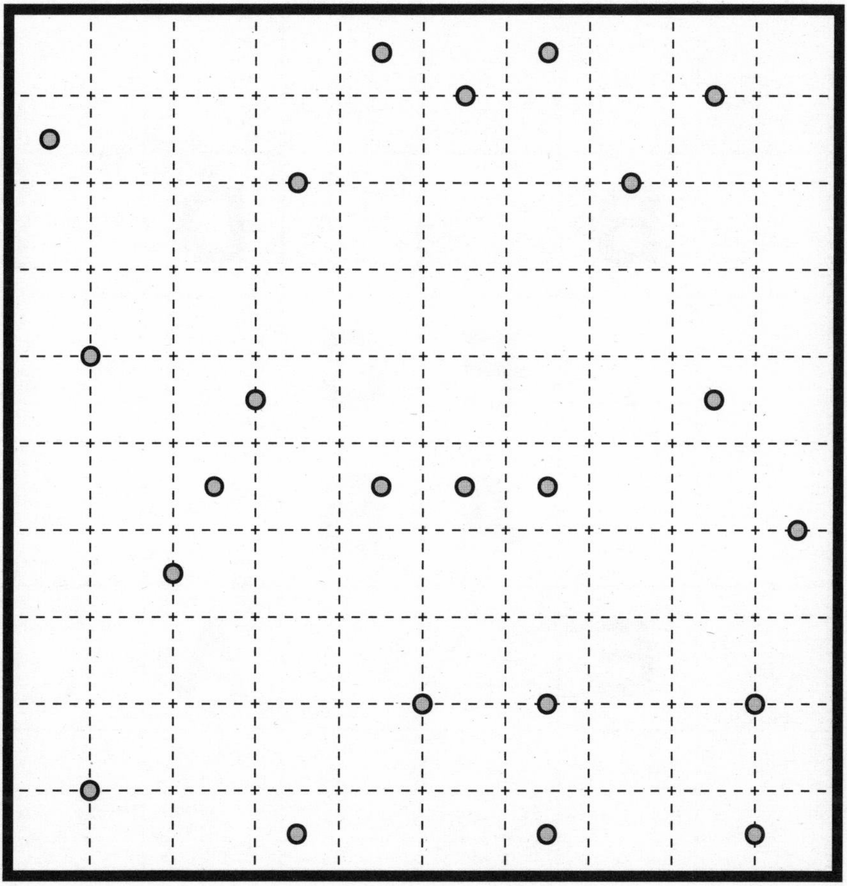

Touchy 1

Mission 41: Fill the square without letters touching

Briefing:

Place a letter from A to F in each empty square so that no letter repeats within any single row or column. Additionally, identical letters cannot be in touching squares – not even diagonally.

	B			D	
		E	C		
		A	B		
	E			A	

Touchy 2

Mission 42: Fill the square without letters touching

Briefing:

Place a letter from A to F in each empty square so that no letter repeats within any single row or column. Additionally, identical letters cannot be in touching squares – not even diagonally.

	F			E	
C					D
		C	E		
		D	A		
E					A
	D			F	

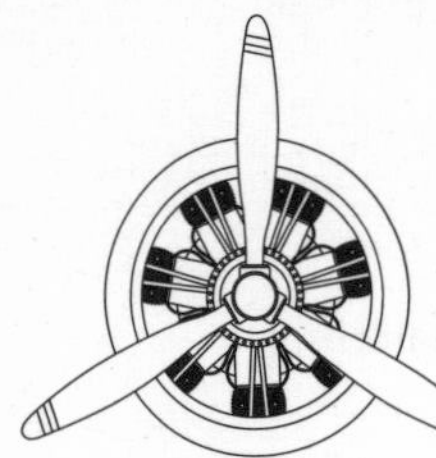

Touchy 3

Mission 43: Fill the square without letters touching

Briefing:

Place a letter from A to G in each empty square so that no letter repeats within any single row or column. Additionally, identical letters cannot be in touching squares – not even diagonally.

	B	F		D	A	
C						G
A						B
F						D
B						F
	E	C		G	B	

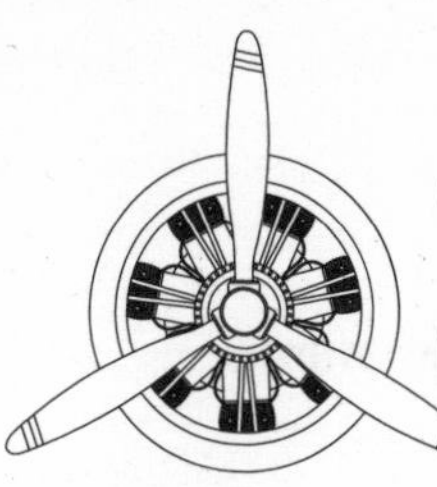

Touchy 4

Mission 44: Fill the square without letters touching

Briefing:

Place a letter from A to H in each empty square so that no letter repeats within any single row or column. Additionally, identical letters cannot be in touching squares – not even diagonally.

			E	B			
		B			D		
	C					A	
A			B	G			E
E			C	A			G
	G					B	
		E			C		
			F	D			

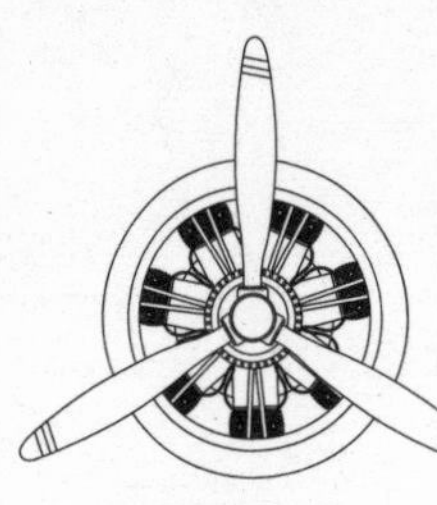

Slitherlink I

Mission 45: Draw a loop past every non-zero number

Briefing:

Connect some of the dots to draw a single loop, using only horizontal and vertical lines. The loop must pass by each given clue the stated number of times. So, for example, three sides of a '3' clue must be visited by the loop. Unless you are already familiar with the puzzle, you'll need to experiment and learn quickly to successfully solve it.

2	1	2	1	1	2	3	3
1	2		2				1
2	2			3		3	3
3	1	0	2		2		
		2		1	3	1	3
0	2		0			3	2
2				1		1	2
3	1	1	2	3	2	2	2

Slitherlink 2

Mission 46: Draw a loop past every number

Briefing:

Connect some of the dots to draw a single loop, using only horizontal and vertical lines. The loop must pass by each given clue the stated number of times. So, for example, three sides of a '3' clue must be visited by the loop.

3	3	2	2	2	3	2	3
2			3		1		3
2		2		3	1	1	2
	2		3			3	3
3	2			2		2	
3	2	2	3		1		2
2		3		2			1
2	1	2	2	3	3	3	3

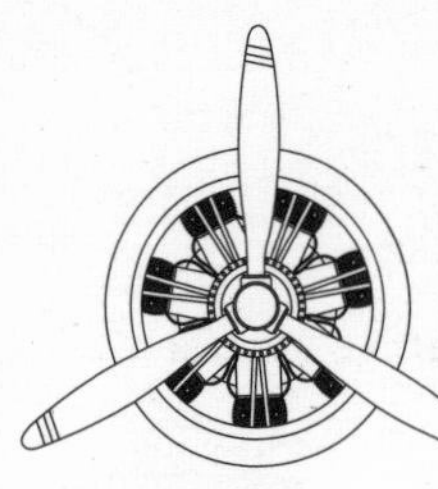

Slitherlink 3

Mission 47: Draw a loop past every non-zero number

Briefing:

Connect some of the dots to draw a single loop, using only horizontal and vertical lines. The loop must pass by each given clue the stated number of times. So, for example, three sides of a '3' clue must be visited by the loop.

3	3	2	3	2	2	2			
2		1		2		0	2	2	
2	3		2		0		0	3	
2			2	3		3	2		
1	1		2	3	2	2	2		3
3		3	1	2	1	1		3	2
		1	2		1	2			1
	0	1		1		2		0	1
	0	0	3		3		0		2
			3	1	2	1	2	2	1

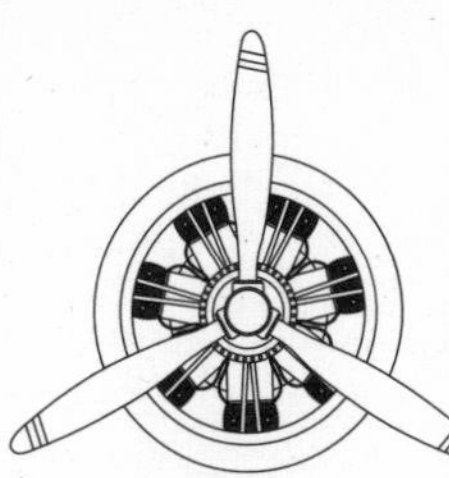

Slitherlink 4

Mission 48: Draw a loop past every non-zero number

Briefing:

Connect some of the dots to draw a single loop, using only horizontal and vertical lines. The loop must pass by each given clue the stated number of times. So, for example, three sides of a '3' clue must be visited by the loop.

3	3	3	3	3	3	3	2	2	3
1		0			1		3		3
1	1		2	3					3
3		3	2	1		3			2
1			0	0	2		2	3	
	3	2		2	3	2			3
2			3		1	2	2		3
1					1	2		1	2
2		0		3			1		1
1	2	2	2	2	2	1	2	3	3

CHAPTER 2

SURVIVAL SKILLS

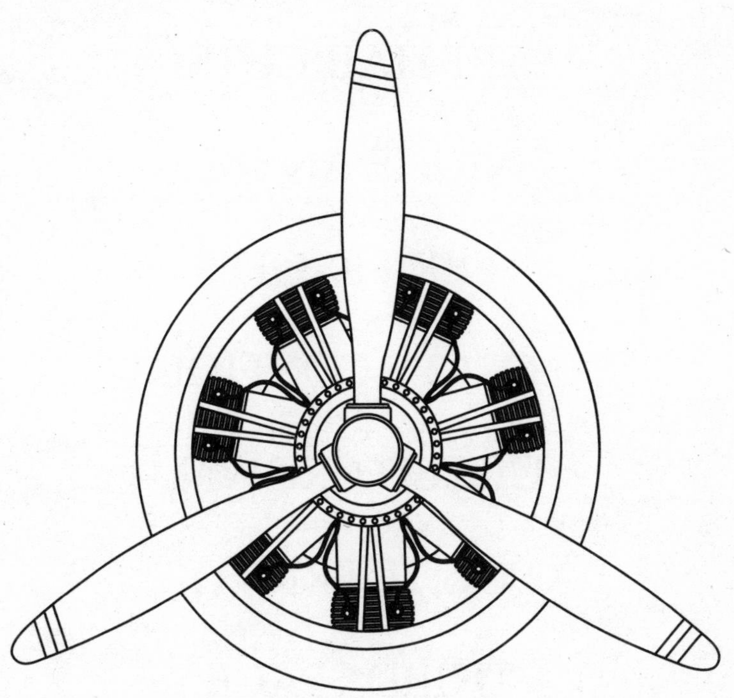

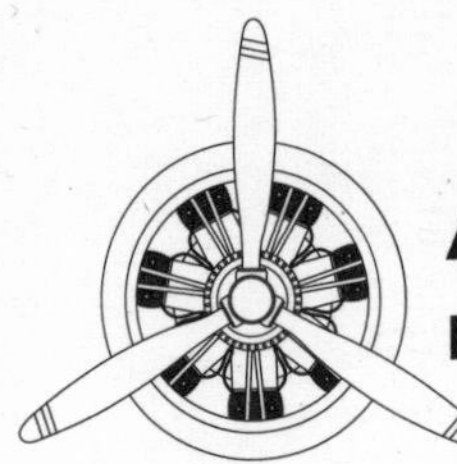

Aviation Occupations

Mission 1: Reveal the hidden aviation job titles

Briefing:

Can you reveal the names of eleven occupations in the field of aviation by unscrambling the anagrams below? Note that the spacing may not match that of the original words.

GENE REIN

VARIANT GO

APT HAIRCUTS

NICHE ANTIC

TERRIFIC OFFS

FORCES CONFIDE

URGED CROWN

POLITE FRIGHT

THIRD SPACE

CHIC NAME

DAFT NIGHT TALENT

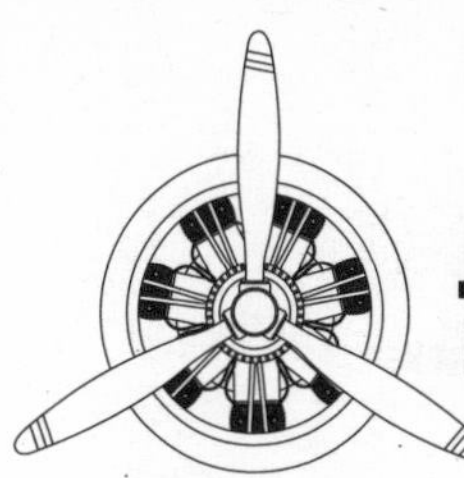

Job Search

Mission 2: Find the job titles as quickly as possible

Briefing:

Complete the mission on the opposite page first. Once you have revealed the names, can you now locate them in the grid below? The occupations may read forward or backward in any direction, including diagonally.

F	L	I	G	H	T	A	T	T	E	N	D	A	N	T
F	Z	Q	E	Y	Q	Q	E	O	C	X	I	K	A	R
K	V	H	B	G	J	Y	W	I	P	N	S	C	O	B
F	H	L	D	X	V	Q	N	F	A	P	P	T	G	F
I	L	N	H	I	W	A	X	I	V	S	A	A	R	P
R	U	K	S	J	H	G	C	S	A	G	T	N	O	A
S	E	I	I	C	Q	I	W	F	I	W	C	X	U	R
T	X	N	E	B	N	F	F	V	I	W	H	Q	N	A
O	U	M	G	H	W	X	A	Z	K	T	E	N	D	C
F	H	F	C	I	U	N	X	P	V	S	R	I	C	H
F	S	E	C	O	N	D	O	F	F	I	C	E	R	U
I	T	P	K	R	R	E	D	K	N	V	R	G	E	T
C	C	K	J	Z	L	K	E	Z	E	P	F	B	W	I
E	I	F	I	G	H	T	E	R	P	I	L	O	T	S
R	M	X	E	F	I	J	O	G	V	S	W	P	E	T

Mini Codeword

Mission 3: Crack the code by solving the clues

Briefing:

Reveal five aviation terms by using the clues to crack the number code, in which each letter has been replaced by a number. A grid is provided beneath for you to keep track of your deductions.

Add additional combustible

4	11	2	7	11	14

Become airborne

9	1	13	11		5	2	2

Stop between two flights

14	1	3	5	10	11	4

Speed in a given direction

10	11	14	5	6	8	9	3

Area of pressure difference, often causing turbulence

1	8	4		12	5	6	13	11	9

Keep track of your deductions here:

1	2	3	4	5	6	7

8	9	10	11	12	13	14

Aviation Phrases

Mission 4: Reveal the anagrammed sayings

Briefing:

Can you restore these six phrases which all have their origins in aviation? The letters in each word have been rearranged into a different order, and a clue to the meaning of each phrase is provided immediately beneath.

AADEH FO EHT CERUV
Forward-thinking and progressive

ABLLS OT EHT ALLW
Full throttle

HPSU EHT EEELNOPV
Test the limits of possibility

AEKT EHT AFKL
Endure criticism

LFY YB EHT AEST FO ORUY ANPST
Act or operate using instinct

AGIMNNW
A supportive associate

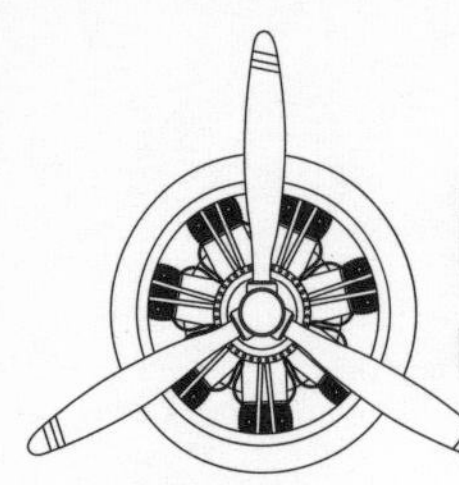

Encoded Quotes

Mission 5: Decode the letter-shifted quotes

Briefing:

Decode these sentences to reveal six quotes about aviation, by shifting each letter backward by a fixed number of positions in the alphabet, wrapping around from A to Z. For example, the text CXKCVG, shifted back by two, would become AVIATE. Each quote uses a different shift, of one to six places.

EZMEXMSR MW TVSSJ XLEX, KMZIR XLI AMPP, AI LEZI XLI GETEGMXC XS EGLMIZI XLI MQTSWWMFPI

FANFYNTS NX YMJ GWFSHM TK JSLNSJJWNSL YMFY NX QJFXY KTWLNANSL TK RNXYFPJX

UIF BFSPQMBOF IBT VOWFJMFE GPS VT UIF USVF GBDF PG UIF FBSUI

VJG CKT KU VJG QPNA RNCEG HTGG HTQO RTGLWFKEGU

VORUZY ZGQK TU YVKIOGR PUE OT CGRQOTM. VORUZY ROQK LREOTM

WKHUH'V QR VXFK WKLQJ DV D QDWXUDO-ERUQ SLORW

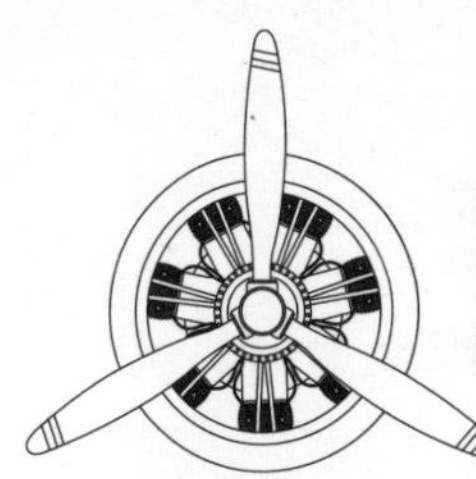

Encoded Speakers

Mission 6: Decode and match the speakers

Briefing:

You must have completed the previous mission first. Once you have decoded the quotes on the opposite page, can you match each one to the name of the person to whom it is attributed? The six encrypted names are given below, and the size of shift used to encrypt each name is the same as that used to encrypt their quotation opposite.

TKOR GXSYZXUTM

IHHMI VMGOIRFEGOIV

DGUUKG EQNGOCP

KWJJRFS IDXTS

FKXFN BHDJHU

BOUPJOF EF TBJOU-FYVQFSZ

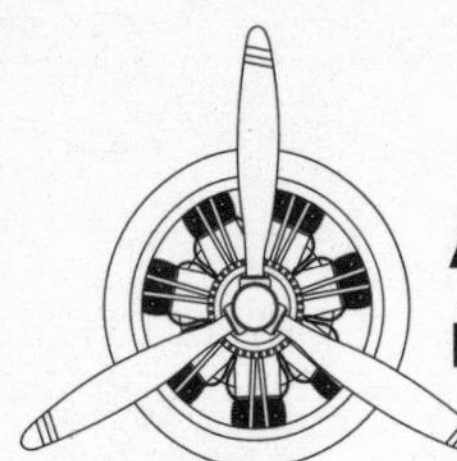

Aviation Physics I

Mission 7: Solve the clues to reveal the physics terms

Briefing:

Can you fill in the gaps below with words related to the physics of aviation by solving the clues on the left? The final letter of each entry is the same as the initial letter of the following entry, as indicated by the arrows. Underlines indicate the number of letters needed for each word.

Force that acts to slow down a plane _ _ _ _

Attractive force _ _ _ _ _ _ _ _

Movement about a vertical axis _ _ _

Downward force related to mass _ _ _ _ _ _

Propulsive, forward force _ _ _ _ _ _

Rear part of a wing _ _ _ _ _ _ _ _ _ _ _ _ _ _

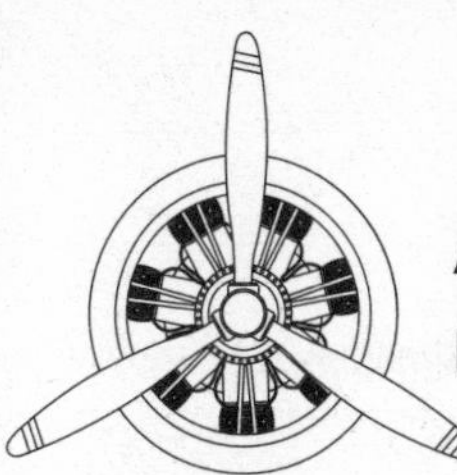

Aviation Physics 2

Mission 8: Solve further clues for more physics terms

Briefing:

Try this puzzle, using the same rules as on the opposite page, by solving these clues to fill in the gaps below. The final letter of each entry is the same as the initial letter of the following entry, as indicated by the arrows. Underlines indicate the number of letters needed for each word.

Steepness of an angle relative to the horizontal axis _ _ _ _ _

Operated using liquid _ _ _ _ _ _ _ _ _ _

Slightly convex shape, required for wings _ _ _ _ _ _

Movement about a plane's longitudinal axis _ _ _ _

Upward force needed for flight _ _ _ _

Unsteady movement within a fluid _ _ _ _ _ _ _ _ _ _ _

Mixed Clouds

Mission 9: Unscramble the cloud-related terms

Briefing:

Can you restore these six words used to describe clouds, which have each had their letters arranged into alphabetical order? All of the solutions consist of one word.

CLMSUUU

ACEILLNRTU

BIMNSU

ALOPR

AFIMORRSTT

EGINORTW

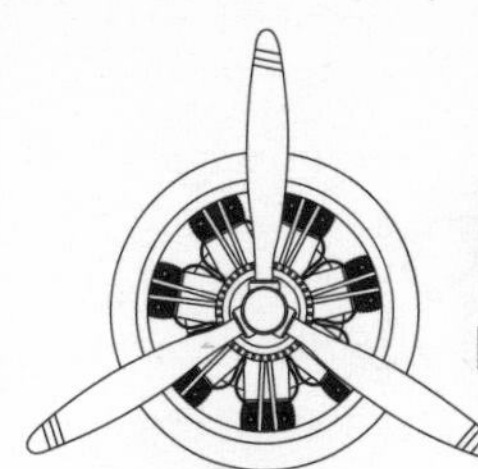

Fragmented Clouds

Mission 10: Reassemble the cloud fragments

Briefing:

Can you reconstruct five words used to describe clouds from the pieces below? Eah word has been split into fragments, and the fragments listed in alphabetical order. All solutions consist of one word.

AN	OR
EL	RO
FU	ROT
LF	SHE
LL	VIL
NN	

Hidden Meteorology

Mission 11: Find the hidden meteorological words

Briefing:

Can you find six meteorological terms hidden in the sentences below? For example, the word 'wind' is hidden in the sentence 'They have twin daughters'. One word is hidden in each sentence.

Will they bring us to the entrance?

We can put the autopilot system on soon.

There's no way we'll be able to get there now.

We're just doing our final safety checks in the aisle; ETA into Boston is 11am local time.

Having safely landed, I will now eat here.

Is it a bird? Is it a plane? Is it a flying dinosaur? Or a hang glider?

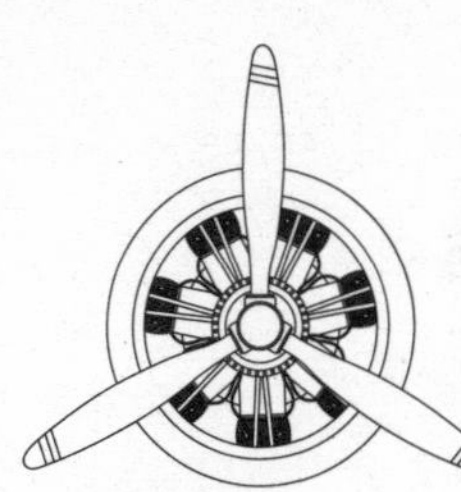

Hidden Aviation

Mission 12: Find the hidden aviation words

Briefing:

Can you find five aviation terms hidden in the sentences below? For example, the word 'flight' is hidden in the sentence 'I want to know i<u>f light</u> clothing is sensible'. Each sentence contains one hidden word, and a clue to that word is given beneath.

I don't think I could afford the repairs I'd eventually need on that vehicle.

Clue: Beyond customs and passport control

You can't take more than 10 cl. I'm being serious.

Clue: An ascent

You need to speak, not shout, over the tannoy.

Clue: Unit of measurement

There's a main meal and side dish for all First Class passengers.

Clue: Opposite of one of the other answers on this page

It's going to be awful if Terminal 5 is really busy.

Clue: Upward force

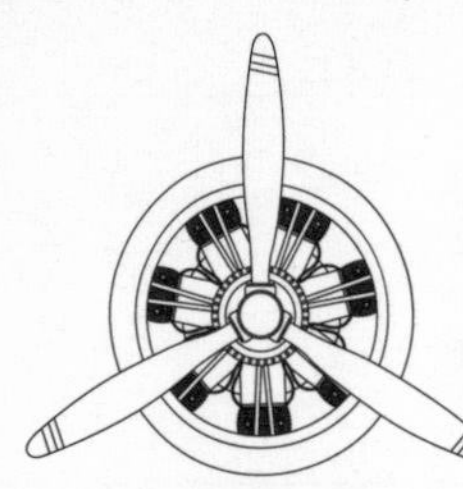

Hidden Plane Parts

Mission 13: Locate the hidden aeroplane parts

Briefing:

Can you find six parts of an aeroplane hidden in the sentences below? For example, the word 'wing' is hidden in the sentence 'I want to win gold medals'. One word is hidden in each sentence.

I don't know how he electrocuted himself.

There's no service flying out to Toronto today.

We dropped all the way down and got a great view of the Grand Canyon.

Do you have a pin in your lapel? Eva tore a button off my coat and I need to disguise it.

Everybody ok? Everyone sitting comfortably?

Make sure the catering staff use lager instead of ale in the officers' mess.

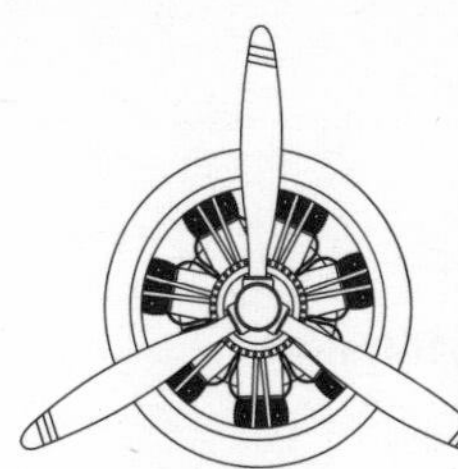

Aviation Links

Mission 14: Find each hidden link between the words

Briefing:

Place a word in each gap below to form two further words per line, one by joining with the preceding word, and the second by joining with the following word. For example, 'GRID _ _ _ _ SMITH' could be filled in with the word LOCK, to create 'GRIDLOCK' and 'LOCKSMITH'. In the puzzle itself, one word in each new pair will be linked to aviation.

TORN _ _ _ RATION

INK _ _ _ LINER

COCK _ _ _ FALL

WING _ _ _ POWER

AIR _ _ _ _ LIGHT

SLEDGE _ _ _ _ _ _ HEAD

Missing Phrases

Mission 15: Solve the clues and find the hidden link

Briefing:

Solve the clues below to reveal six idioms, such as 'over the moon'. The number of letters in each solution is given. Once you have revealed the idioms, can you identify something that connects them all?

Dreamily happy (2, 5, 4)

Feeling unwell (5, 3, 7)

Fit and well (5, 2, 4)

Trivial event prompting a disproportionate reaction (5, 2, 1, 6)

Refuse an invitation, with the implication of accepting it later (4, 1, 4, 5)

Behave recklessly (5, 7, 2, 3, 4)

Coded Communication

Mission 16: Decrypt the concealed details

Briefing:

You receive the following notes, which you have been told contain the concealed surname of a contact you need to meet and the country where they are located. Can you crack the codes and reveal the name and country?

Surname

Bravo, comrade.

Current mission over Lima still active, await instruction.

You will likely be flying an Alpha jet model; pending confirmation.

Personal effects are limited to one kilo per pilot.

Let me echo the sentiments of our commanders in congratulating you thus far.

Country

4th November

Time to get photos. Carry out mission as instructed.

Don't turn back unless you hear from the maestro (me) or HQ.

Trust your wingman now; his key objective is to cover you.

This will be the final phase of this mission.

Your code name: Yankee Doodle.

(NB You will need NATO on your side)

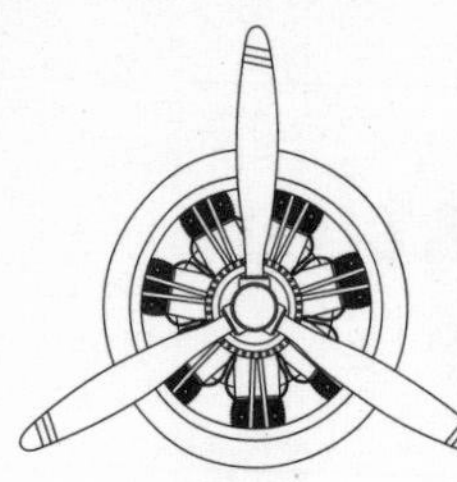

Missing Words

Mission 17: Solve the clues and find the hidden link

Briefing:

Can you solve the clues below to reveal six words related to aviation? The number of letters in each solution is given. Once you have solved the clues, can you find the specific aviation connection which links the solutions together?

A single piece of grass (5)

Slides on its tyres, as a car (5)

Ursine foot (4, 3)

Be buoyant in water (5)

Landing stage (7)

A word that sounds like a 'duty schedule' (5)

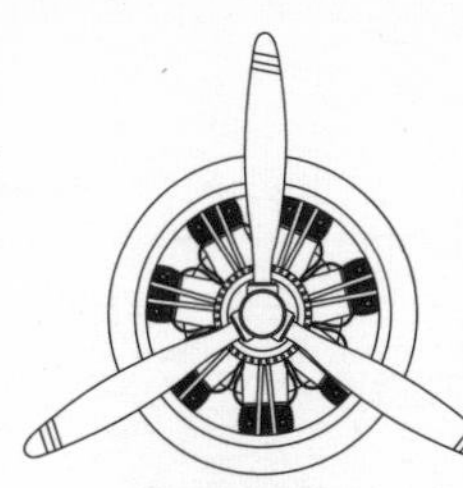

Word Circle 1

Mission 18: Find words within the circle

Briefing:

Solve these clues using only letters found within the word circle below. Each word must use three or more of the letters in the circle, and must include the centre letter. Letters can't be used more times than they appear in the circle, and the number of letters in each word is given. Once you have solved the clues, see how many other words you can find.

Atmosphere; where flight occurs (3)

Related to birds (5)

Letter T in NATO Phonetic Alphabet (5)

By way of (3)

A pilot, for example (7)

Someone who finds the way (9)

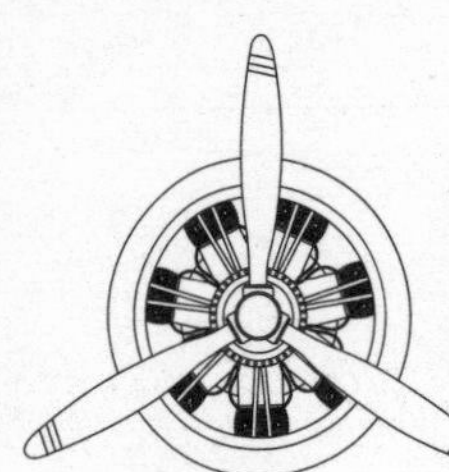

Word Circle 2

Mission 19: Find words within the circle

Briefing:

Solve these clues using only letters found within the word circle below. Each word must use three or more of the letters in the circle, and must include the centre letter. Letters can't be used more times than they appear in the circle, and the number of letters in each word is given. Once you have solved the clues, see how many other words you can find.

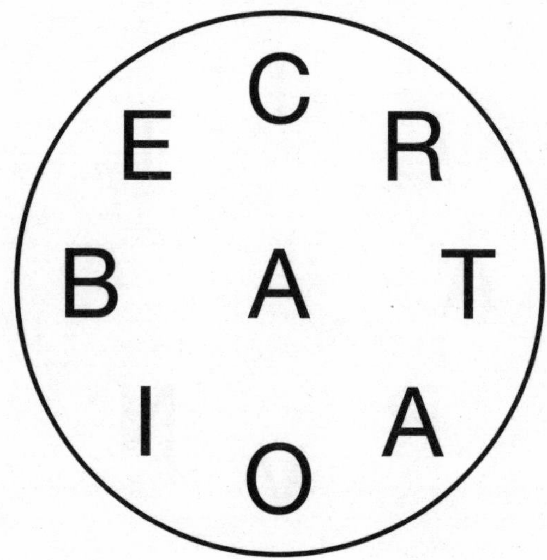

Fighter pilot with several confirmed successes (3)

Terminate a task or mission, often prematurely (5)

Position adopted in emergency (5)

Capital of Egypt (5)

Flying stunt; venomous snake (5)

Related to stunt flying (9)

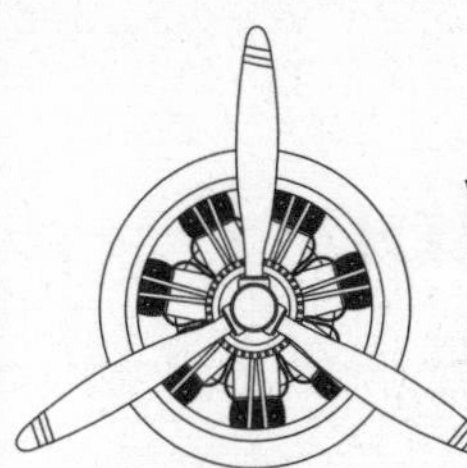

Word Circle 3

Mission 20: Find words within the circle

Briefing:

Solve these clues using only letters found within the word circle below. Each word must use three or more of the letters in the circle, and must include the centre letter. Letters can't be used more times than they appear in the circle, and the number of letters in each word is given. Once you have solved the clues, see how many other words you can find.

Prefix used in naming middle-altitude clouds (4)

Rear end of a plane (4)

Related to the sun; renewable energy (5)

Wind local to southern France (7)

Russian mountain range (5)

Machine used in aviation training (9)

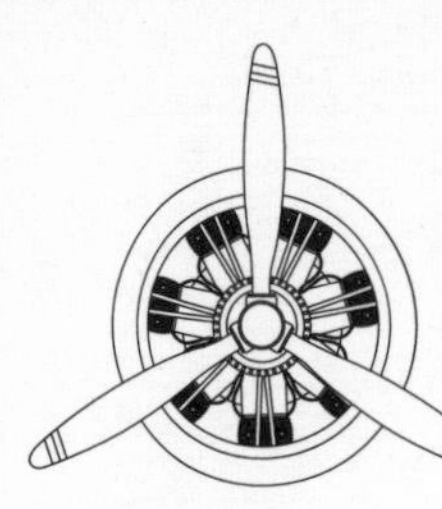

Speed and Navigation I

Mission 21: Complete these flight calculations

Briefing:

Answer the following questions about flight speed, time and distance. Distance is measured in nautical miles (nm), and speed is measured in knots (kn), with 1 kn equivalent to 1 nm per hour. For reference, a nautical mile is approximately 1.15 miles in length.

1. Which of these flights will travel at the greatest average speed?

   a. A 14 nm flight with a duration of 36 minutes

   b. An 18 nm flight with a duration of 42 minutes

   c. A 15 nm flight with a duration of 30 minutes

2. At what average speed would each of the following flights need to travel, to be able to set off from London at midday GMT and land at their destination at 3am GMT, to the nearest knot? The distances are an approximation of the real-world distance.

   a. A flight to New York, a distance of 3,000 nm

   b. A flight to Johannesburg, a distance of 5,000 nm

   c. A flight to Vancouver, a distance of 4,000 nm

   d. A flight to Buenos Aires, a distance of 6,000 nm

3. A flight leaves London Heathrow at 9am GMT, travelling to Shanghai (GMT+8), a distance of approximately 4,900 nm. If the plane travels at an average speed of 700 kn, at what local time does it arrive in Shanghai?

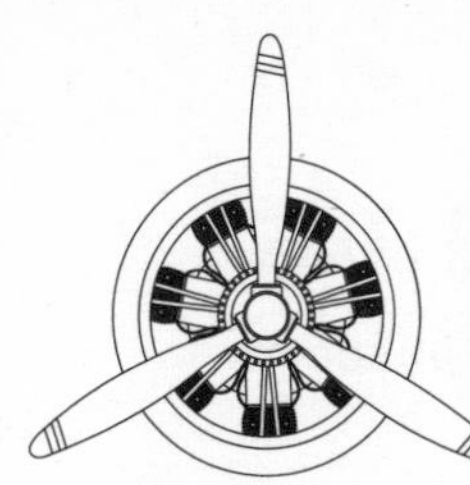

Speed and Navigation 2

Mission 22: Complete these further flight calculations

Briefing:

Answer these additional questions about flight speed, time and distance. It may be helpful to refer to the mission opposite for a definition of knots and nautical miles.

1. Two flights leave Manchester airport. One is travelling to Seattle, the other to Mumbai. Taking into account the following figures, which plane will land first?

   a. The Seattle flight is travelling at an average speed of 500 kn, to cover a distance of approximately 3,300 nm

   b. The Mumbai flight is travelling at an average speed of 600 kn, to cover a distance of approximately 3,900 nm

2. A flight leaves Edinburgh at 10am GMT and lands in Toronto at 1pm local time. If the distance travelled is approximately 2,800 nm, and the plane was travelling at an average speed of 400 kn, what is the current time difference between Edinburgh and Toronto?

3. Two planes leave London Gatwick at 12pm GMT. The first is travelling to Minsk (GMT+3), and the second to Moscow (GMT+4). If both planes travel at an average speed of 600 kn, at what local times will they land in Minsk and Moscow respectively, given the following approximations?

   - The distance between London and Minsk is 1,000 nm
   - The distance between London and Moscow is 1,350 nm

Simple Loop I

Mission 23: Test your loop-finding instincts at speed

Briefing:

Draw a single loop which visits every unshaded square, without entering any square more than once. The loop can only travel horizontally and vertically. Try to do this as quickly as you can, using your instinct if necessary.

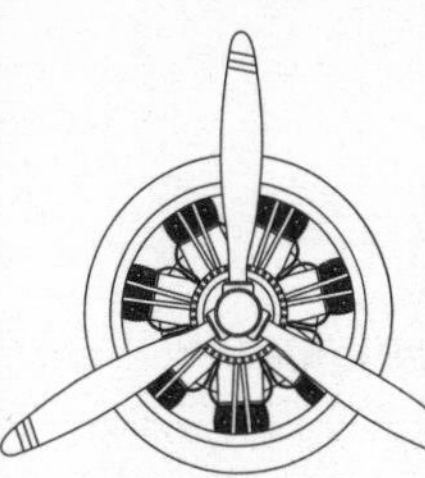

Simple Loop 2

Mission 24: Test your loop-finding instincts at speed

Briefing:

Draw a single loop which visits every unshaded square, without entering any square more than once. The loop can only travel horizontally and vertically. Try to do this as quickly as you can, using your instinct if necessary.

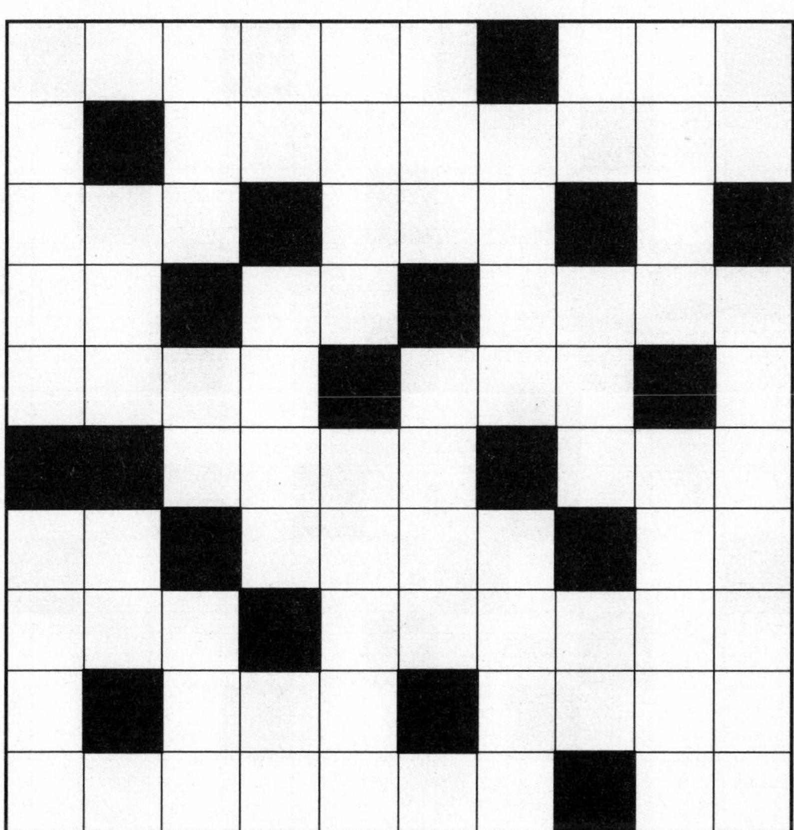

Simple Loop 3

Mission 25: Test your loop-finding instincts at speed

Briefing:

Draw a single loop which visits every unshaded square, without entering any square more than once. The loop can only travel horizontally and vertically. Try to do this as quickly as you can, using your instinct if necessary.

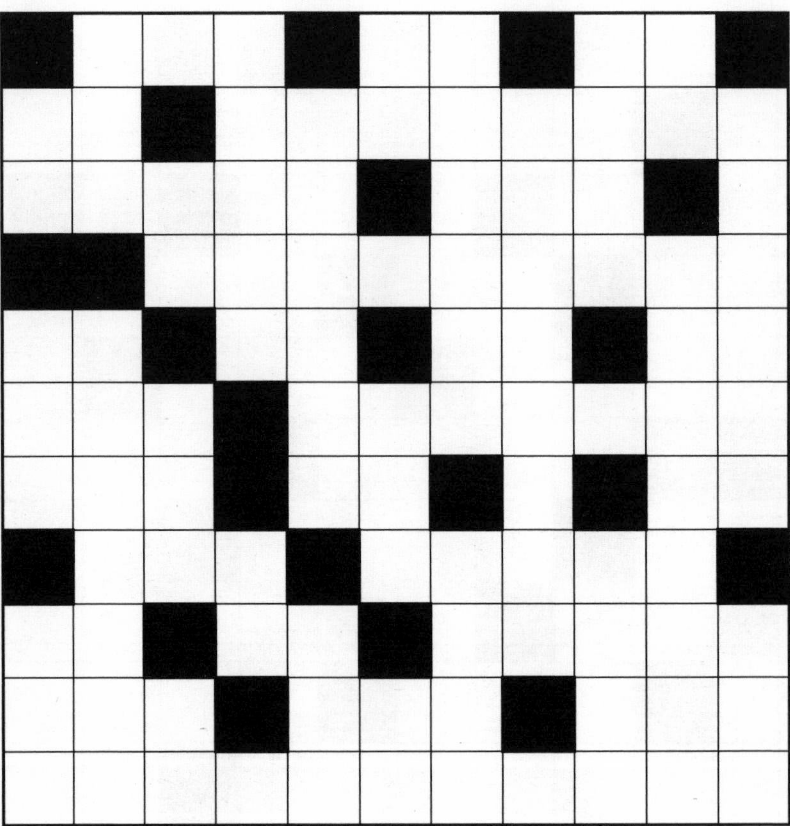

Simple Loop 4

Mission 26: Test your loop-finding instincts at speed

Briefing:

Draw a single loop which visits every unshaded square, without entering any square more than once. The loop can only travel horizontally and vertically. Try to do this as quickly as you can, using your instinct if necessary.

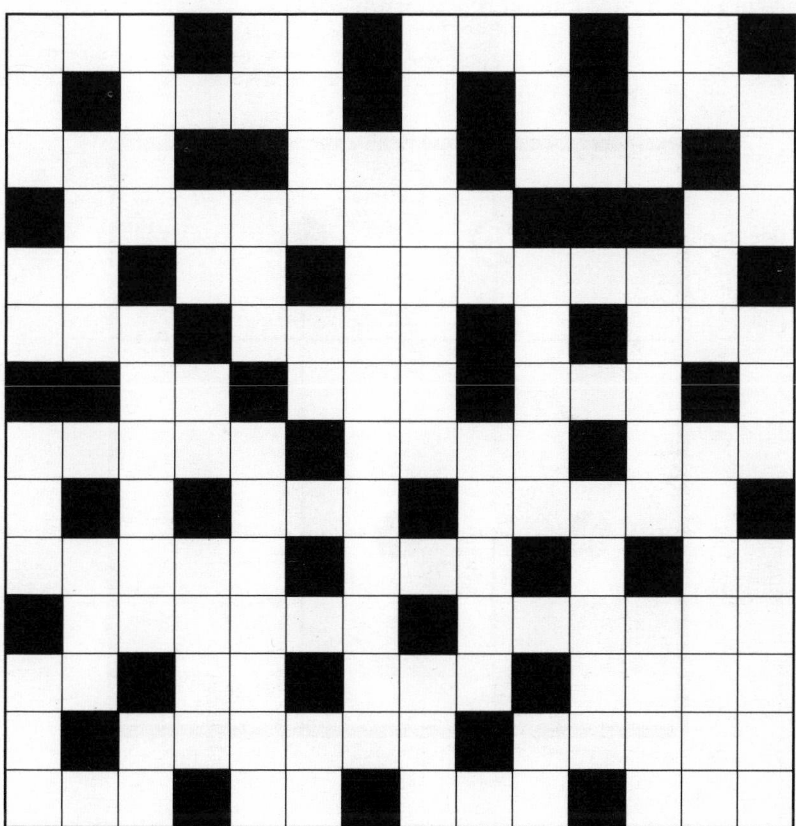

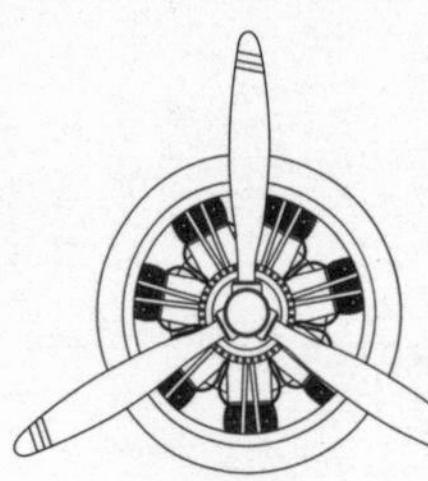

Kropki Square I

Mission 27: Test your reasoning at speed

Briefing:

See how quickly you can solve this puzzle, which involves placing just nine numbers. Specifically, place a number from 1 to 9 in each empty square, so no number repeats in the grid. Squares joined by a white dot contain consecutive digits, meaning that they have a numerical difference of 1. Squares joined by a black dot contain digits where one is exactly twice the value of the other. The absence of a dot means neither relationship applies.

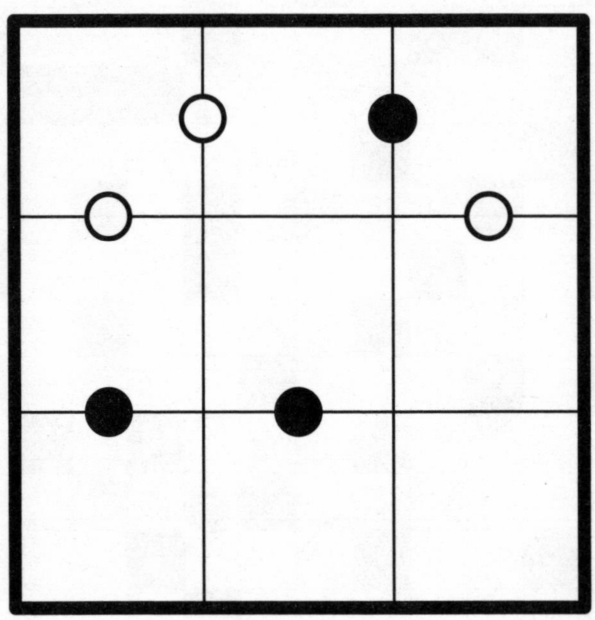

Kropki Square 2

Mission 28: Test your reasoning at speed

Briefing:

See how quickly you can solve this puzzle, which involves placing just nine numbers. Specifically, place a number from 1 to 9 in each empty square, so no number repeats in the grid. Squares joined by a white dot contain consecutive digits, meaning that they have a numerical difference of 1. Squares joined by a black dot contain digits where one is exactly twice the value of the other. The absence of a dot means neither relationship applies.

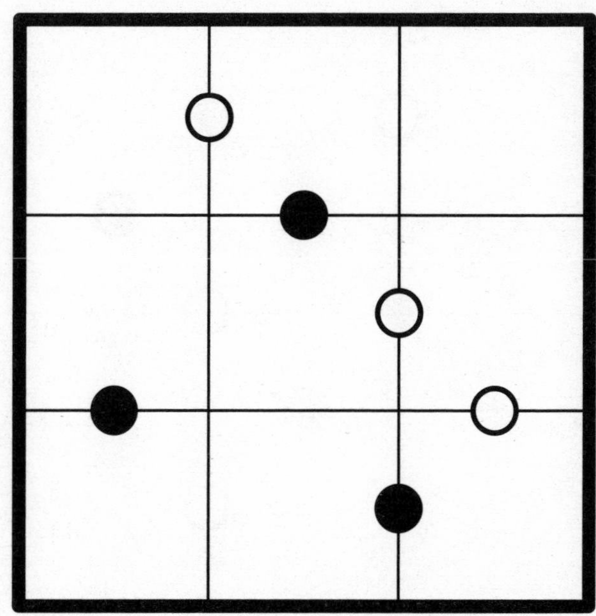

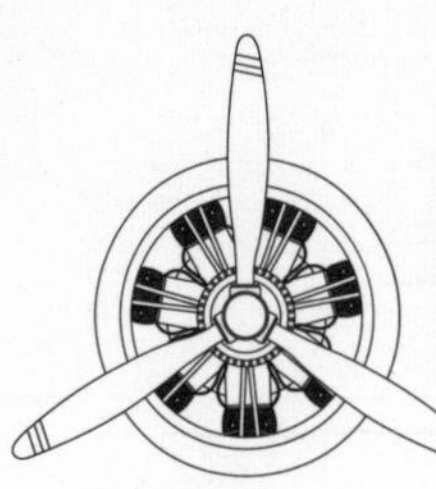

Kropki Square 3

Mission 29: Test your reasoning at speed

Briefing:

See how quickly you can solve this puzzle, which involves placing just nine numbers. Specifically, place a number from 1 to 9 in each empty square, so no number repeats in the grid. Squares joined by a white dot contain consecutive digits, meaning that they have a numerical difference of 1. Squares joined by a black dot contain digits where one is exactly twice the value of the other. The absence of a dot means neither relationship applies.

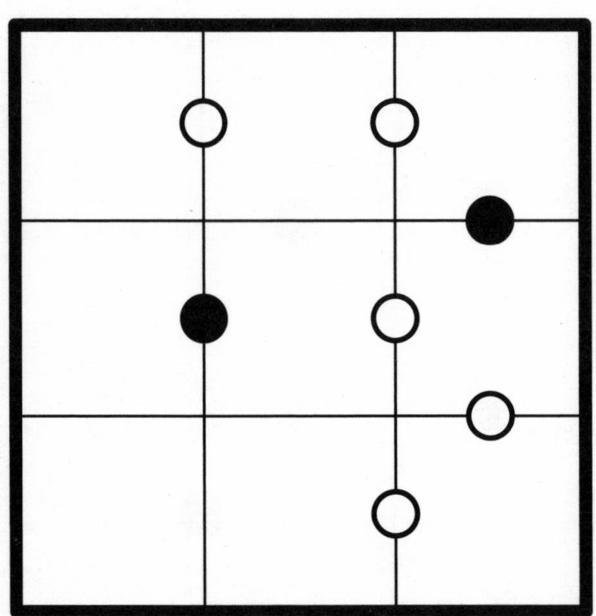

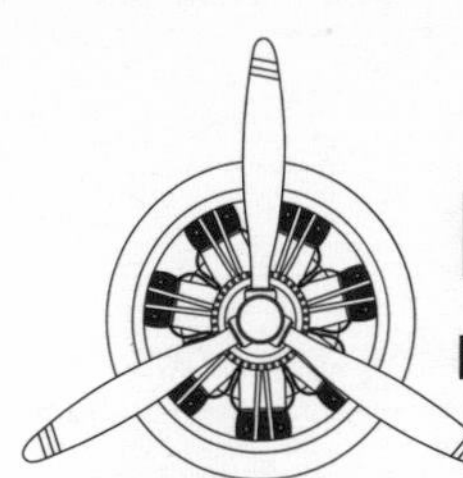

Kropki Square 4

Mission 30: Test your reasoning at speed

Briefing:

See how quickly you can solve this puzzle, which involves placing just nine numbers. Specifically, place a number from 1 to 9 in each empty square, so no number repeats in the grid. Squares joined by a white dot contain consecutive digits, meaning that they have a numerical difference of 1. Squares joined by a black dot contain digits where one is exactly twice the value of the other. The absence of a dot means neither relationship applies.

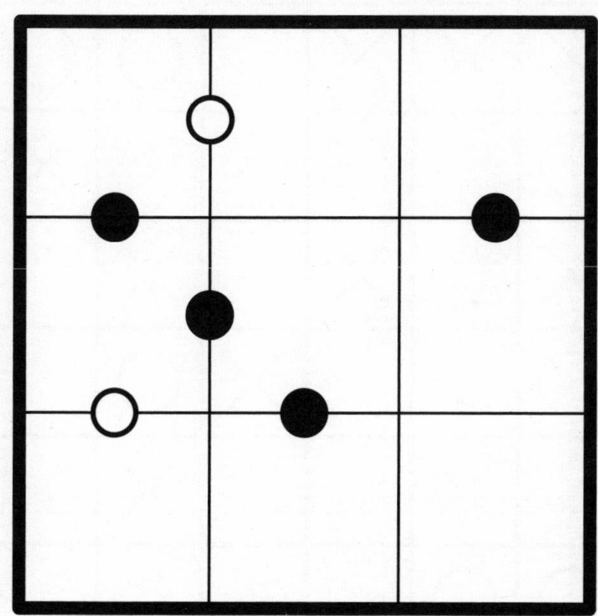

No Four in a Row 1

Mission 31: Complete the grid without forming any lines

Briefing:

Place either an 'X' or an 'O' in each empty square so that no lines of four or more 'X's or 'O's are formed in any direction, including diagonally.

				O	O		
	X	X	X		O	O	
O	O					X	X
X	X		X		X		X
O	O			X	O		
X		X			X		X
	O	O					
		O	O	O			

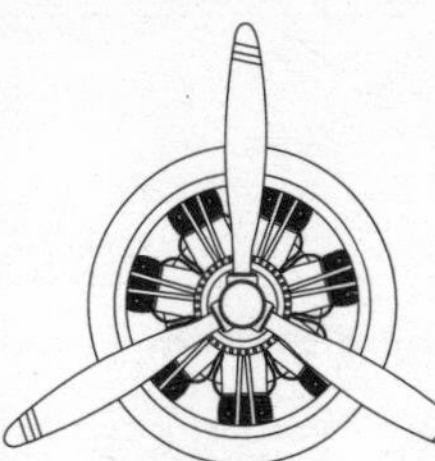

No Four in a Row 2

Mission 32: Complete the grid without forming any lines

Briefing:

Place either an 'X' or an 'O' in each empty square so that no lines of four or more 'X's or 'O's are formed in any direction, including diagonally.

			O	O			
	O			O		X	
X			O			O	
O	X	O				O	O
X				X			O
O	X					O	O
				O		X	
		X	X	X			

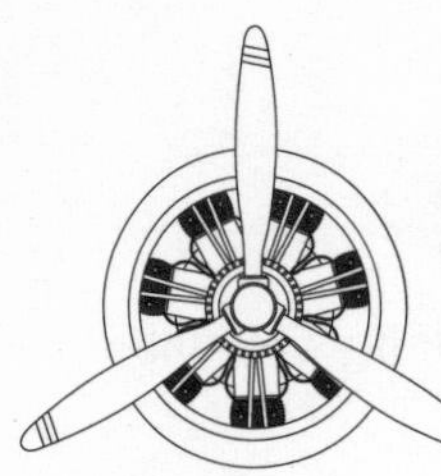

No Four in a Row 3

Mission 33: Complete the grid without forming any lines

Briefing:

Place either an 'X' or an 'O' in each empty square so that no lines of four or more 'X's or 'O's are formed in any direction, including diagonally.

			O			O			
		X	X			O	O		
				X				O	
	X	O	X	X	O	O		X	
X	O				X			X	X
		X	O	O		O		O	
							X	O	
	O	O		X		O			
		O	X				X		
			O		O				

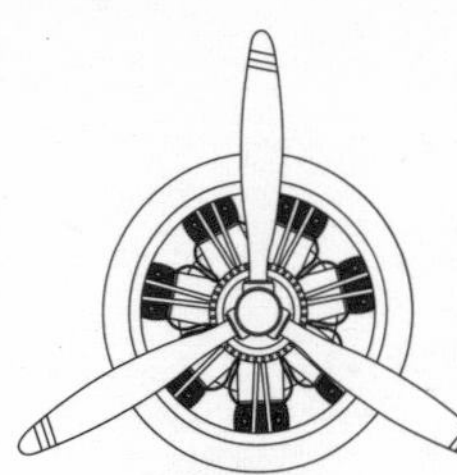

No Four in a Row 4

Mission 34: Complete the grid without forming any lines

Briefing:

Place either an 'X' or an 'O' in each empty square so that no lines of four or more 'X's or 'O's are formed in touching squares in any direction, including diagonally. The centre of the puzzle is hollow and should not have any symbol placed in it.

				O		O	O				
			X					X			
		O		O		O	X		X		
	X				O					O	
O	O	O								X	O
X		O	X					O	X	O	
X	X										O
O							O		O	O	O
		X	X	X						O	
			X	O			O	O	O		
							O				
				X			X				

Entries and Exits I

Mission 35: Find a route through every region

Briefing:

Draw a loop which visits every square. The loop should only travel horizontally or vertically, and cannot visit any square more than once. The loop can only enter and exit each bold-lined region once. These puzzles may require experimentation to solve, so are a great test of your concentration.

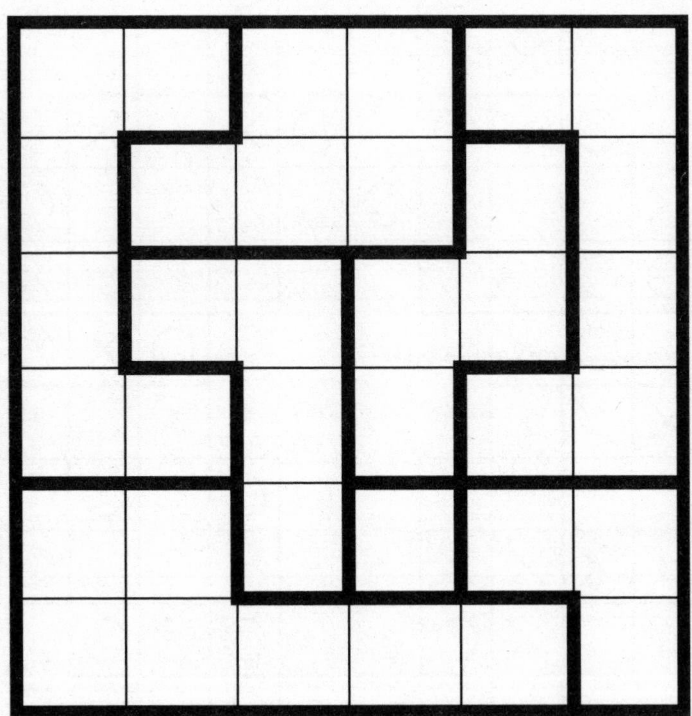

Entries and Exits 2

Mission 36: Find a route through every region

Briefing:

Draw a loop which visits every square. The loop should only travel horizontally or vertically, and cannot visit any square more than once. The loop can only enter and exit each bold-lined region once.

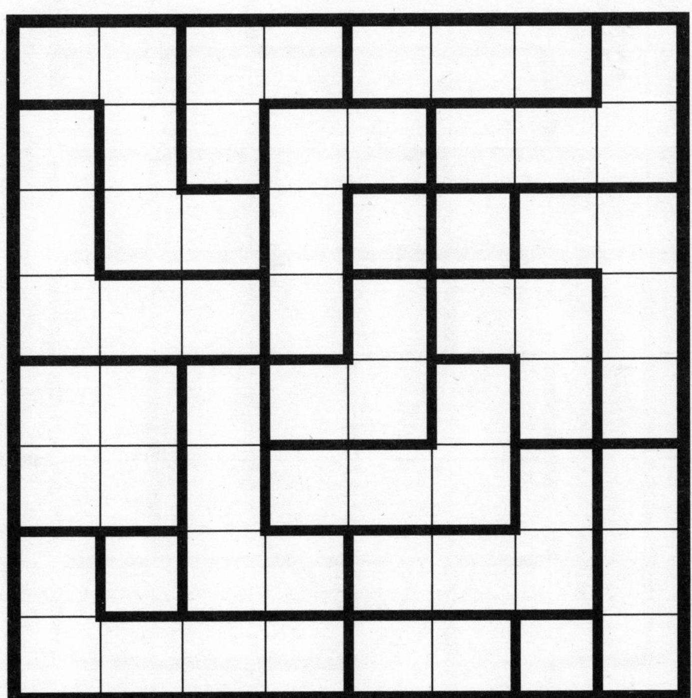

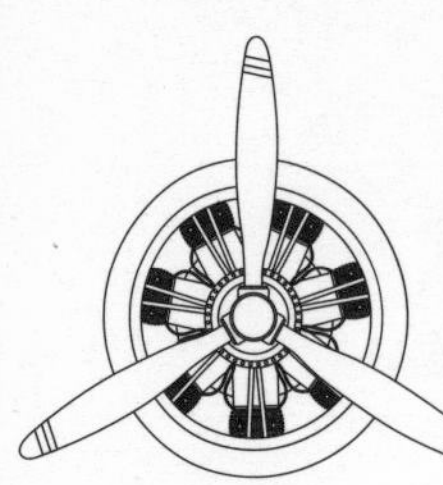

Entries and Exits 3

Mission 37: Find a route through every region

Briefing:

Draw a loop which visits every square. The loop should only travel horizontally or vertically, and cannot visit any square more than once. The loop can only enter and exit each bold-lined region once.

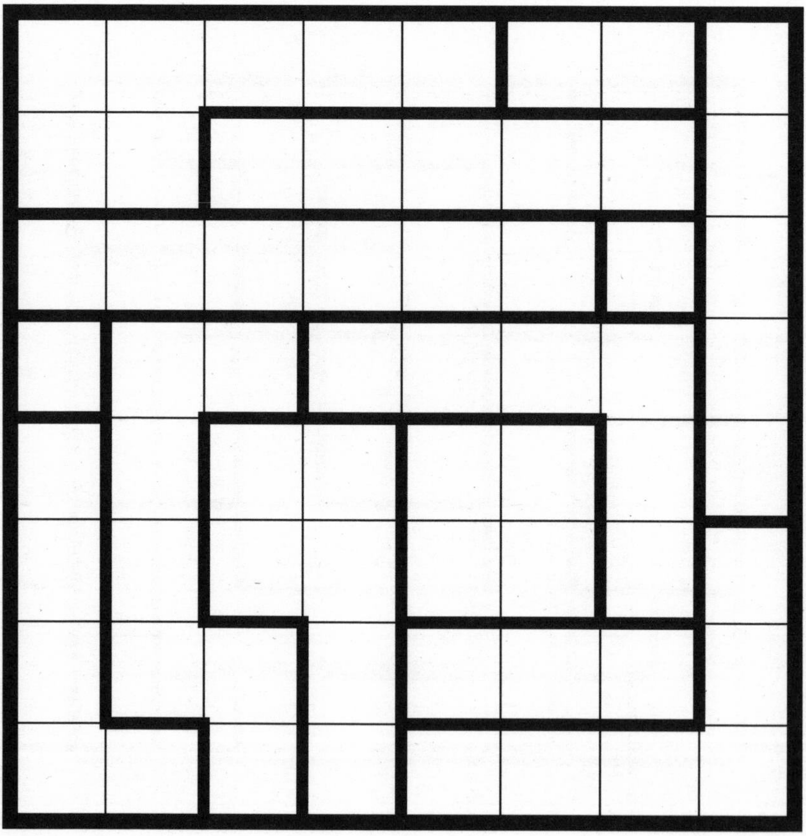

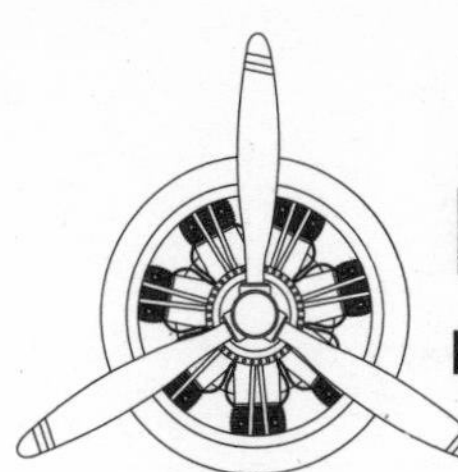

Entries and Exits 4

Mission 38: Find a route through every region

Briefing:

Draw a loop which visits every square. The loop should only travel horizontally or vertically, and cannot visit any square more than once. The loop can only enter and exit each bold-lined region once.

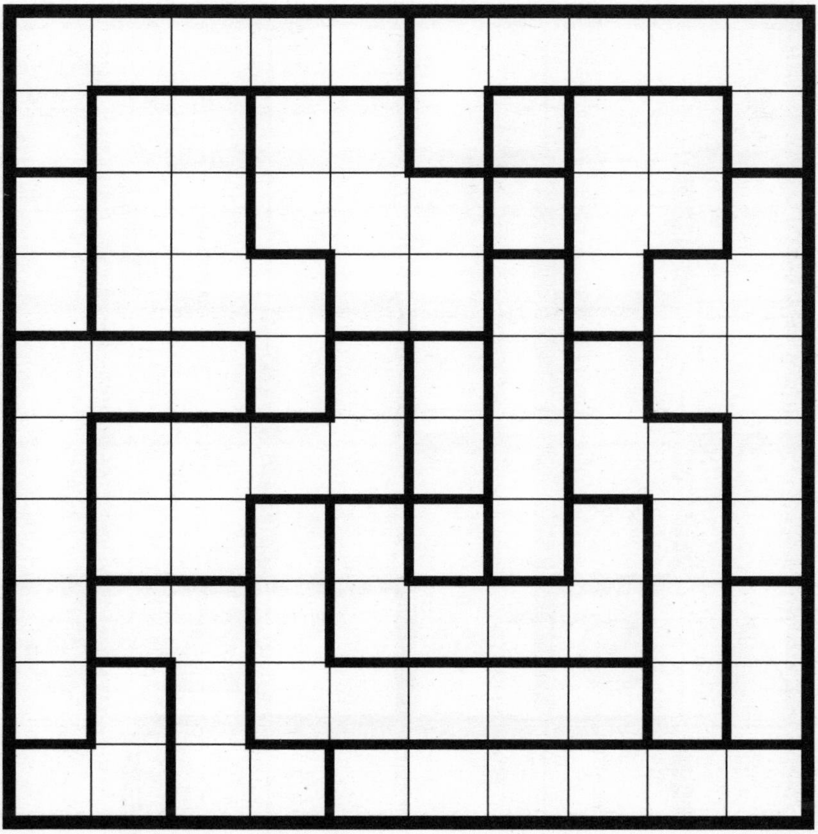

Shape Fit I

Mission 39: Place one of each shape into every region

Briefing:

Place circles and triangles so every bold-lined shape contains exactly one circle and exactly one triangle. Two identical shapes cannot be in touching grid cells – not even diagonally. To solve these puzzles you may need to make sensible guesses, and then keep track of the ensuing implications in case the guess fails.

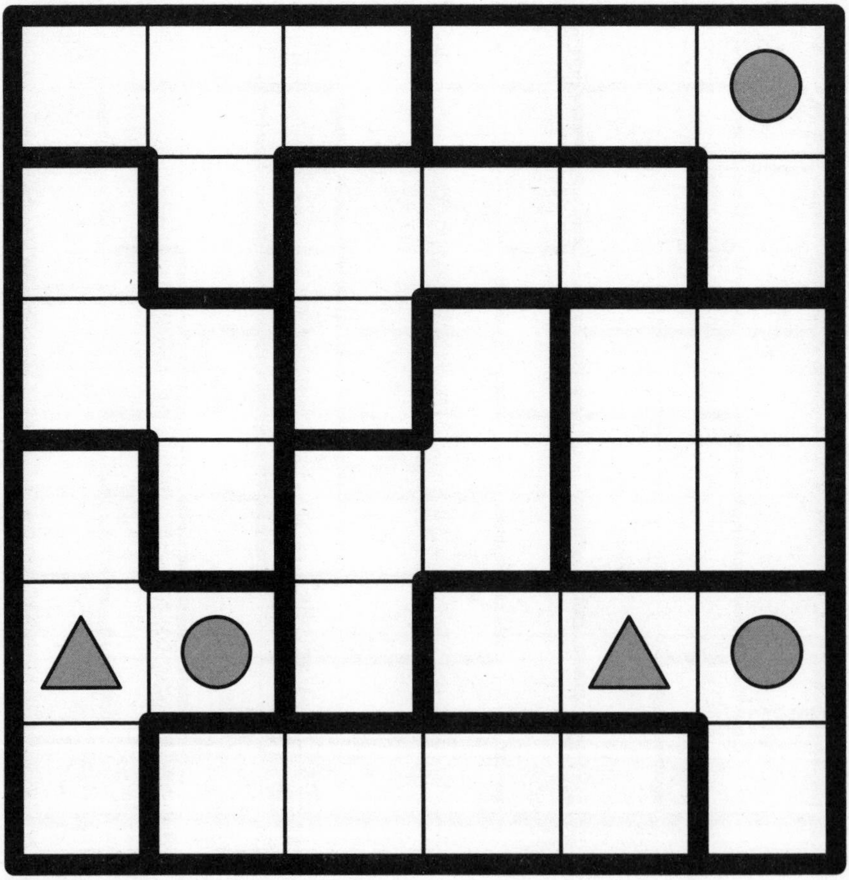

					●
▲	●			▲	●

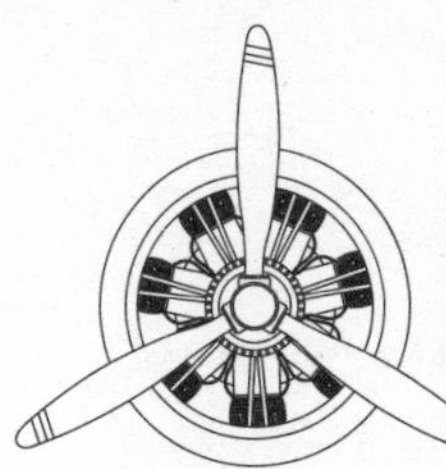

Shape Fit 2

Mission 40: Place one of each shape into every region

Briefing:

Place circles and triangles so every bold-lined shape contains exactly one circle and exactly one triangle. Two identical shapes cannot be in touching grid cells – not even diagonally.

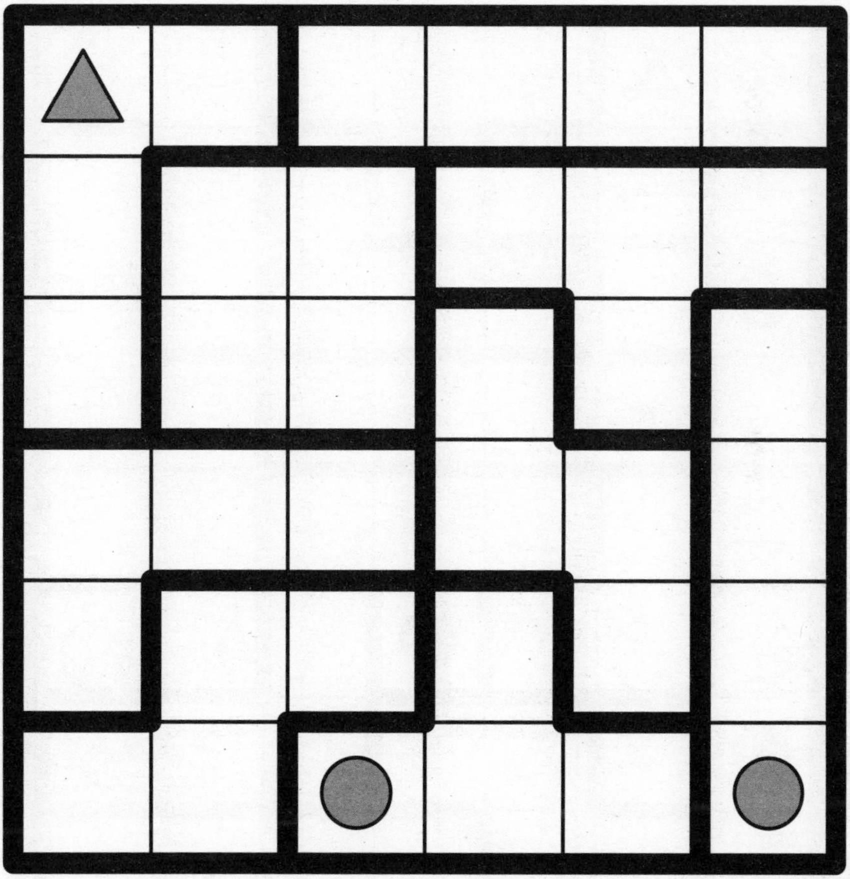

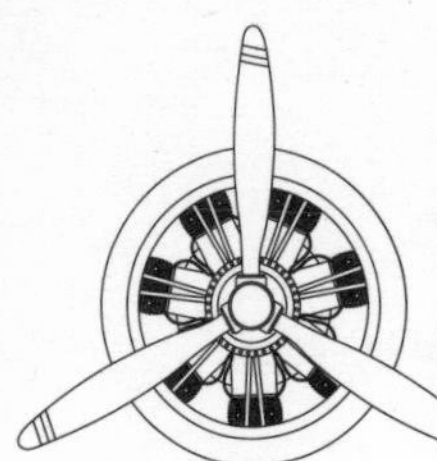

Shape Fit 3

Mission 41: Place one of each shape into every region

Briefing:

Place circles and triangles so every bold-lined shape contains exactly one circle and exactly one triangle. Two identical shapes cannot be in touching grid cells – not even diagonally.

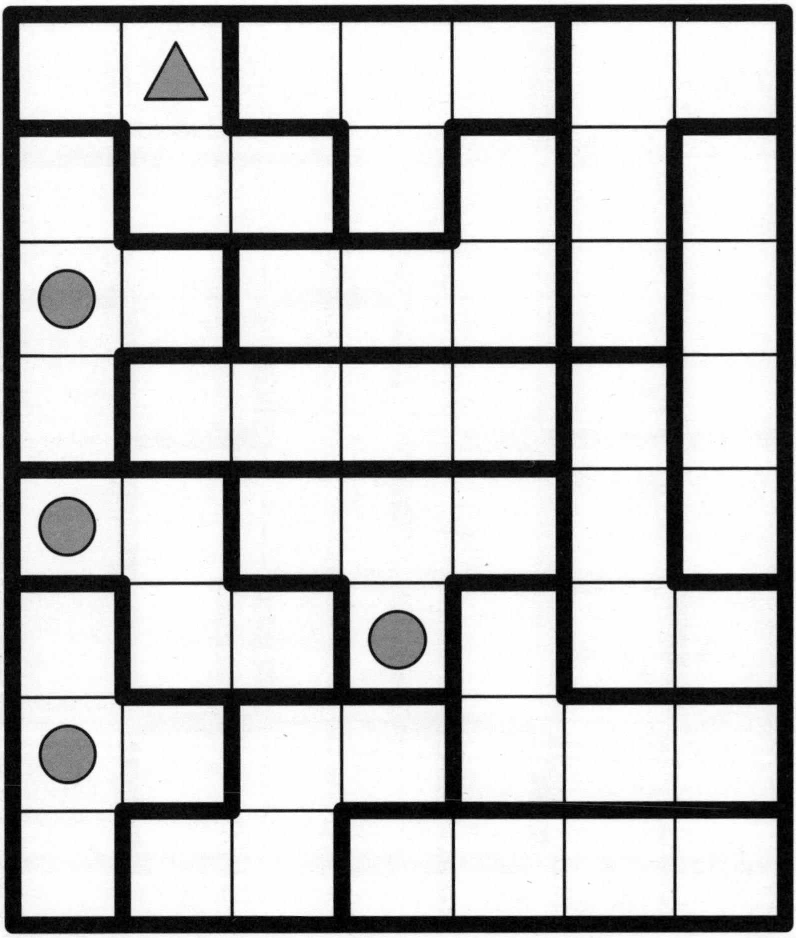

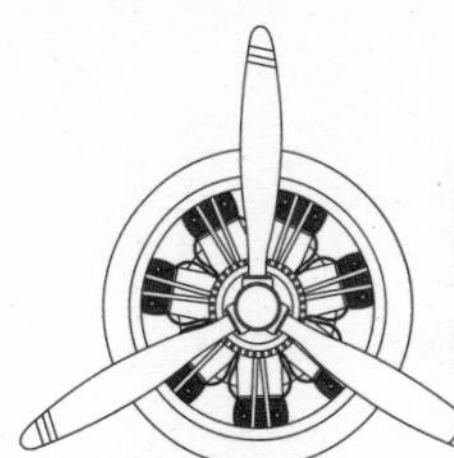

Shape Fit 4

Mission 42: Place one of each shape into every region

Briefing:

Place circles and triangles so every bold-lined shape contains exactly one circle and exactly one triangle. Two identical shapes cannot be in touching grid cells – not even diagonally.

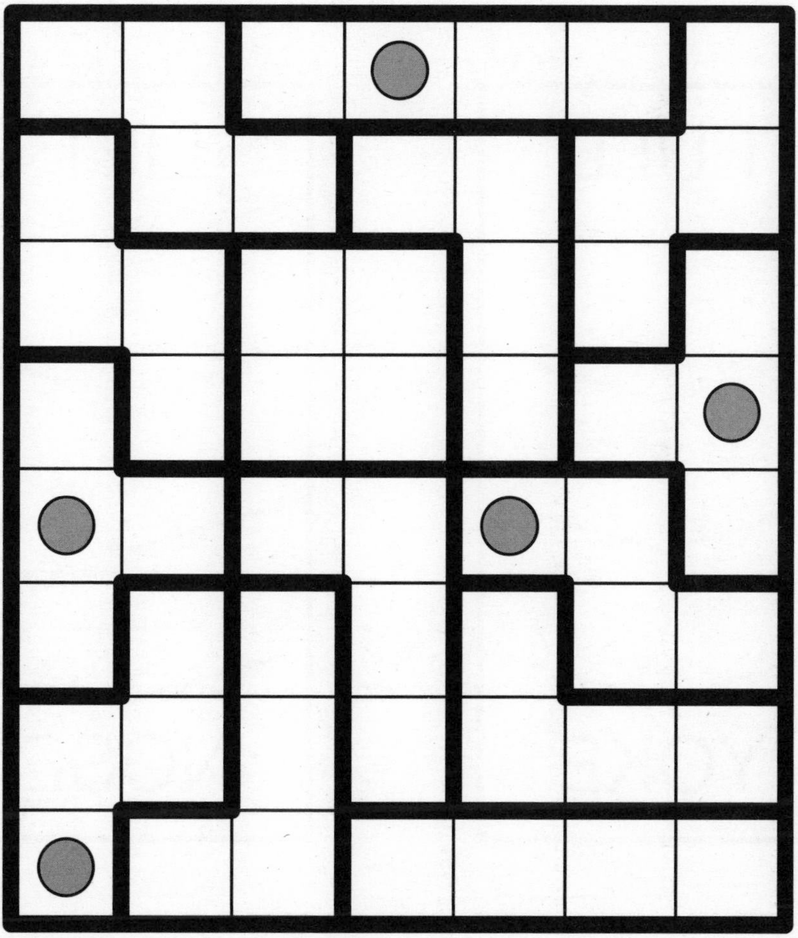

Word Chains I

Mission 43: Fill the missing links on each chain

Briefing:

Complete each of these word chains by writing a regular English word at each step. Each word must use the exact same letters in the same order as the word above, except with a single letter changed.

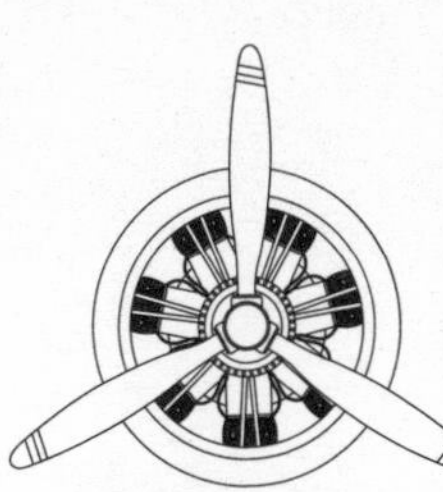

Word Chains 2

Mission 44: Fill the missing links on each chain

Briefing:

Complete each of these word chains by writing a regular English word at each step. Each word must use the exact same letters in the same order as the word above, except with a single letter changed.

CHAPTER 3

VISUAL ABILITIES

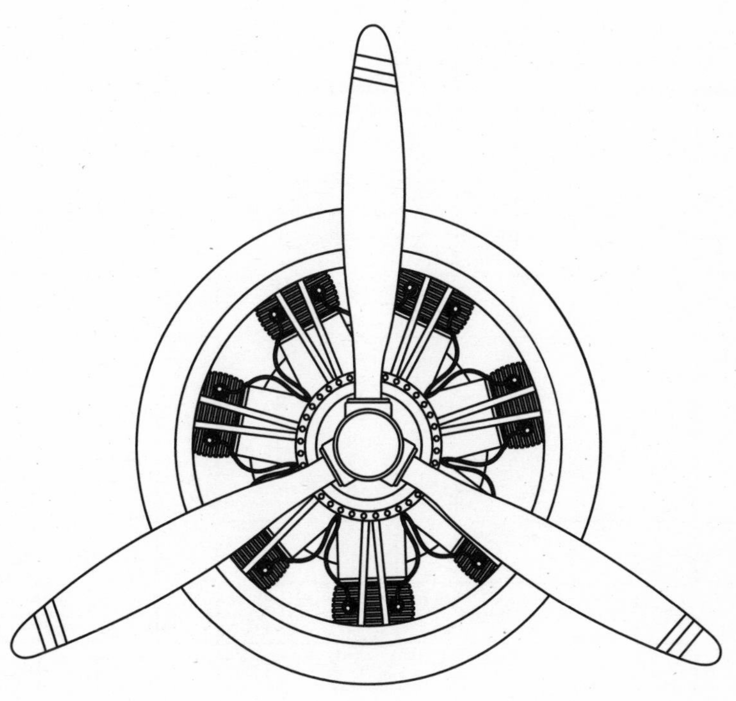

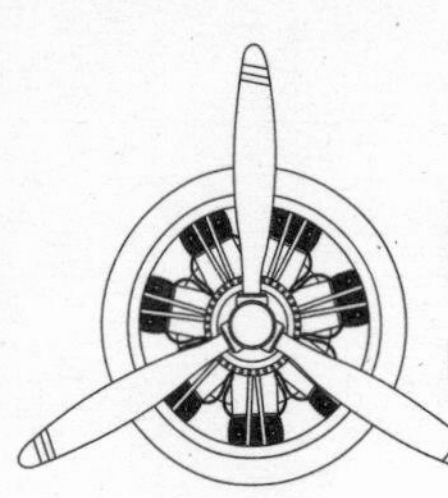

Left To Count

Mission 1: Keep track of the essential left turns

Briefing:

Find your way through this maze, starting at the entrance at the top and finishing at the exit at the bottom. Keep a mental note of the number of left turns you need to make on your journey, updating this count appropriately if you need to retrace your steps at any point. How many left turns are needed?

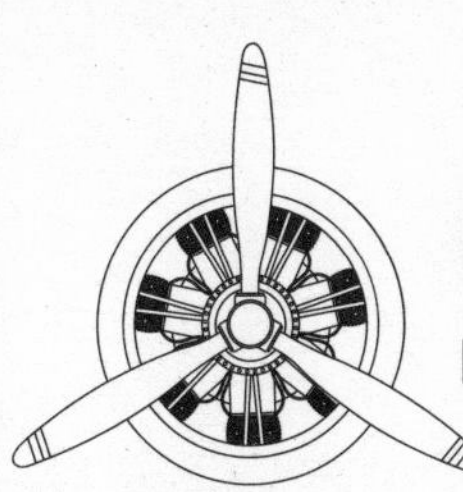

Right Way

Mission 2: Keep track of the essential right turns

Briefing:

Find your way through this maze, entering at the top and exiting at the bottom. Keep a mental note of the number of right turns you need to make on your journey, updating this count appropriately if you need to retrace your steps at any point. How many right turns are needed?

Cloudy Count

Mission 3: Keep track of all essential turns

Briefing:

Find your way through this turbulent cloud maze, entering at the top and exiting at the bottom. Keep a mental note of the total number of all turns you need to make on your journey, updating this count appropriately if you need to retrace your steps at any point. How many turns are needed?

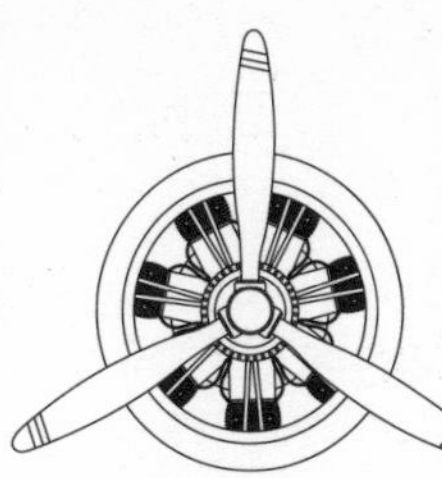

Under the Bridge

Mission 4: Count each time you pass under a bridge

Briefing:

Find your way through this maze, entering at the top and exiting at the bottom. The path can cross over and under itself, using the marked bridges. Keep a mental note of the number of bridges you *must* pass **under** on your journey, updating this count if retracing steps from a dead end.

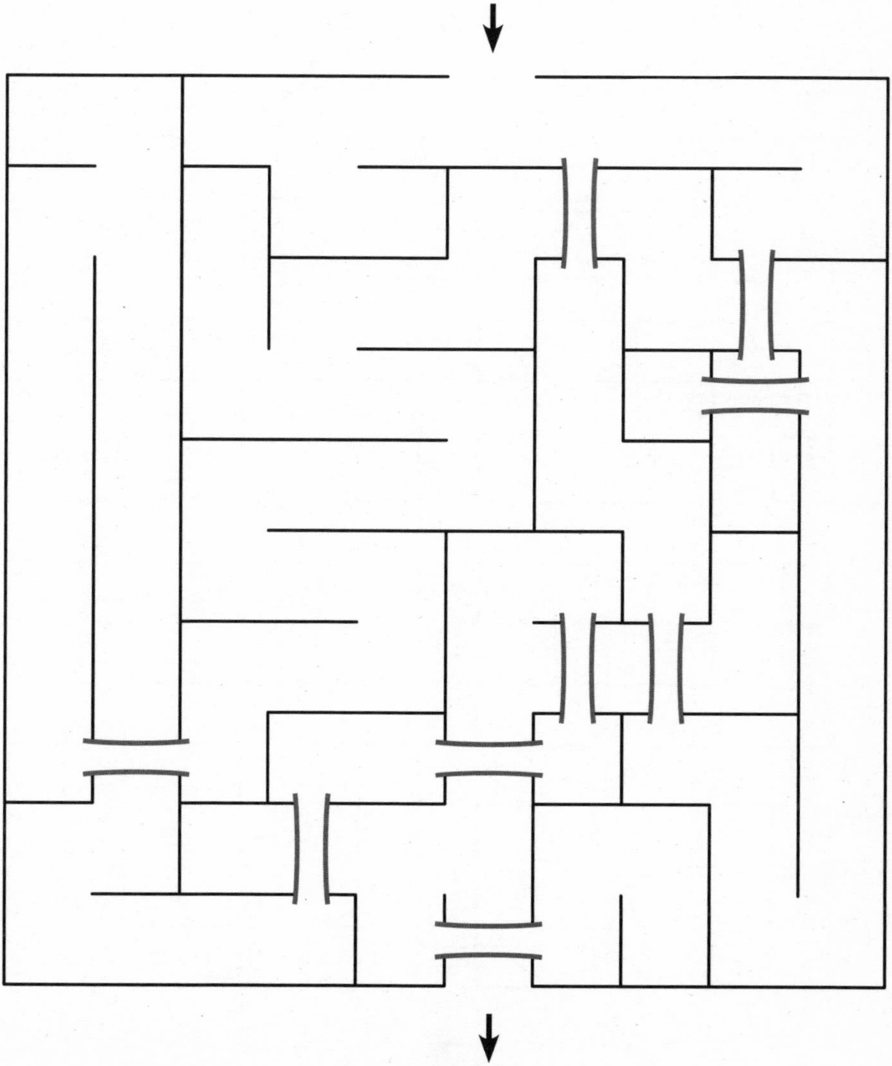

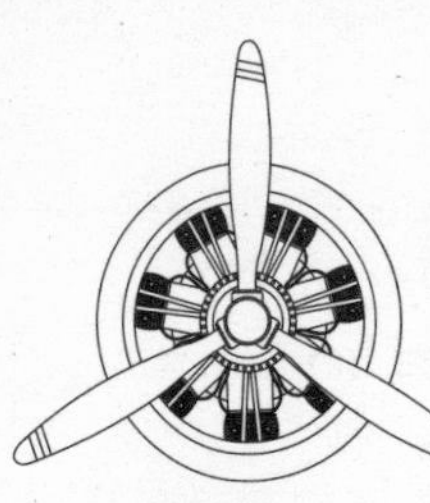

Over the Bridge

Mission 5: Count each time you pass over a bridge

Briefing:

Find your way through this maze, entering at the top and exiting at the bottom. The path can cross over and under itself, using the marked bridges. Keep a mental note of the number of bridges you *must* pass **over** on your journey, updating this count if retracing steps from a dead end.

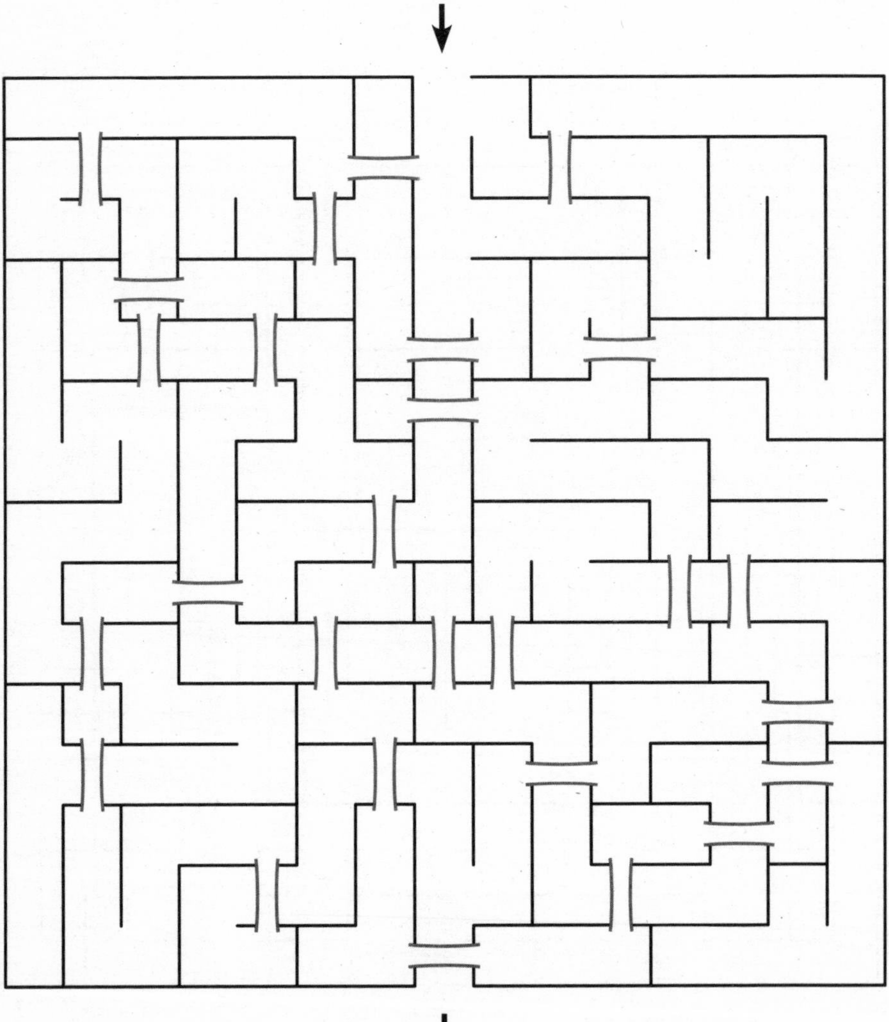

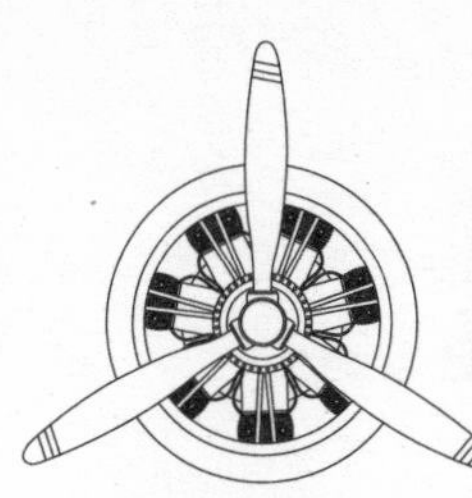

Over and Under

Mission 6: Count every bridge you pass over *and* under

Briefing:

Find your way through this maze, entering at the top and exiting at the bottom. The path can cross over and under itself, using the marked bridges. Keep a mental note of the number of bridges you *must* pass ***both* over and under** on your journey, updating this count if retracing steps from a dead end.

Ground Division I

Mission 7: Divide the plan into four identical areas

Briefing:

Can you draw along the dashed lines below to split this ground plan into four identical areas? All four areas must be of equal size and shape. Rotations are allowed, but reflections that are not also rotations are not considered valid.

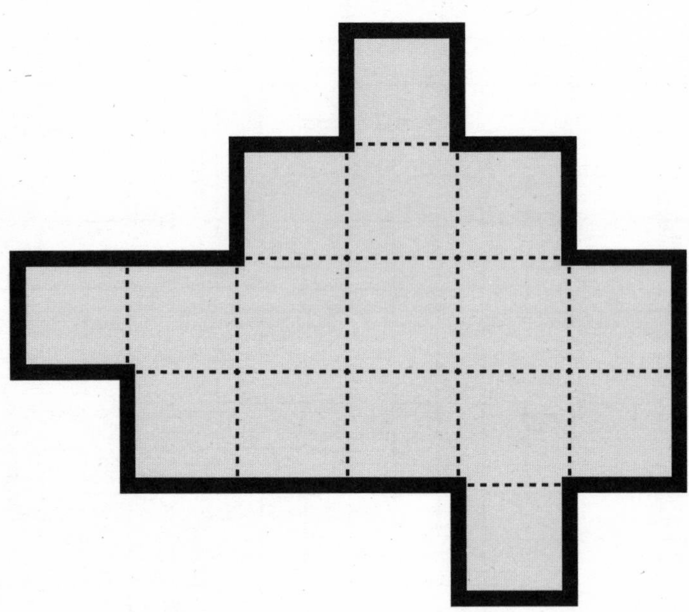

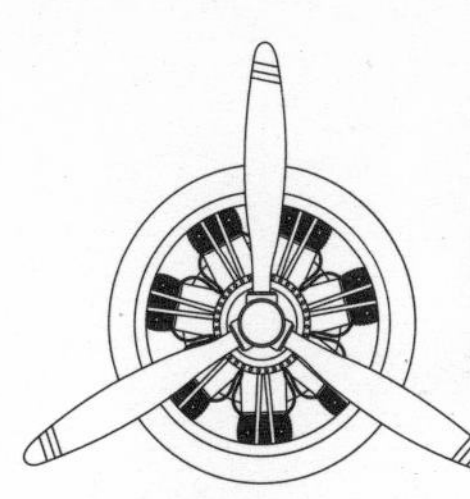

Ground Division 2

Mission 8: Divide the plan into four identical areas

Briefing:

Can you draw along the dashed lines below to split this ground plan into four identical areas? All four areas must be of equal size and shape. Rotations are allowed, but reflections that are not also rotations are not considered valid.

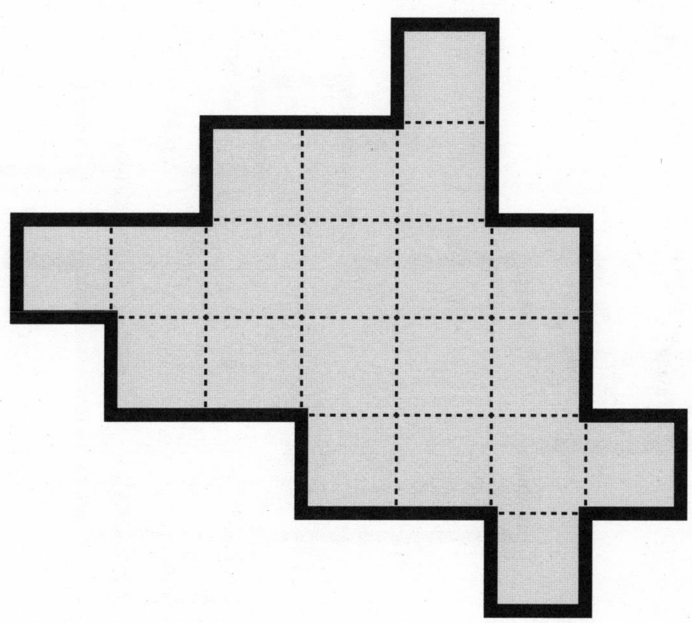

Ground Division 3

Mission 9: Divide the plan into four identical areas

Briefing:

Can you draw along the dashed lines below to split this ground plan into four identical areas? All four areas must be of equal size and shape. Rotations are allowed, but reflections that are not also rotations are not considered valid.

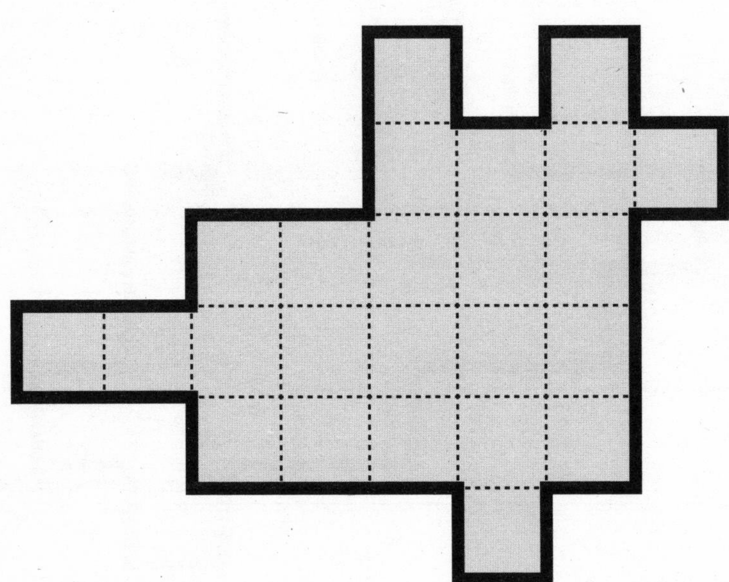

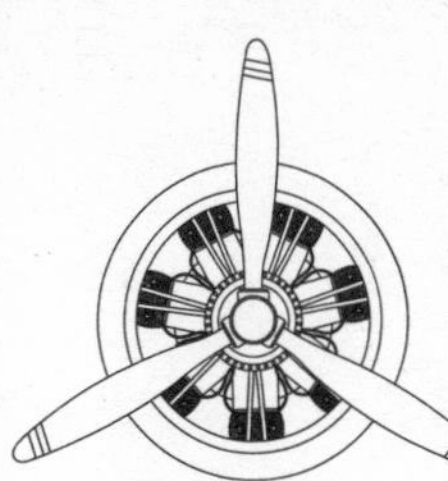

Ground Division 4

Mission 10: Divide the plan into four identical areas

Briefing:

Can you draw along the dashed lines below to split this ground plan into four identical areas? All four areas must be of equal size and shape. Rotations are allowed, but reflections that are not also rotations are not considered valid.

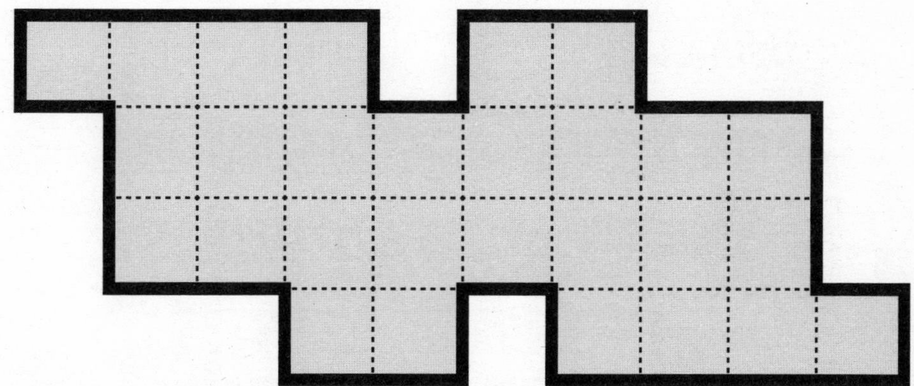

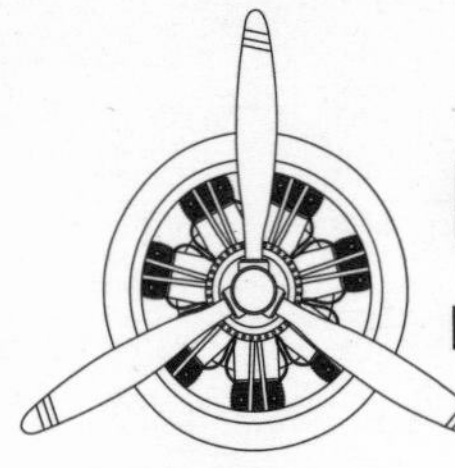

NATO Coordinates 1

Mission 11: Follow the spoken instructions

Briefing:

The NATO phonetic alphabet is used in aviation to ensure individual letters and numbers are clear when spoken. Bearing this in mind, can you decode the list of spoken coordinates on this page, and shade the squares described? For example, a code of 'HOTEL NINE-ER' would instruct you to shade square H9.

ECHO FOW-ER

ECHO FIFE

BRAVO TOO

BRAVO SIX

FOXTROT SIX

CHARLIE TREE

DELTA FIFE

DELTA TREE

CHARLIE FOW-ER

ECHO TREE

CHARLIE FIFE

FOXTROT TOO

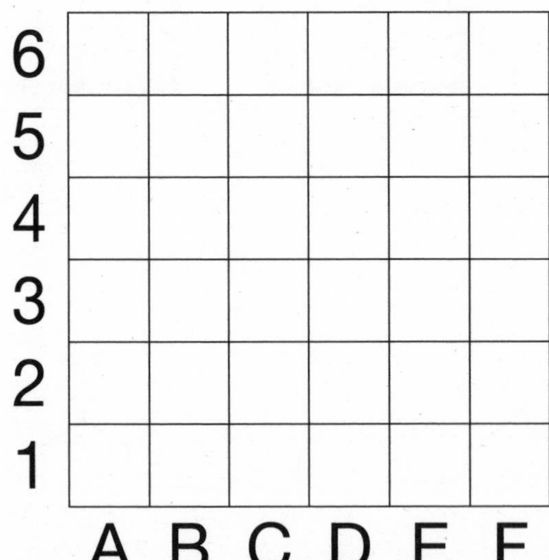

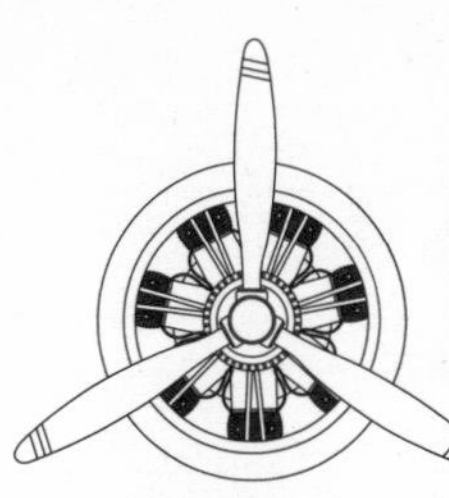

NATO Coordinates 2

Mission 12: Follow further spoken instructions

Briefing:

Complete the mission on the opposite page first. Once you have done so, try this similar mission. This time the coded speech is given slightly differently, and the shading must take place on a hexagonal grid.

AIT: ALPHA, BRAVO, CHARLIE, DELTA

FIFE: ALPHA, CHARLIE, DELTA, ECHO, GOLF

FOW-ER: BRAVO, DELTA, ECHO, GOLF

SEV-EN: ALPHA, ECHO

SIX: ALPHA, CHARLIE, DELTA, FOXTROT

TOO: DELTA, ECHO, FOXTROT, GOLF

TREE: CHARLIE, GOLF

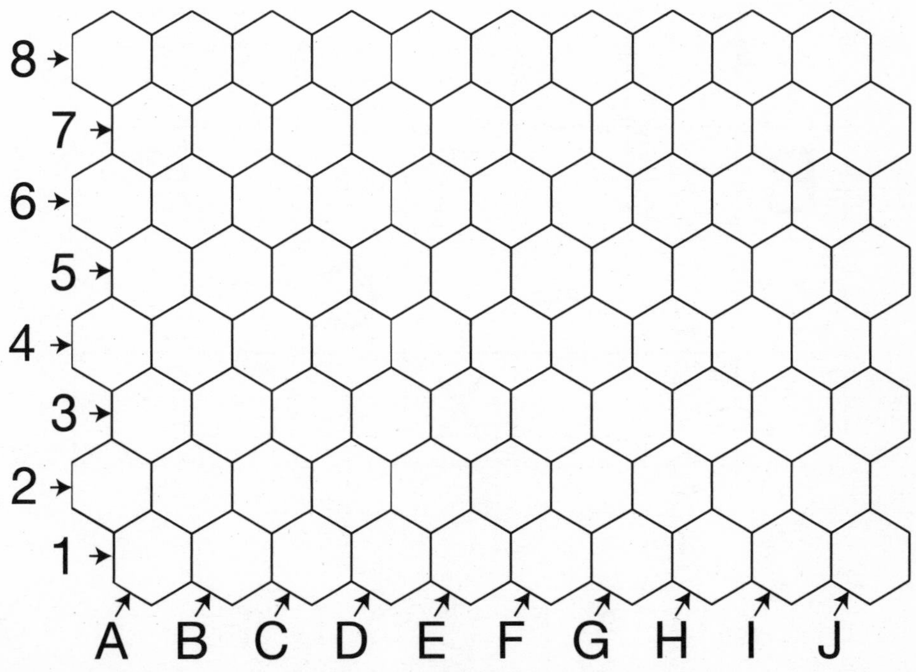

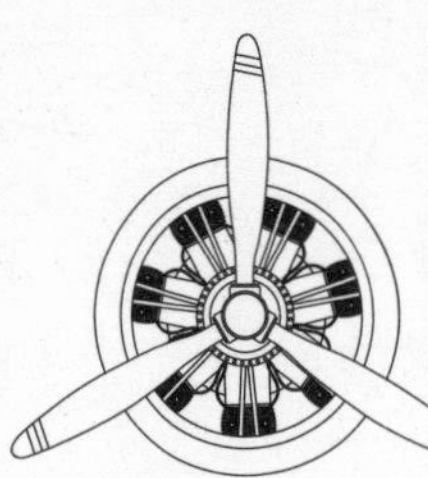

Arrow Directions

Mission 13: Follow the route without drawing

Briefing:

Without drawing on the page, map out the path of an aircraft on the grid below by following the given directions. Starting at the 'X', will you end up at A, B or C? Assume that all steps travel horizontally or vertically between the centres of grid squares, and all arrows point in the literal direction to move.

<table>
<tr><td></td><td></td><td></td><td></td><td></td><td></td><td></td></tr>
<tr><td></td><td></td><td></td><td></td><td>A</td><td></td><td></td></tr>
<tr><td></td><td></td><td></td><td></td><td></td><td></td><td></td></tr>
<tr><td>B</td><td></td><td></td><td></td><td></td><td></td><td></td></tr>
<tr><td></td><td></td><td></td><td></td><td>C</td><td></td><td></td></tr>
<tr><td></td><td></td><td></td><td>X</td><td></td><td></td><td></td></tr>
</table>

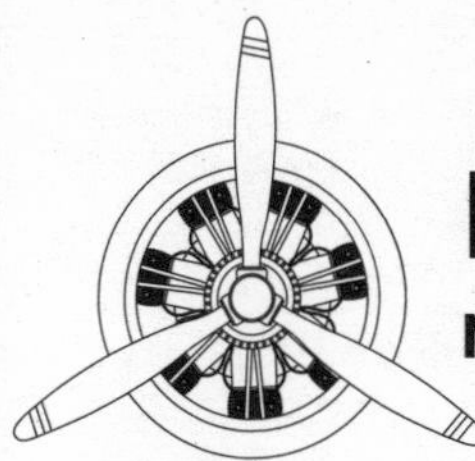

Relative Directions

Mission 14: Follow the further route without drawing

Briefing:

Without drawing on the page, map out the path of an aircraft on the grid below by following the given directions. Start at the arrow, facing in the direction shown. Assume that all turns are through ninety degrees, and each square is one unit wide/tall. Which letter do you finish at?

Move forward two units, then turn right
Move forward one unit, then turn left
Move forward two units, then turn left
Move forward two units, then turn left
Move forward one unit, then turn right
Move forward one unit, then turn left
Move forward one unit, then turn right
Move forward one unit, to reach your destination

	A					
			B			
C						
					D	
			↑			

Full Loop

Mission 15: Identify the flight path that makes a loop

Briefing:

Can you work out which of the three flight paths below forms a loop back to its starting point? Each direction is given as a move of a number of grid squares, using absolute directions – i.e. 'up' always means up the page, and 'left' always means to the left of the page. Use the grid to help you if you wish.

Flight Path A
UP 1
RIGHT 2
UP 1
LEFT 3
UP 1
LEFT 1
DOWN 5
RIGHT 4
UP 1

Flight Path B
LEFT 1
UP 1
RIGHT 1
UP 2
RIGHT 1
UP 1
LEFT 3
DOWN 5
RIGHT 3
UP 1
LEFT 1

Flight Path C
UP 2
LEFT 1
UP 1
RIGHT 4
DOWN 2
LEFT 2
UP 1
RIGHT 1
DOWN 3
RIGHT 1

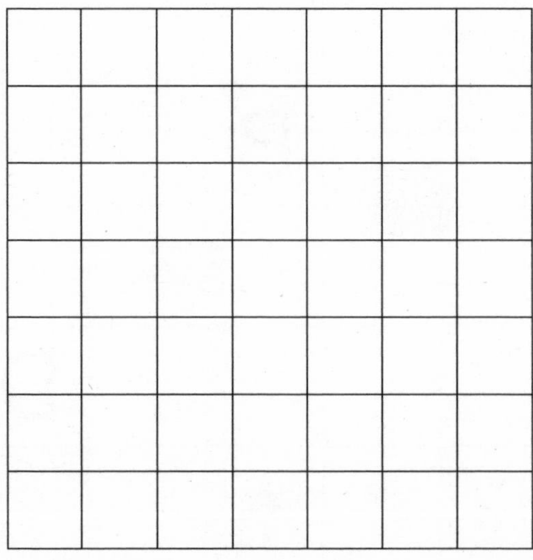

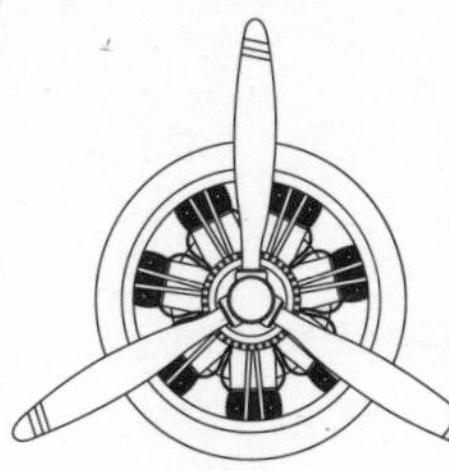

Safe Route 1

Mission 16: Identify the route that avoids blocked areas

Briefing:

Without drawing on the page, work out which of the sets of instructions given below would take you from 'X' to 'Y' on the grid, without passing through a blocked (shaded) square. Assume that all steps travel horizontally or vertically between the centres of grid squares, and move in the literal direction shown.

Flight Path A

Flight Path B

Flight Path C

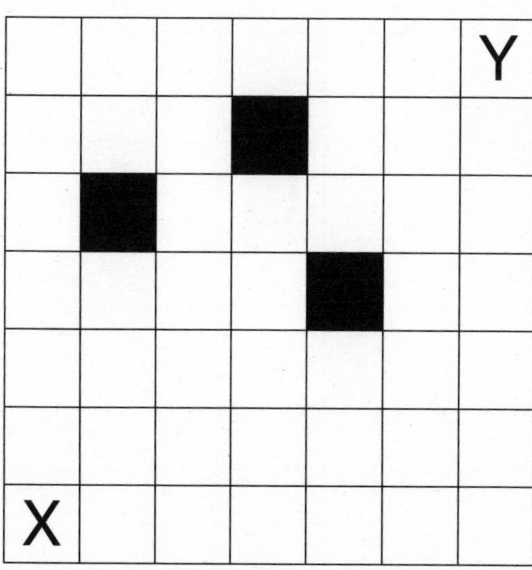

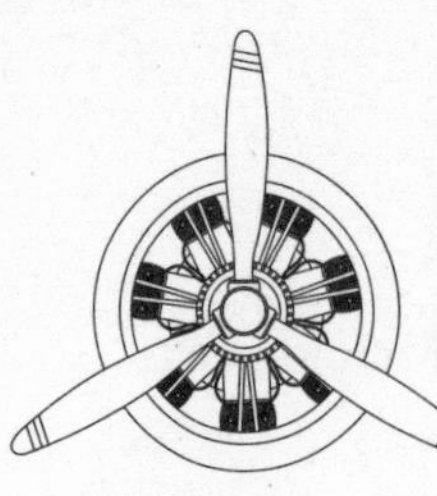

Drone Decision

Mission 17: Trace the path of the drone across the grid

Briefing:

Map out the path of a drone on the grid by decoding the system of directions given. Start at the 'X' and assume the aircraft is facing right, so it only moves from left to right across the grid when it is not moving either up or down. Which letter do you end up at? Each move is exactly one square in length.

1. LIFT
2. THRUST
3. LIFT
4. LIFT
5. LIFT
6. THRUST
7. FALL
8. FALL
9. THRUST
10. LIFT

	A					
		B				
			C			
					D	
X						E

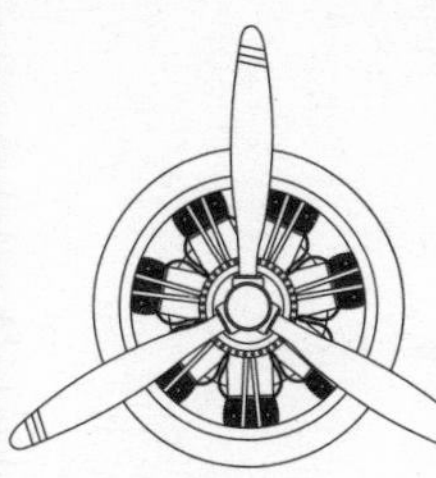

Flight Path

Mission 18: Trace out the given route

Briefing:

Draw a flight path in a particular shape on the airspace grid below by following the directions given. Your flight path should travel along the grid lines, and you should assume that one side of a square in the grid has a length of one nautical mile (nm). Assume that north is directly up the page. What shape do you draw?

Fly north 5 nm
Turn 135 degrees to the left
Fly to a point 2 nm south and 2 nm west of your position
Turn 135 degrees to the left
Fly 4 nm
Turn 135 degrees to the left
Fly north-west until you reach a point you have already visited

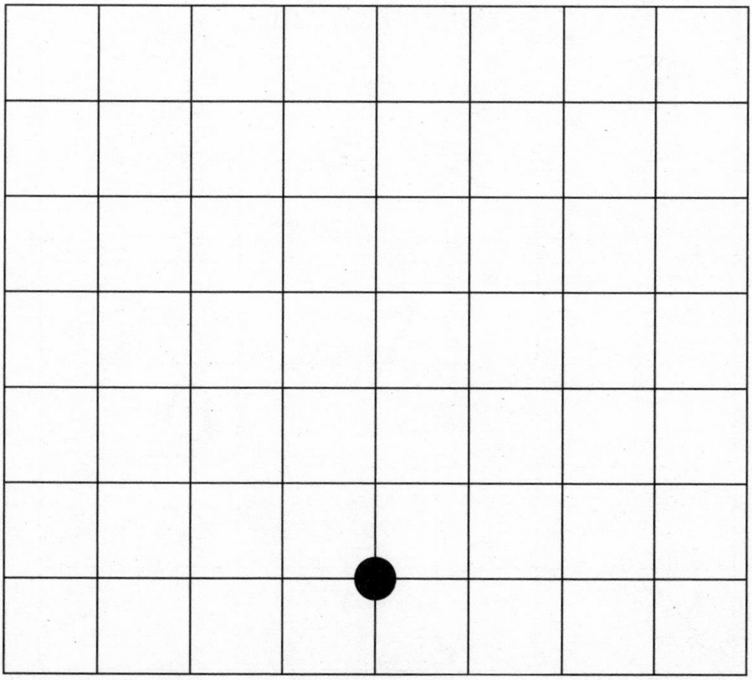

Triangular Route

Mission 19: Follow the directions to reveal a shape

Briefing:

Decode the instructions below to draw out a flight path on the triangular airspace regions below, starting from the black dot. Your route should travel along the grid lines, and you should assume that each side of a grid triangle has a length of one nautical mile (nm). North (0°) is directly up the page.

at 30°: 3 nm

at 330°: 1 nm

at 270°: 2 nm

at 210°: 1 nm

at 150°: 3 nm

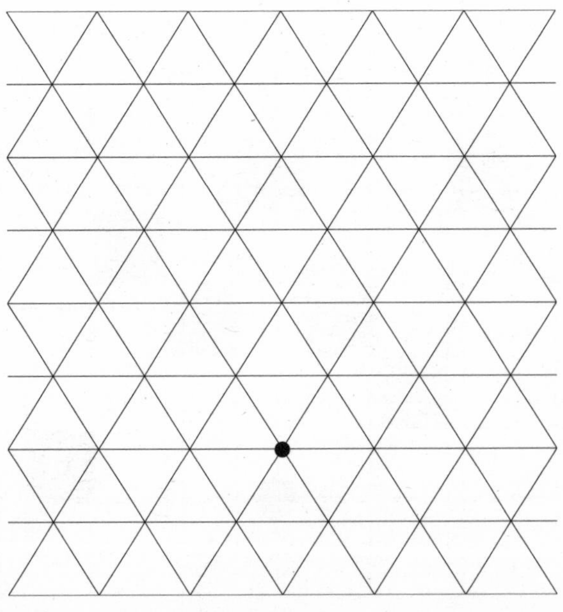

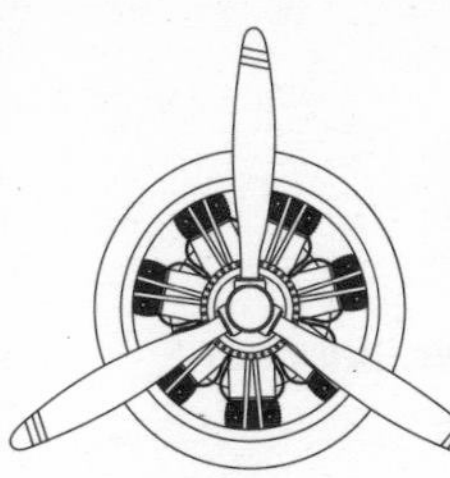

Safe Route 2

Mission 20: Identify the route that avoids blocked areas

Briefing:

Without drawing on the page, work out which of the sets of instructions given below would take you from the arrow to 'X', without passing through a blocked (shaded) square. Directions are either to move one step forward, or to turn 90 degrees *and stay in the same square* while pointing in a new direction. Start at the square marked with the arrow, facing as shown.

Flight Path A

Flight Path B

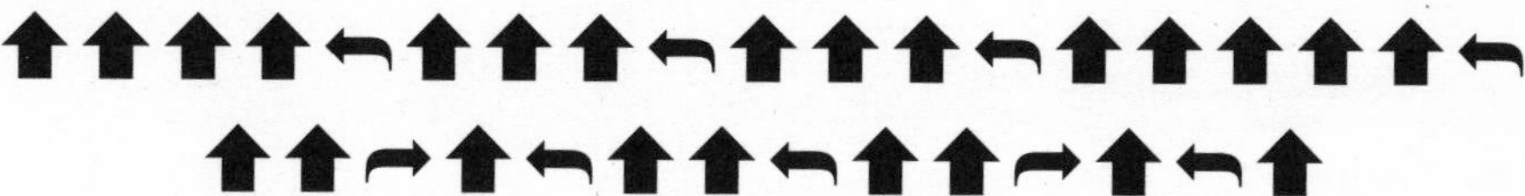

Flight Path C

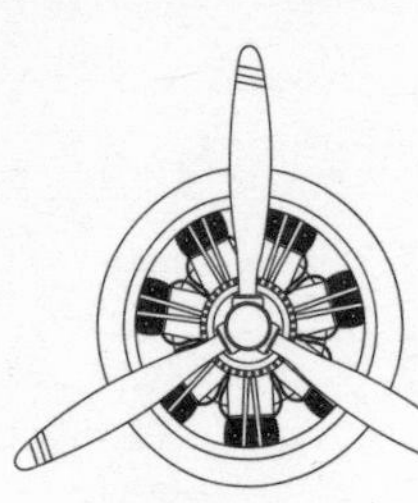

US Flight Paths

Mission 21: Trace the routes and answer the questions

Briefing:

Some major airports have been marked on the US map opposite, although only their three-letter airport codes have been used. Assuming that all flight paths travel in a straight line across the page, answer the following questions.

1. Which of these flight paths between cities crosses over the fewest number of states?

   a. Houston to Los Angeles

   b. Chicago to Miami

   c. Seattle to Minneapolis

2. Which of these flight paths crosses over one of the Great Lakes?

   a. Detroit to Seattle

   b. Boston to Nashville

   c. Denver to New Orleans

3. Which of these flight paths does not involve travelling over sea?

   a. Boston to Miami

   b. Chicago to Miami

   c. Houston to Miami

What NATO codeword corresponds with the following flight path?

Denver ➡ Minneapolis ➡ Chicago ➡ Detroit ➡ Nashville

US Flight Paths (map)

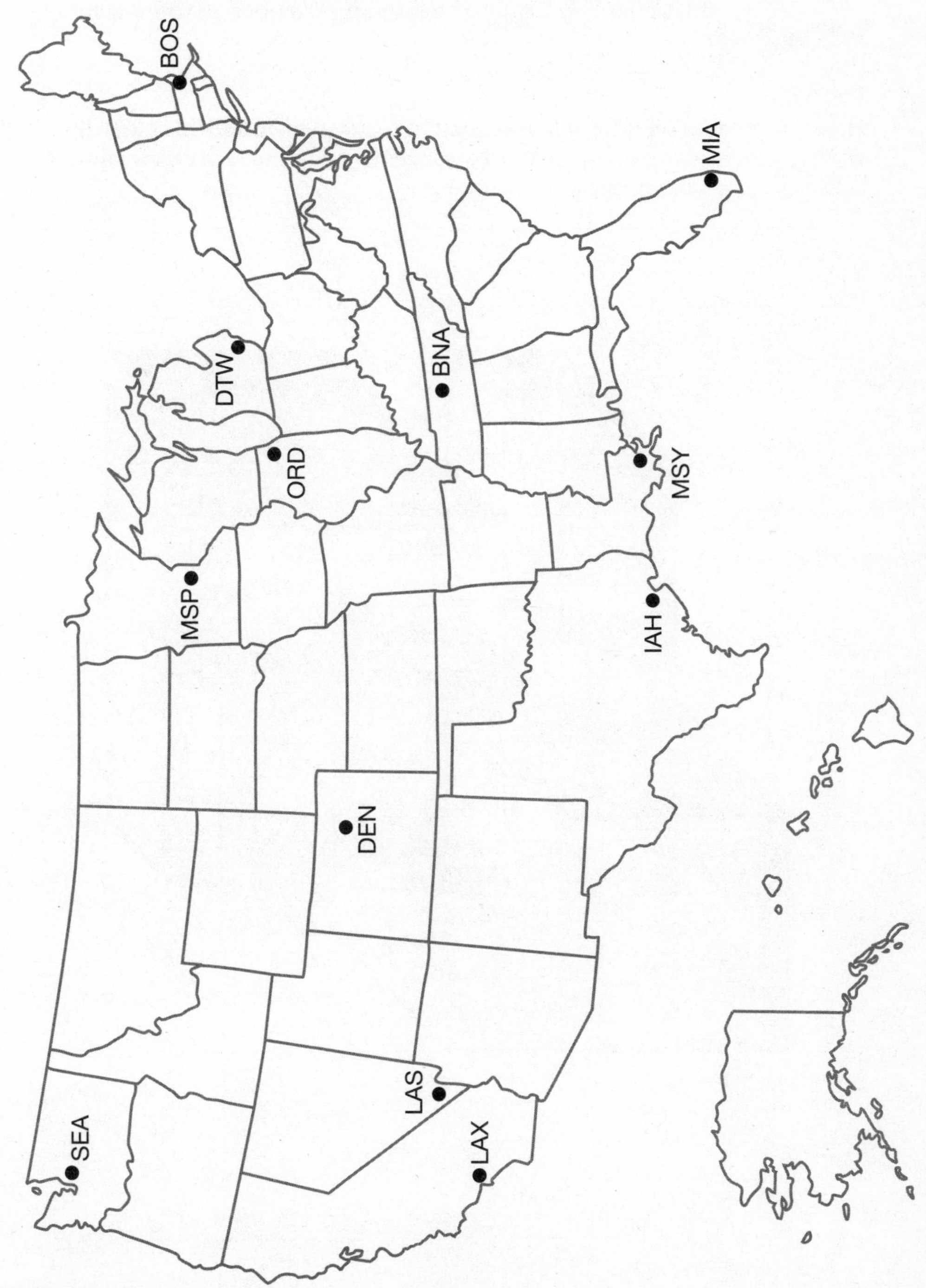

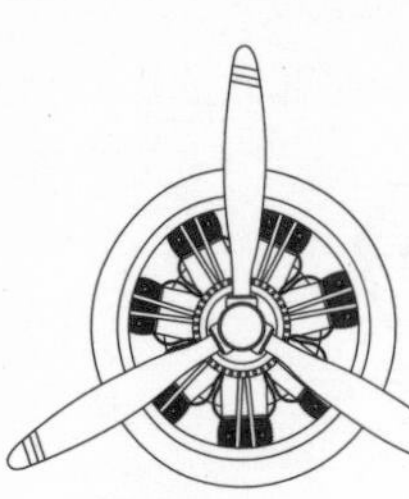

Cube Counting 1

Mission 22: Count the number of cubes in the image

Briefing:

How many cubes were used to construct the arrangement shown below? It was created by starting with a 4×4×4 arrangement and then removing some cubes. No cubes are floating.

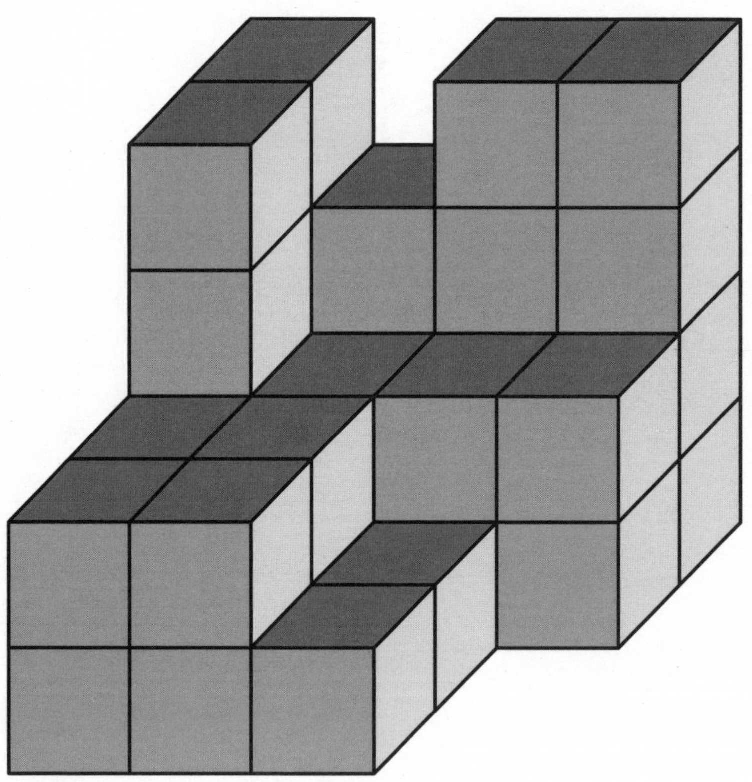

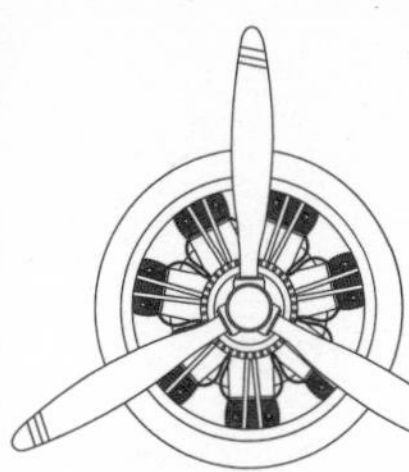

Cube Counting 2

Mission 23: Count the number of cubes in the image

Briefing:

How many cubes were used to construct the arrangement shown below? It was created by starting with a 4×4×4 arrangement and then removing some cubes. No cubes are floating.

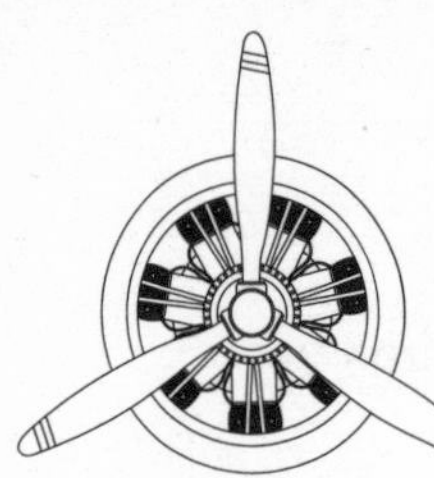

Cube Counting 3

Mission 24: Count the number of cubes in the image

Briefing:

How many cubes were used to construct the arrangement shown below? It was created by starting with a 5×4×5 arrangement and then removing some cubes. No cubes are floating.

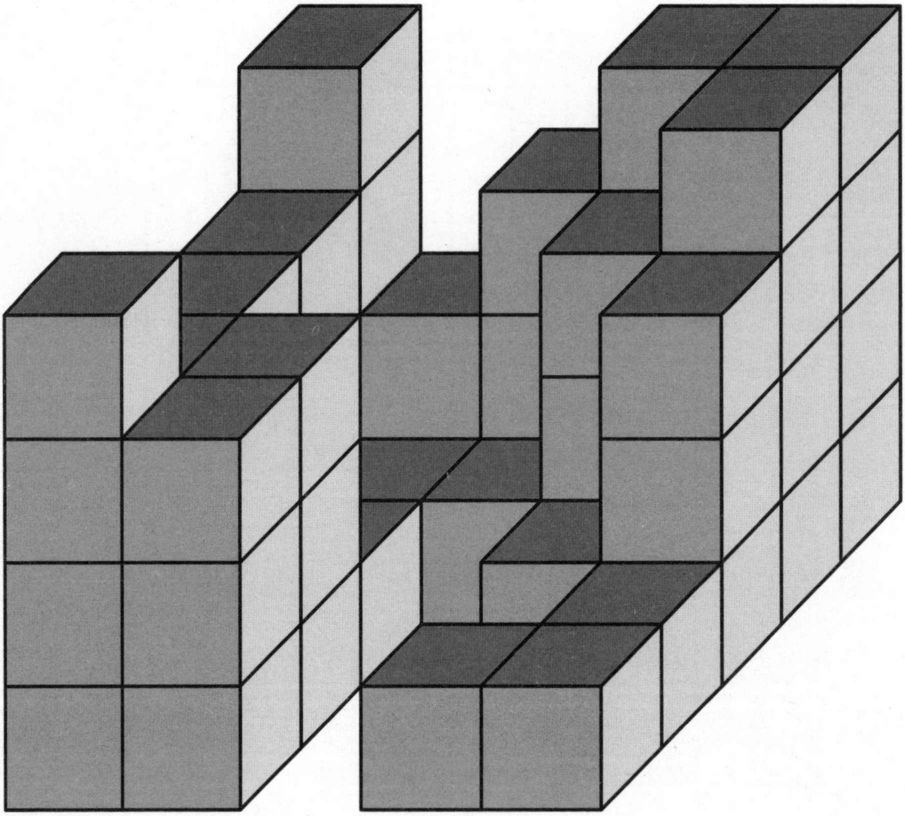

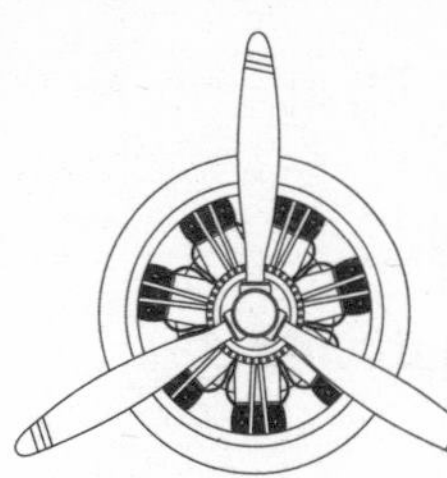

Cube Counting 4

Mission 25: Count the number of cubes in the image

Briefing:

How many cubes were used to construct the arrangement shown below? It was created by starting with a 5×5×5 arrangement and then removing some cubes. No cubes are floating.

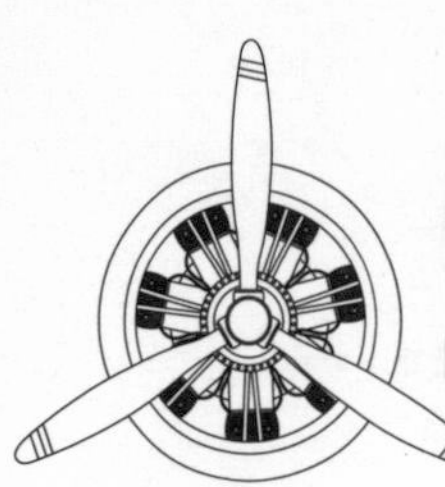

Shape Link 1

Mission 26: Visualize and then draw the shape links

Briefing:

Link each pair of identical shapes by drawing a path from one to the other that travels only horizontally and vertically. No more than one path can enter any square, which also means that paths can't cross.

							●
					■		
		⬟			⬢		
	■		▲				
					◆		
				⬟			
⬢			⯃			●	
▲				◆			⯃

Shape Link 2

Mission 27: Visualize and then draw the shape links

Briefing:

Link each pair of identical shapes by drawing a path from one to the other that travels only horizontally and vertically. No more than one path can enter any square, which also means that paths can't cross.

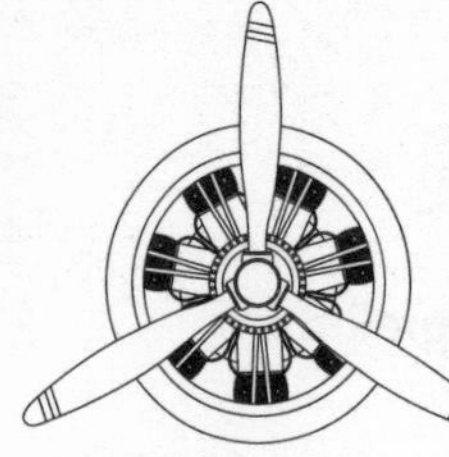

Shape Link 3

Mission 28: Visualize and then draw the shape links

Briefing:

Link each pair of identical shapes by drawing a path from one to the other that travels only horizontally and vertically. No more than one path can enter any square, which also means that paths can't cross.

●	■					⬟			
					■				
⬢				●	▲		◆		
	⯃				⬟		▲		
					○			□	
		○				⬠			
		⬢		◆					
				⯃				□	
						⬠			

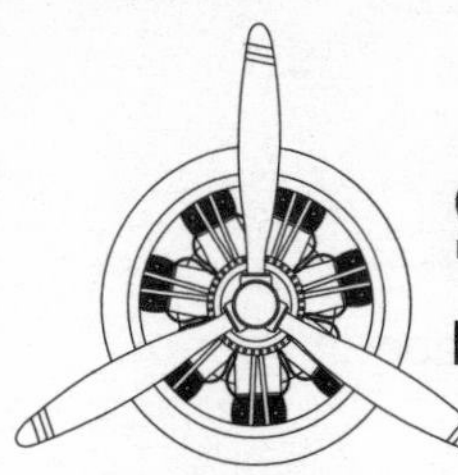

Shape Link 4

Mission 29: Visualize and then draw the shape links

Briefing:

Link each pair of identical shapes by drawing a path from one to the other that travels only horizontally and vertically. No more than one path can enter any square, which also means that paths can't cross.

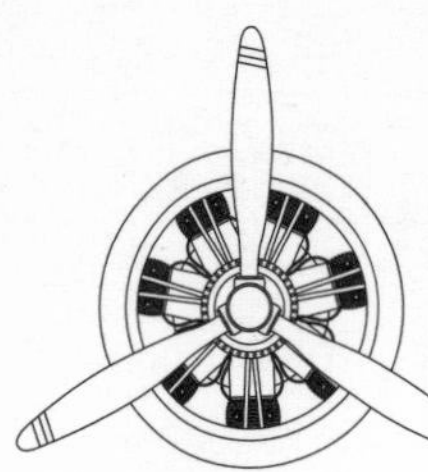

Shady Groups

Mission 30: Crack the code to reveal the correct group

Briefing:

You know you will be flying with one of three code-named groups: Golf, Sierra or Papa. To inform you of your assigned group, you receive the following cryptic diagram and list of cities given below. Can you crack the code and work out which group you should report to?

Bergen	Manchester
Copenhagen	Riga
Geneva	Warsaw
Malaga	Zurich

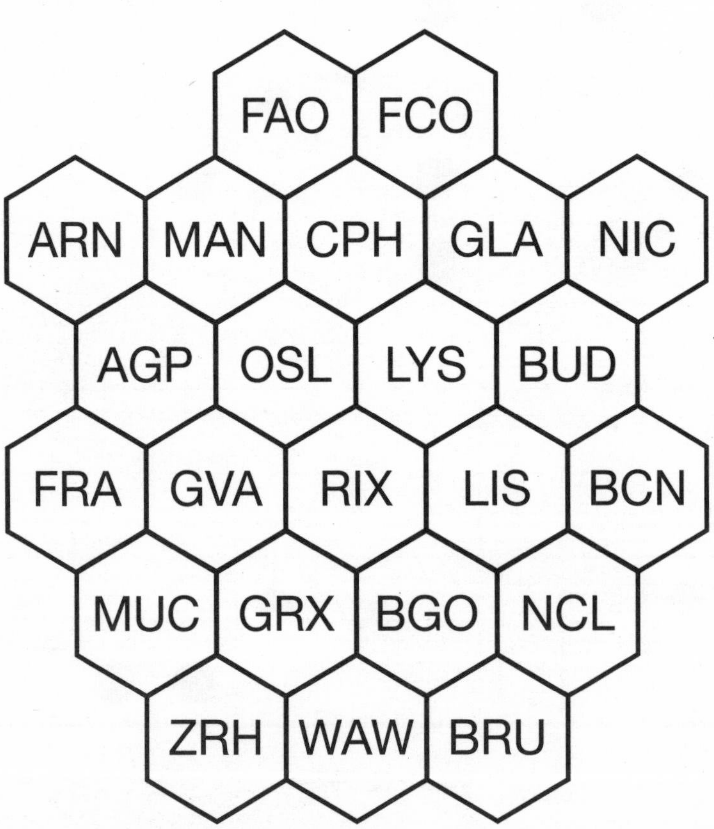

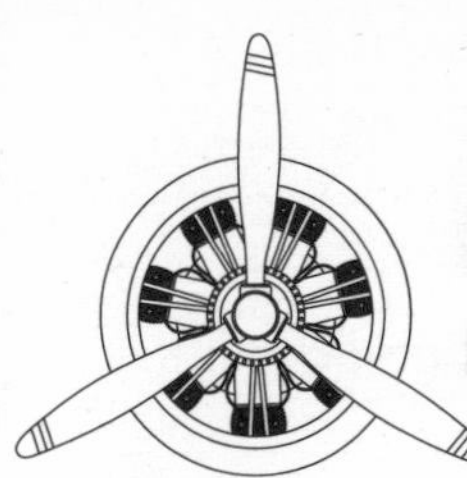

Helicopter Silhouette

Mission 31: Identify the matching image

Briefing:

Which of the four silhouettes exactly matches the helicopter at the top?

A

B

C

D

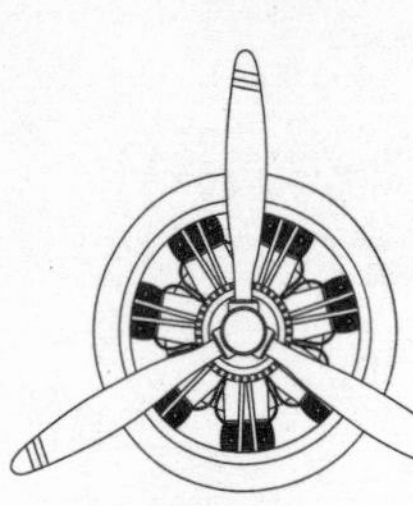

Country Confusion

Mission 32: Identify the reflected country outlines

Briefing:

Six European countries have been reflected horizontally (so east became west, and west became east) and then outlined below, with north to the top of the page. The outlines are not to scale, relative to one another. Can you identify all six countries?

A

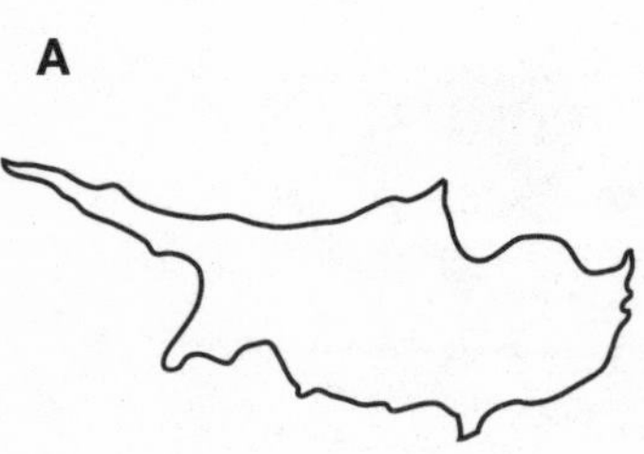

B

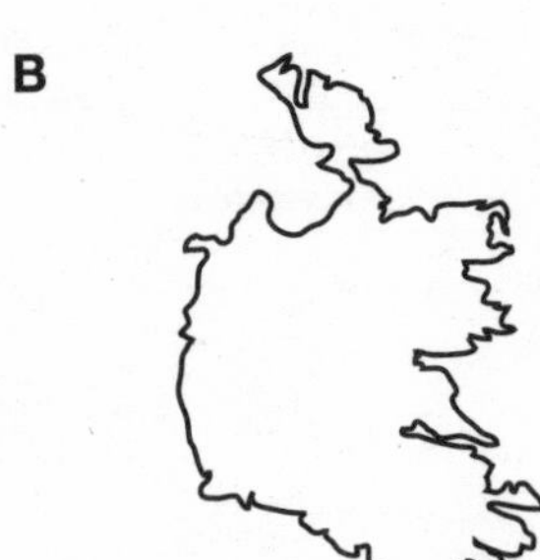

C

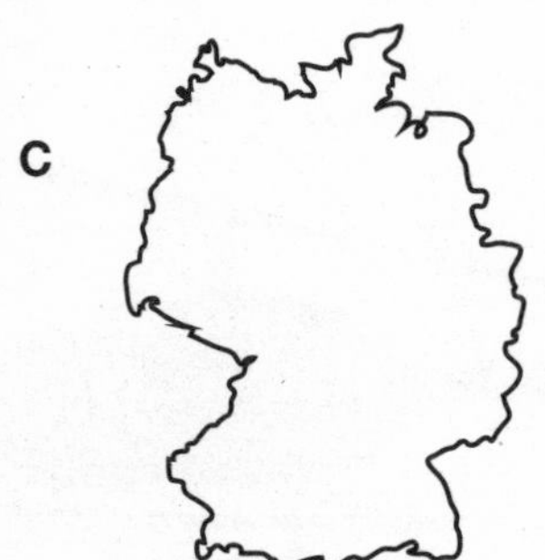

D

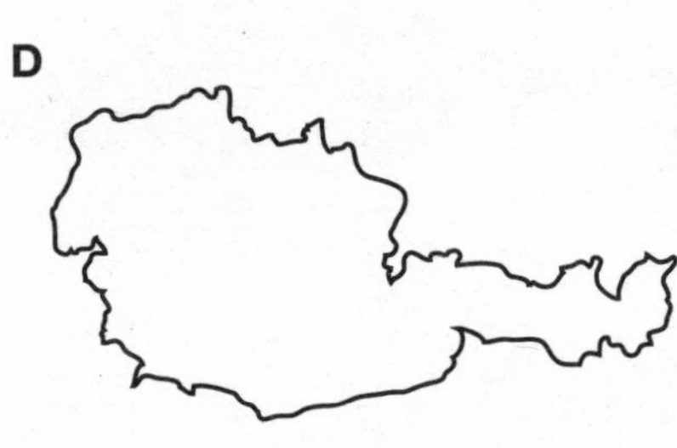

E

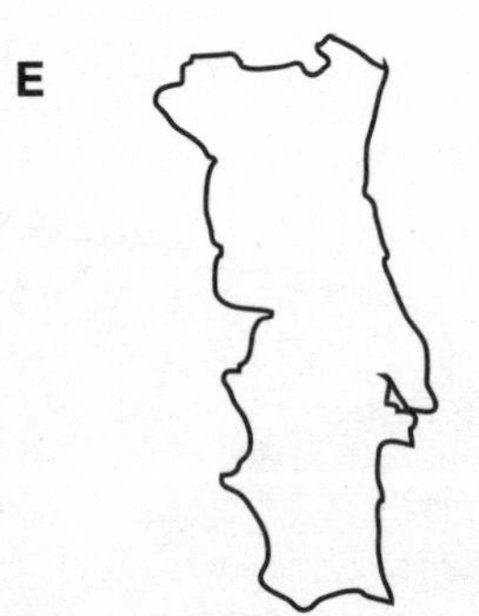

F

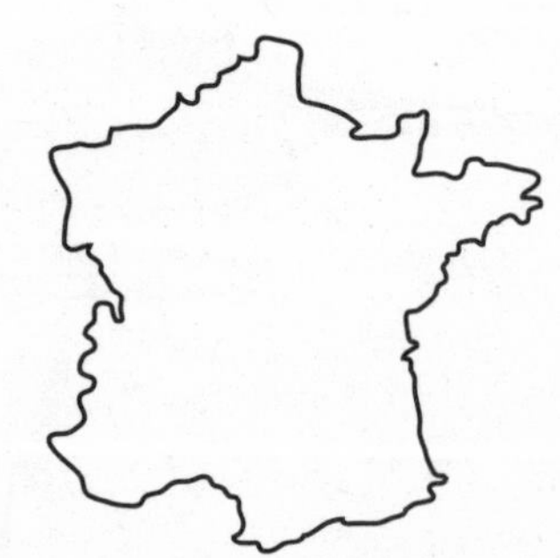

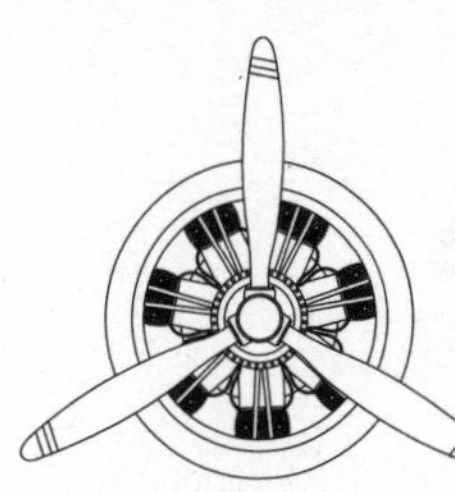

Propeller Pair

Mission 33: Identify the identical propeller images

Briefing:

Can you find the pair of identical propellers beneath, allowing for the fact that each image has been rotated slightly differently?

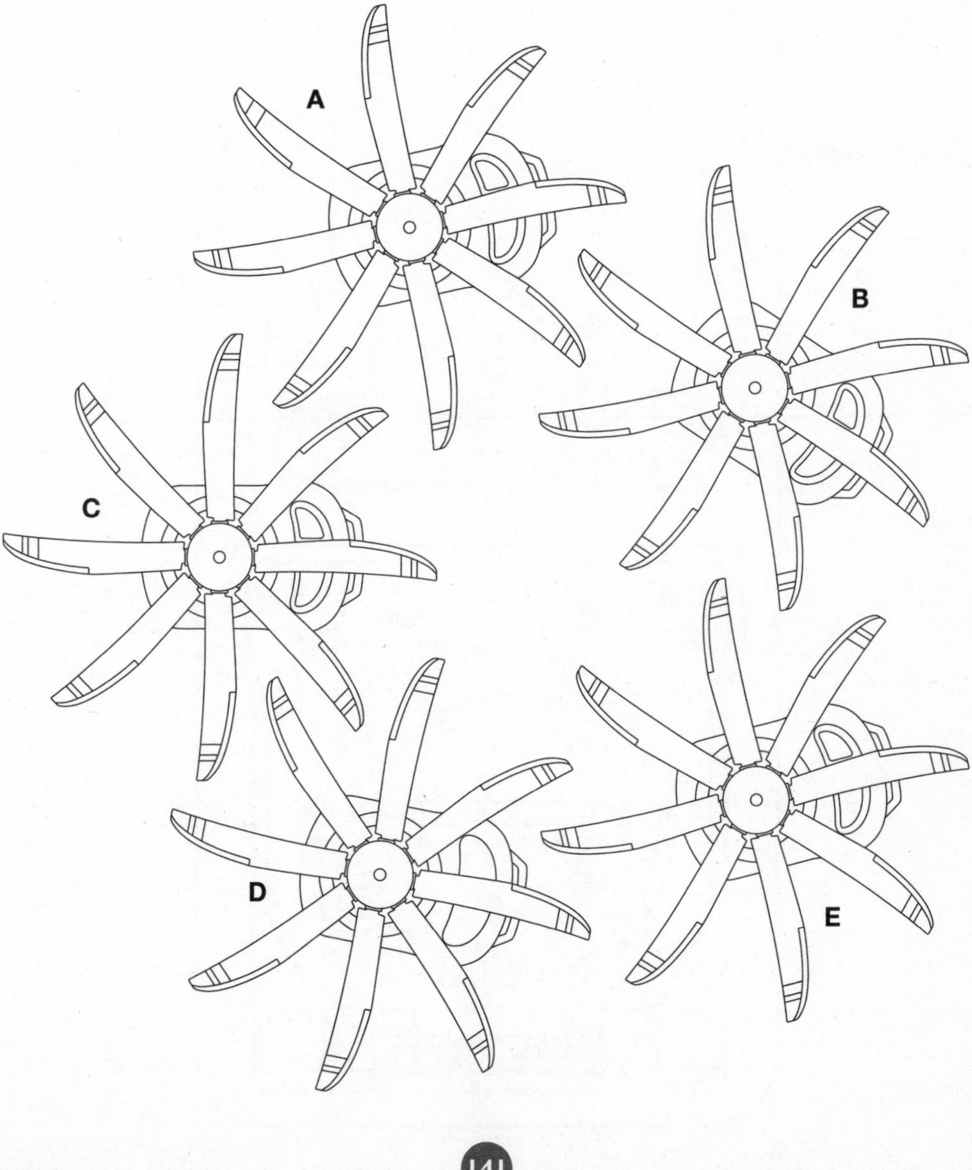

A

B

C

D

E

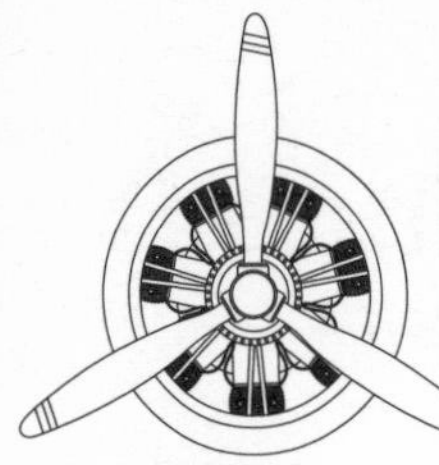

Spot the Difference

Mission 34: Find the changes in the cockpit display

Briefing:

Find ten differences between the image below and its reflection opposite.

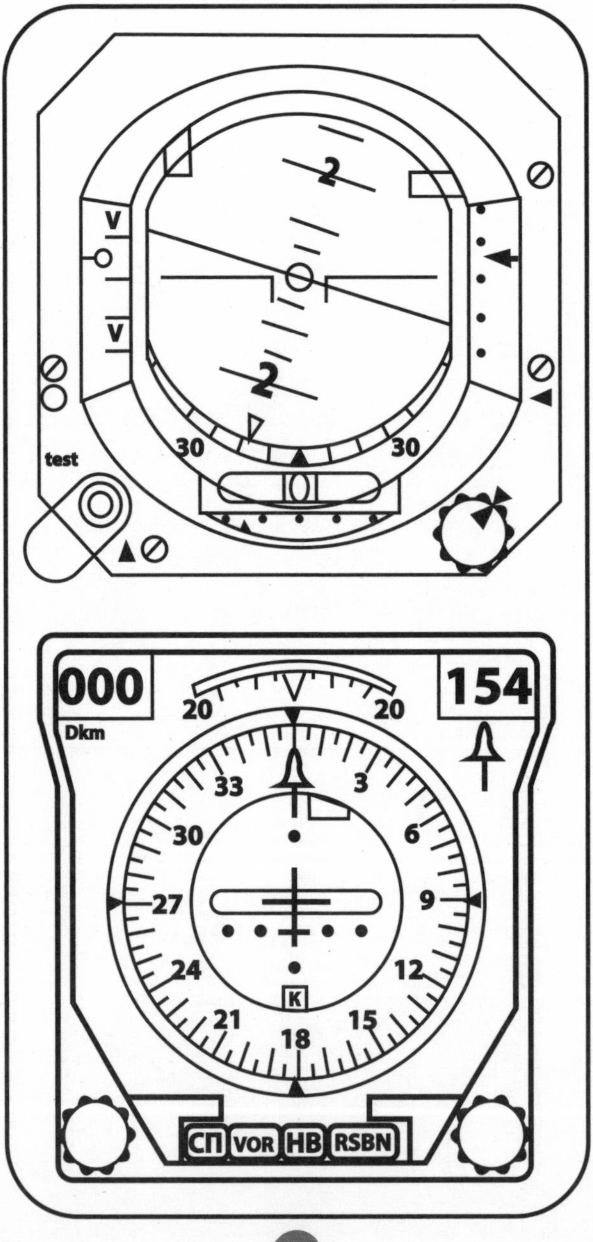

Spot the Difference (continued)

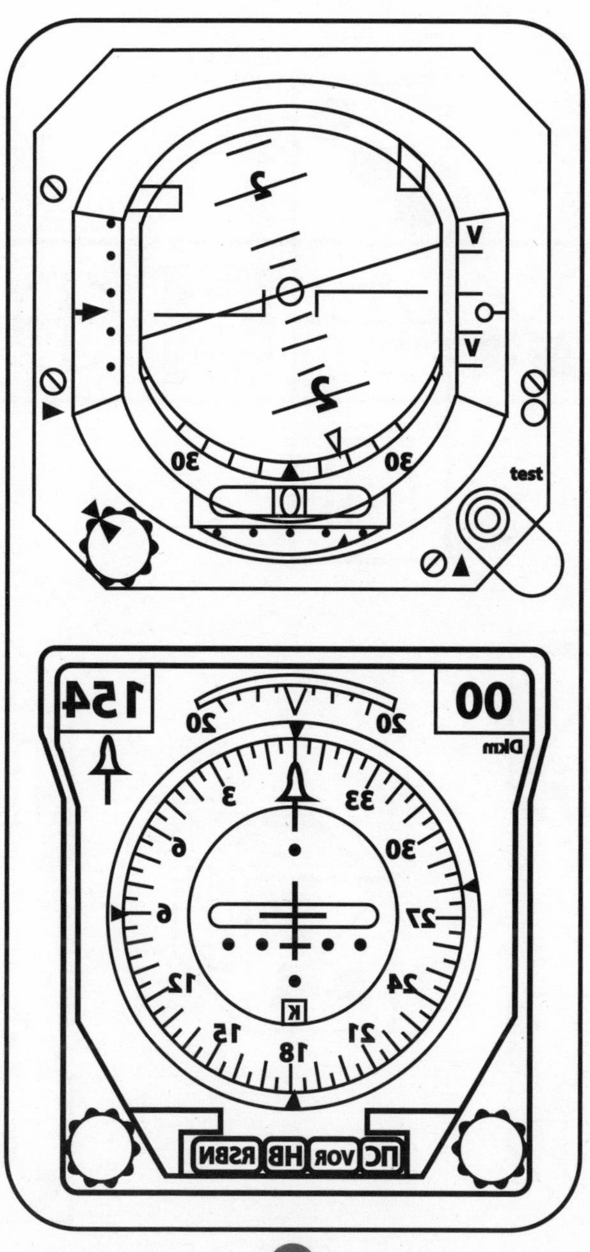

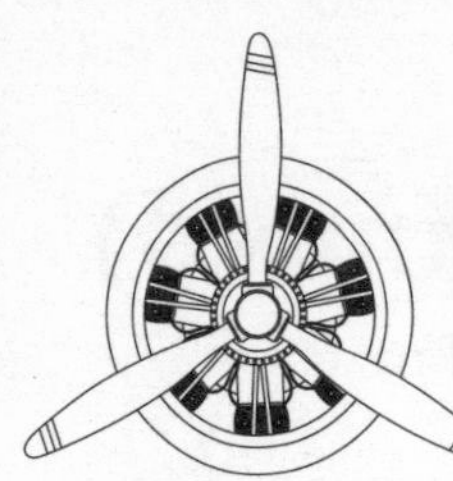

Dicey Decision I

Mission 35: Imagine the result of folding to make a dice

Briefing:

If you were to cut out and fold up the shape shown, which one of the five dice at the bottom of the page would result?

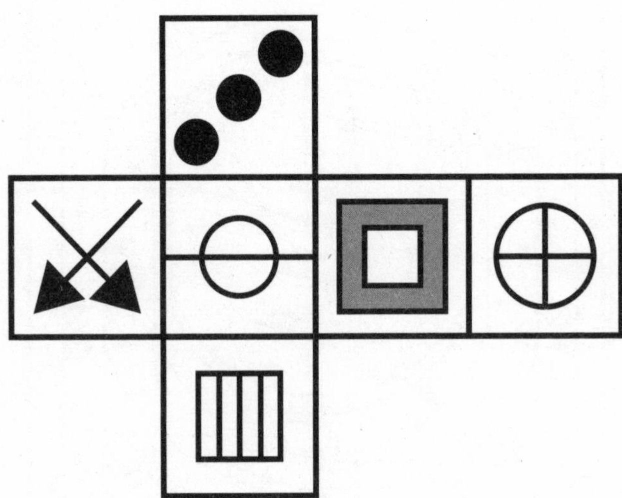

A

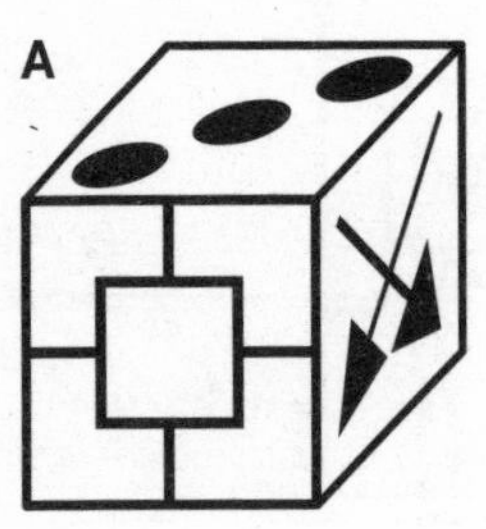

B

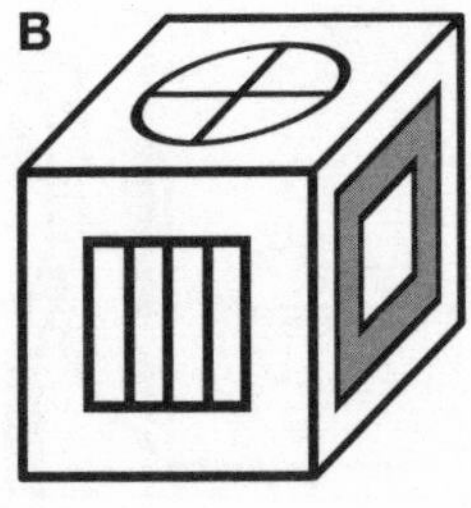

C

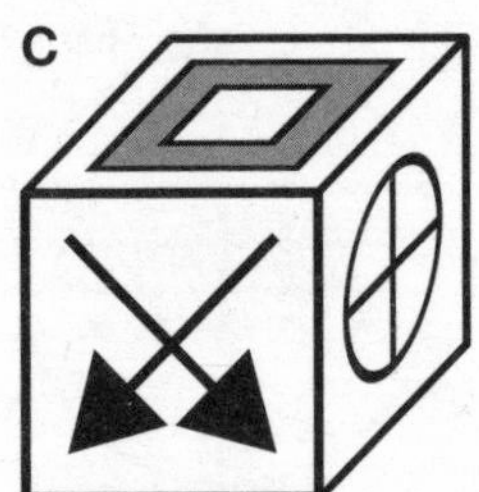

D

E

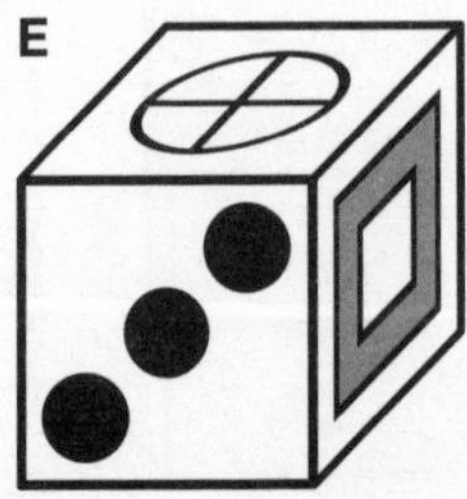

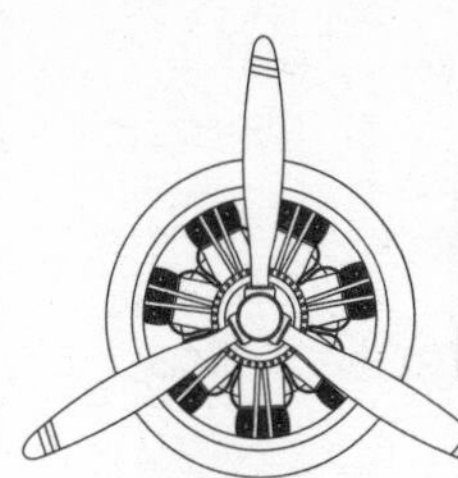

Dicey Decision 2

Mission 36: Imagine the result of folding to make a dice

Briefing:

If you were to cut out and fold up the shape shown, which one of the five dice at the bottom of the page would result?

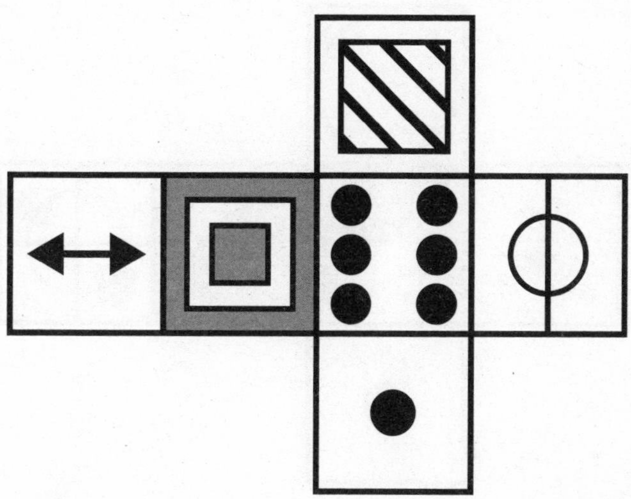

A

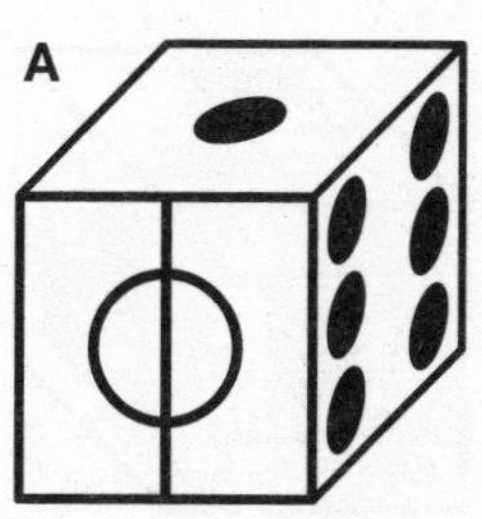

B

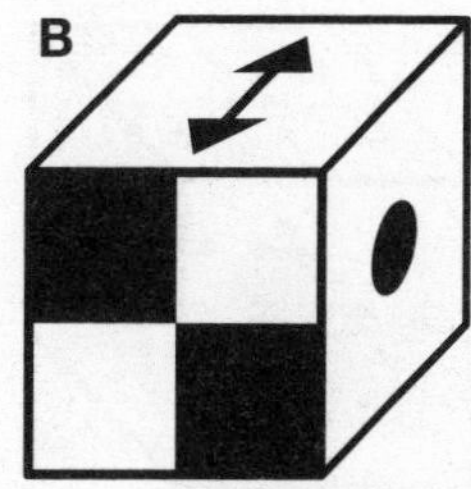

C

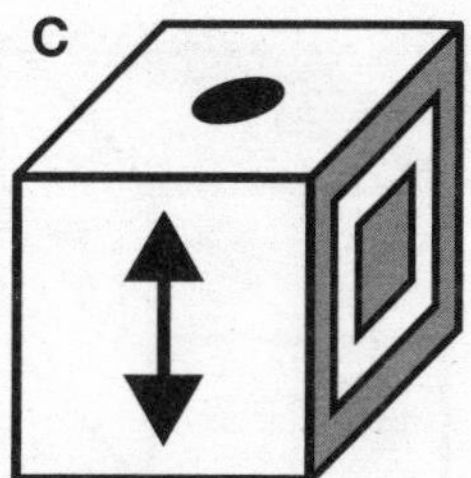

D

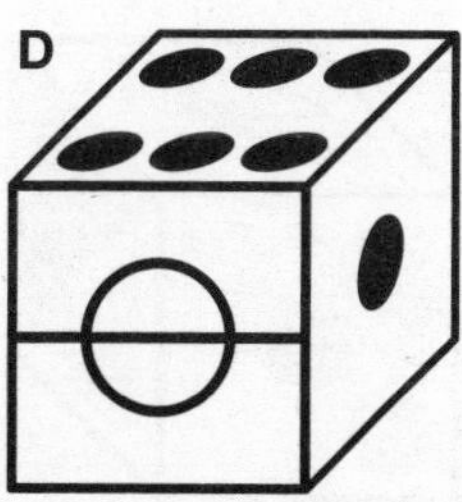

E

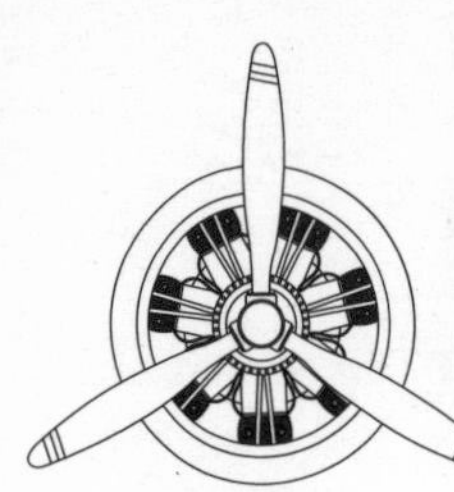

Dicey Decision 3

Mission 37: Imagine the result of folding to make a dice

Briefing:

If you were to cut out and fold up the shape shown, which one of the five dice at the bottom of the page would result?

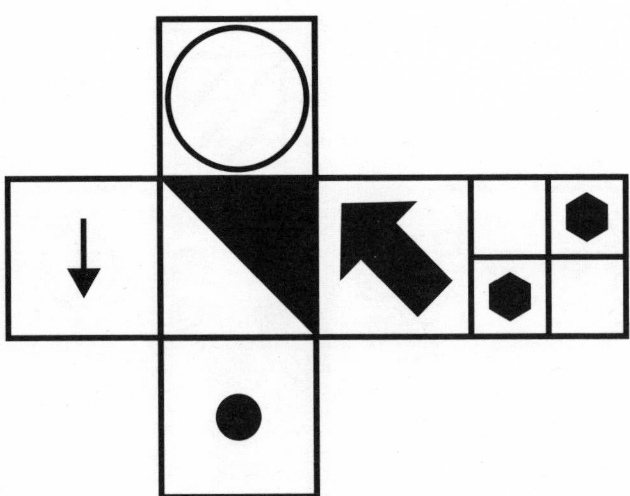

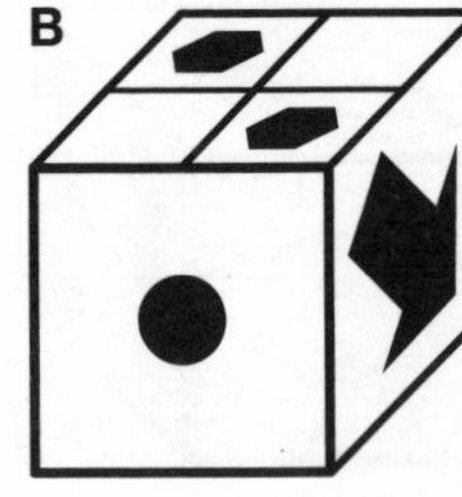

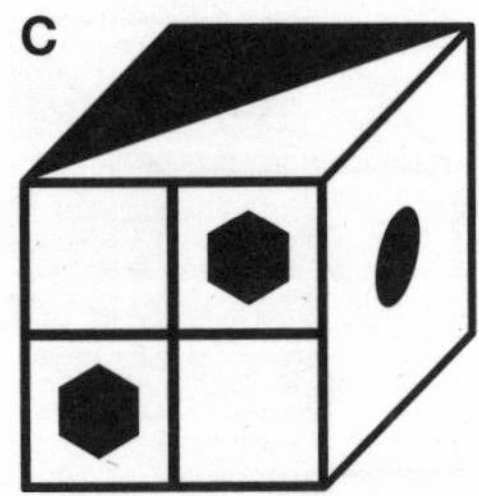

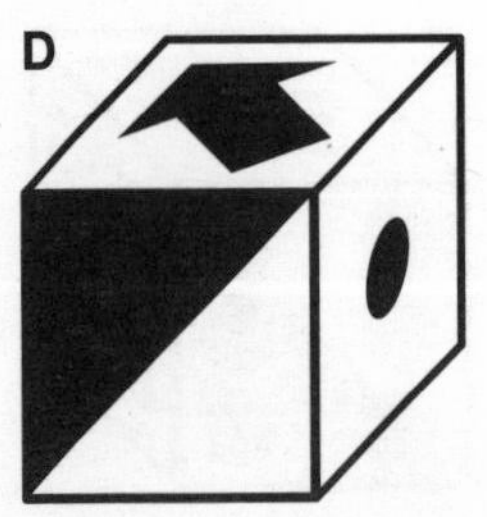

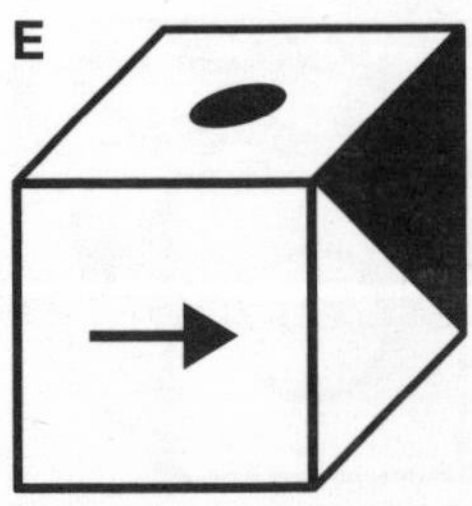

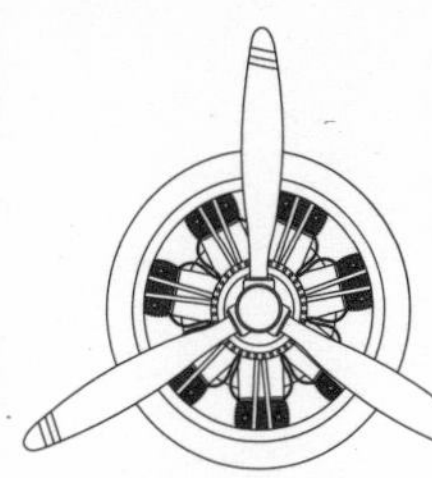

Dicey Decision 4

Mission 38: Imagine the result of folding to make a dice

Briefing:

If you were to cut out and fold up the shape shown, which one of the five dice at the bottom of the page would result?

A

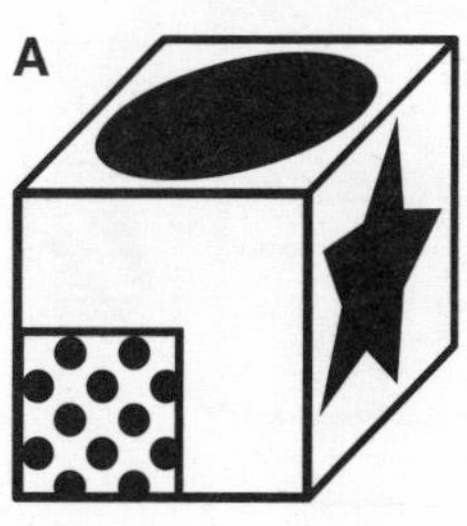

B

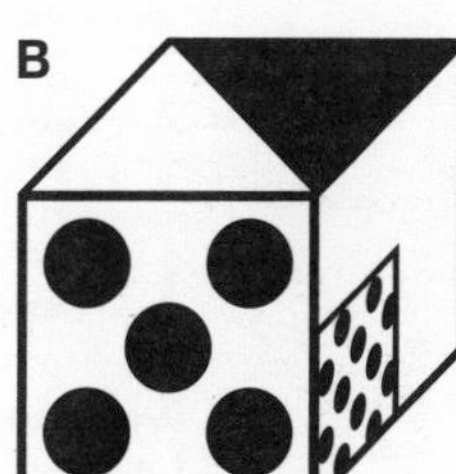

C

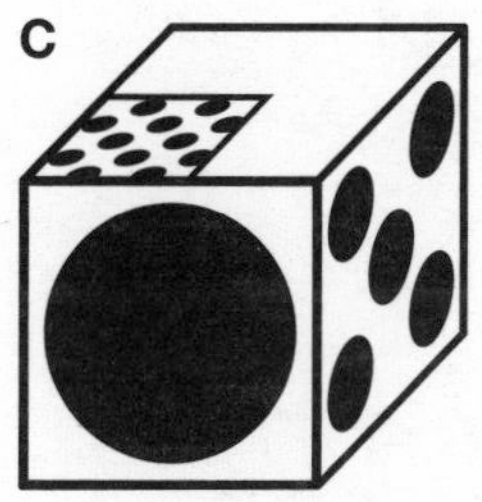

D

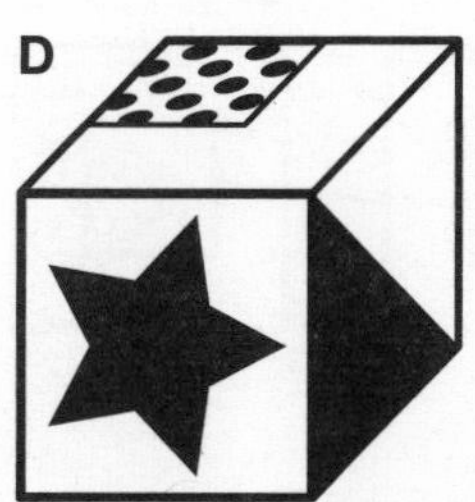

E

Cube Confusion I

Mission 39: Identify the missing face

Briefing:

All four of these dice should be identical, but one of the faces is missing completely from one of the dice. Which of the five options, A to E, should replace the blank face, at some orientation?

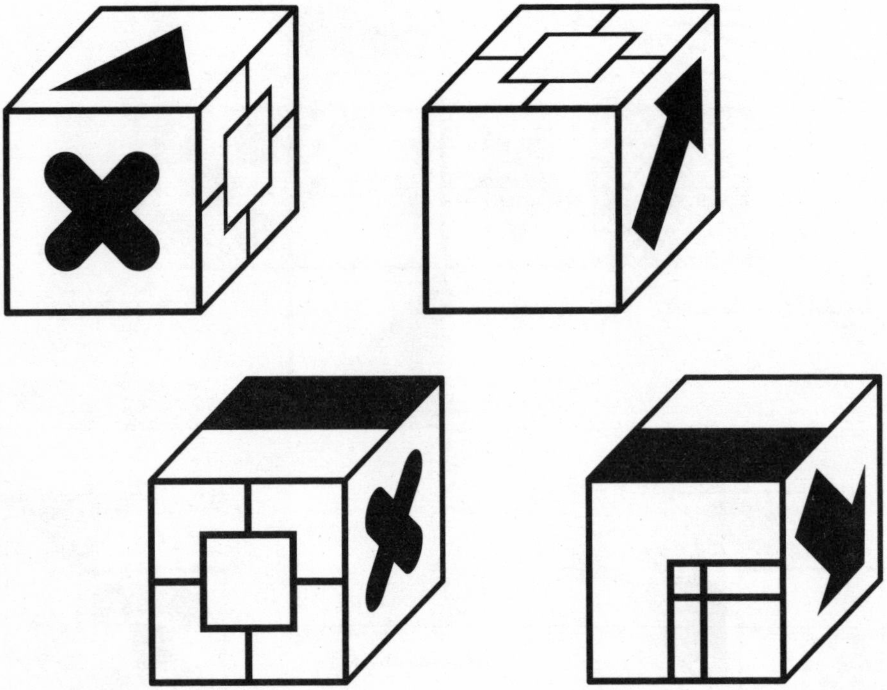

A

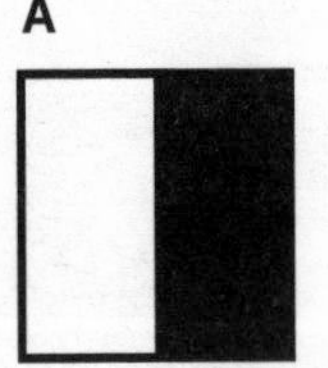

B

C

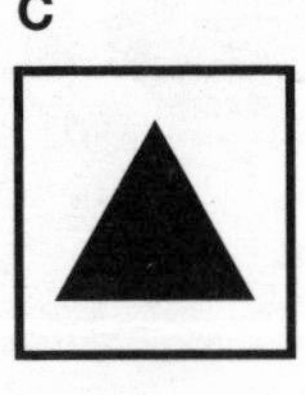

D

E

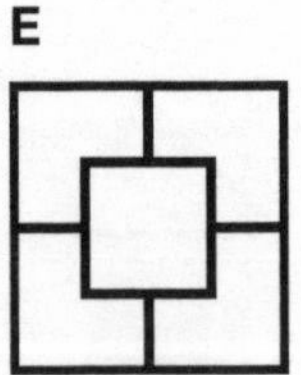

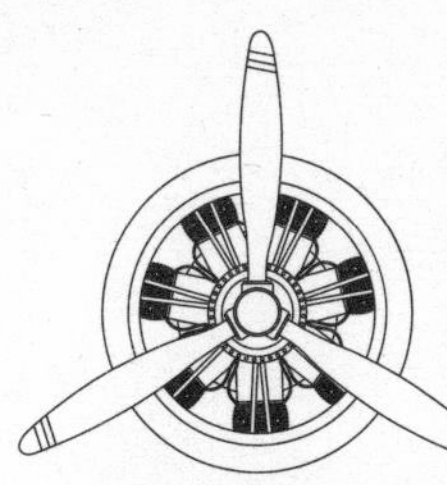

Cube Confusion 2

Mission 40: Identify the missing face

Briefing:

All four of these dice should be identical, but one of the faces is missing completely from one of the dice. Which of the five options, A to E, should replace the blank face, at some orientation?

A

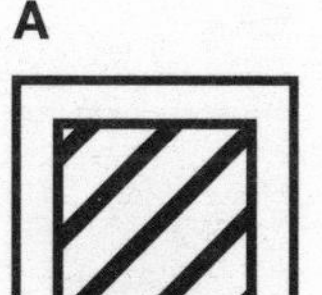

B

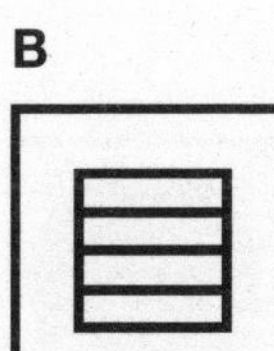

C

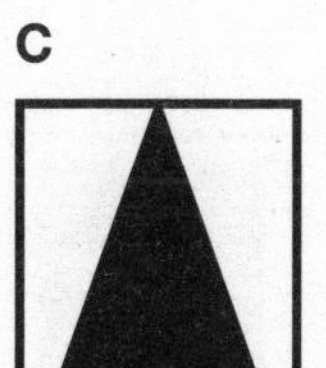

D

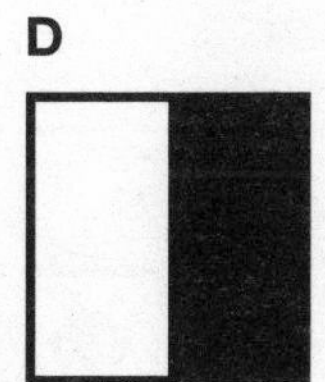

E

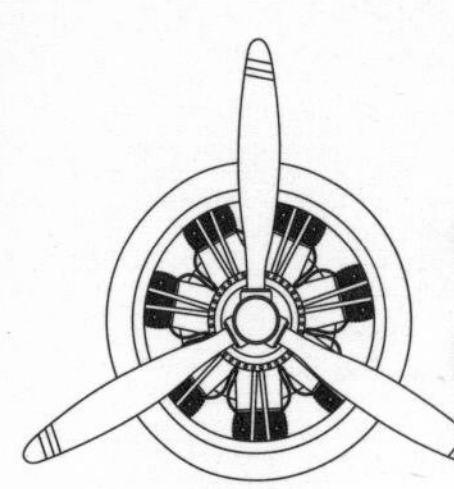

Cube Confusion 3

Mission 41: Identify the missing face

Briefing:

All three of these dice should be identical, but one of the faces is missing completely from one of the dice. Which of the five options, A to E, should replace the blank face, at some orientation?

A

B

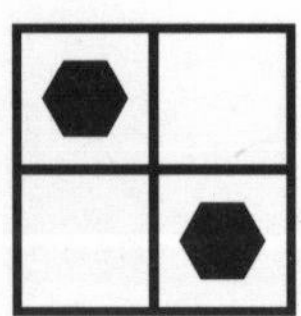

C

D

E

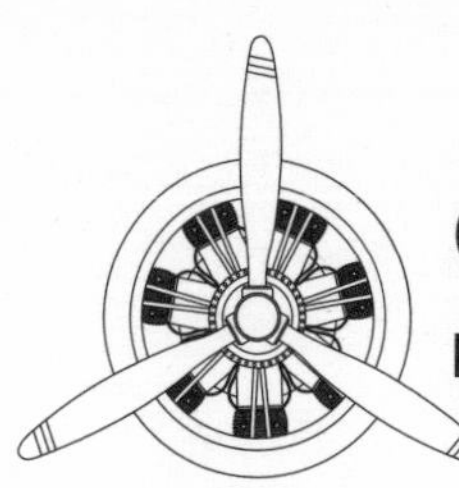

Cube Confusion 4

Mission 42: Identify the missing face

Briefing:

All three of these dice should be identical, but one of the faces is missing completely from one of the dice. Which of the five options, A to E, should replace the blank face, at some orientation?

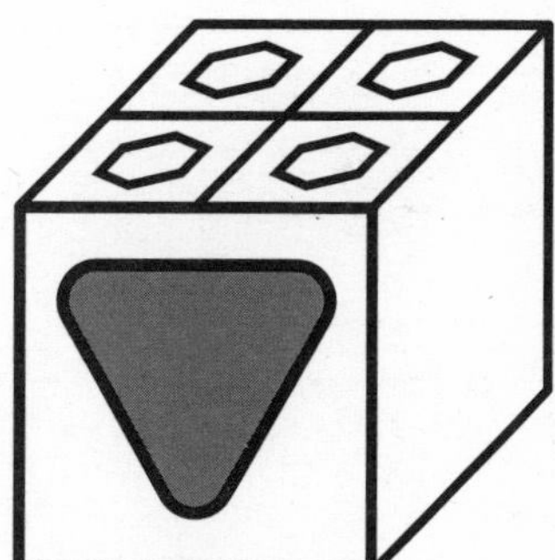

A

B

C

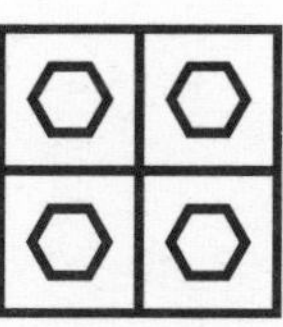

D

E

CHAPTER 4

MEMORY TESTS

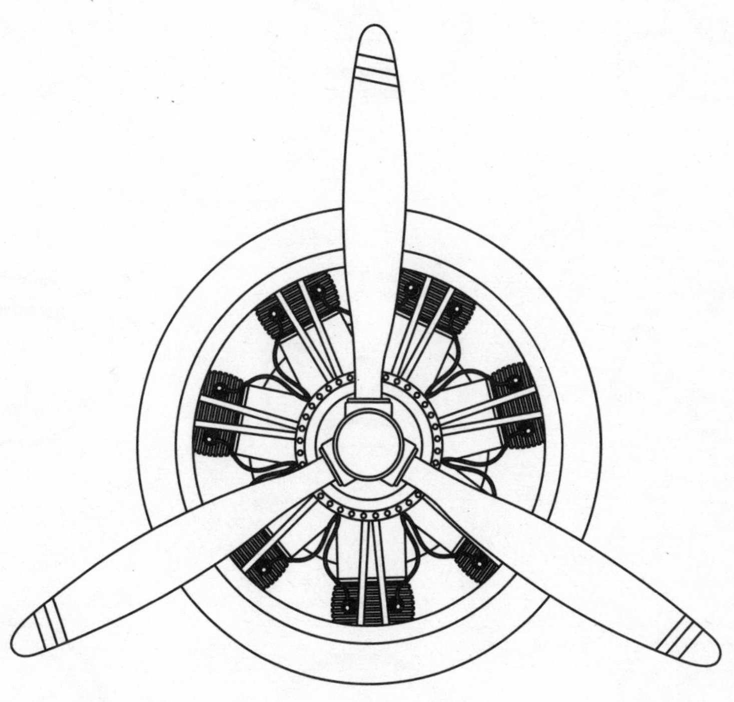

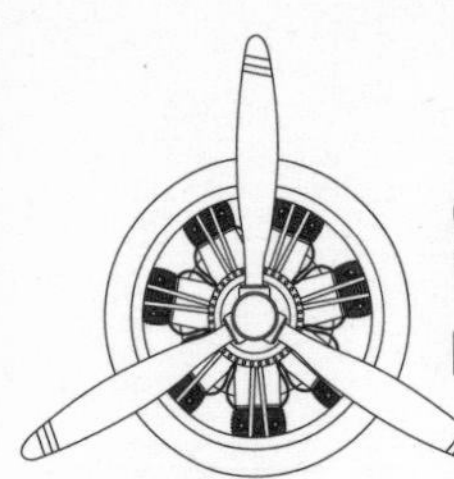

Speed Switch 1

Mission 1: Memorize the following airspeed gauges

Briefing:

Cover the opposite page, then study the aviation-related images below for one minute. When time is up, cover over this page instead, revealing the opposite page in the process, and read the instructions at the top of the page.

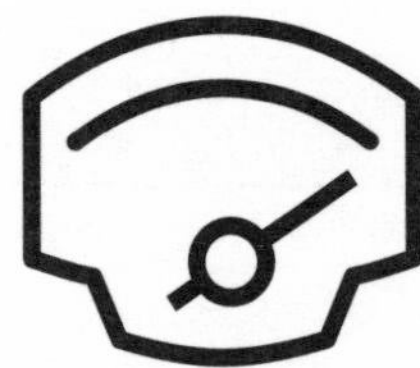

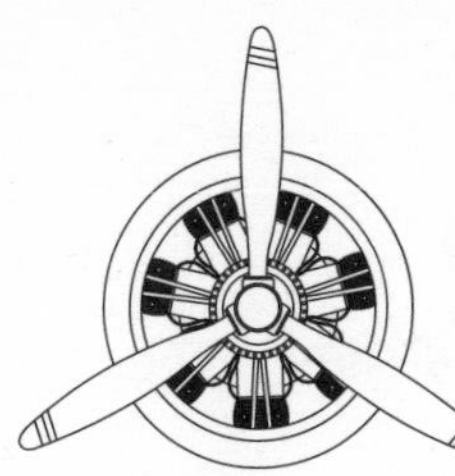

Speed Switch 2

Mission 2: Test your recall of the gauges

Briefing:

If you have not already done so, read the instructions on the previous page first.

Five of the images have been replaced with new images, which are otherwise in the same order. Can you spot all of the *new* images, without referring back to the previous page?

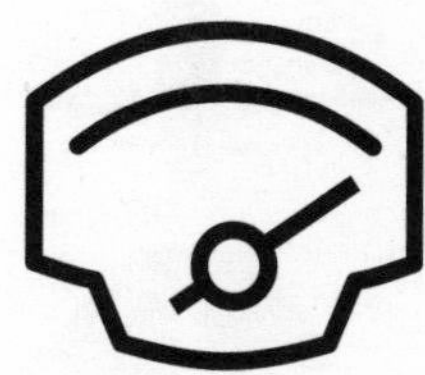

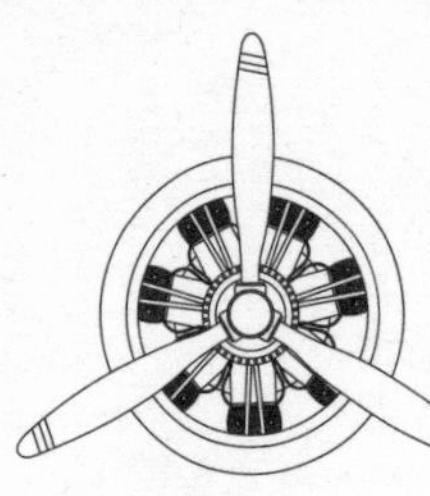

Airport Change 1

Mission 3: Memorize the following airport-related icons

Briefing:

Cover the opposite page, then study the airport-related images below for one minute. When time is up, cover over this page instead, revealing the opposite page in the process, and read the instructions at the top of the page.

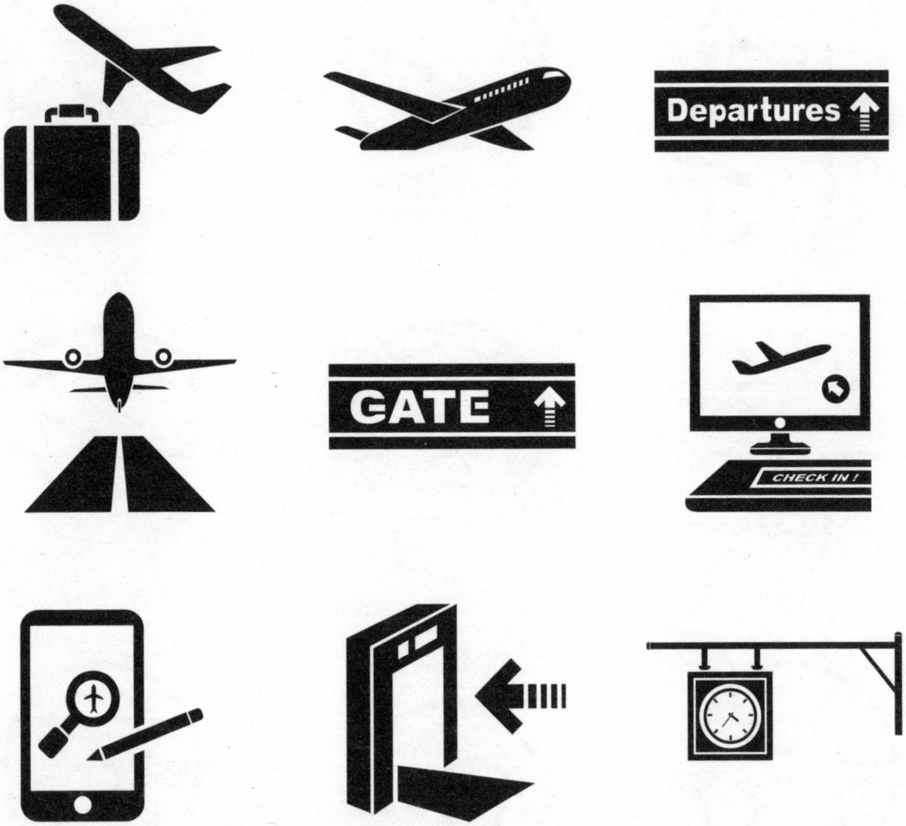

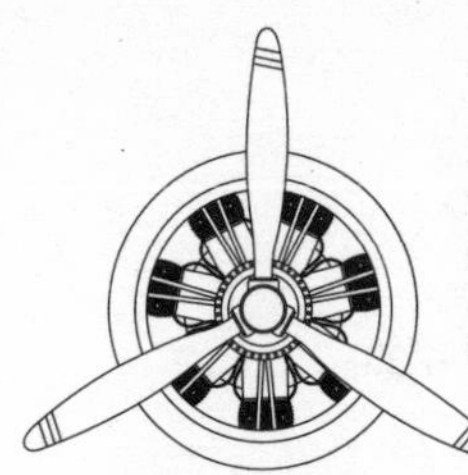

Airport Change 2

Mission 4: Test your recall of the airport icons

Briefing:

If you have not already done so, read the instructions on the previous page first.

Some of the images from the previous page have been replaced, and all of them have been re-ordered. Can you describe all of the *missing* images?

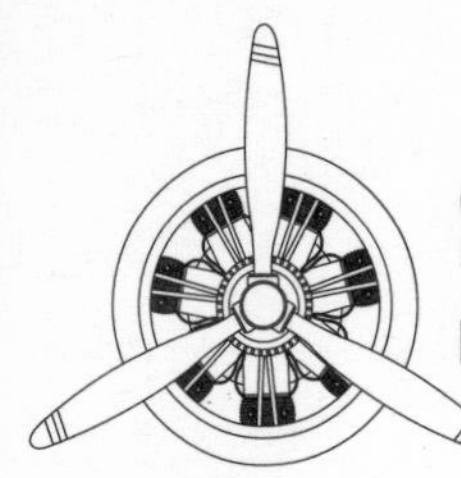

Swapped Pairs I

Mission 5: Memorize the location of each image

Briefing:

Cover the opposite page, then study the airport-related images below for one minute. When time is up, cover over this page instead, revealing the opposite page in the process, and read the instructions at the top of the page – which will ask you about which images have changed locations.

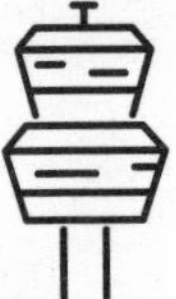

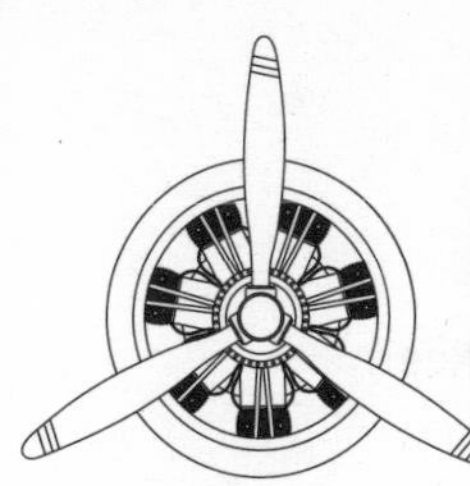

Swapped Pairs 2

Mission 6: Recall the location of each image

Briefing:

If you have not already done so, read the instructions on the previous page first.

Some *pairs* of images from the previous page have swapped places. Can you draw lines to join pairs of images that have taken each other's previous place?

Briefing I

Mission 7: Study and memorize the announcement

Briefing:

Cover the opposite page, then read the passage below, studying each sentence carefully. After two minutes, cover over this page and reveal the opposite page, then read the instructions there.

Good morning, ladies and gentlemen. This is your captain speaking.

We would like to welcome you on board this Boeing 747 flight to Barcelona. We are expecting a flight time of around two hours and five minutes this morning, touching down at around 11am local time.

Flying conditions are looking good. We have a slight breeze coming from the east but are expecting a smooth flight today.

The cabin crew will be performing their final safety checks in a moment, so I'll leave them to it but I'll be in touch a little later with some updates during the flight.

In the meantime, please sit back, relax, and enjoy your flight.

Briefing 2

Mission 8: Find differences in this similar announcement

Briefing:

If you have not already done so, read the instructions on the previous page first.

Can you find ten differences between the passage below and the one you read on the previous page, without checking back?

Good morning, ladies and gentlemen. This is your pilot speaking.

We would like to welcome you on board this Boeing 757 flight to Barcelona. We are expecting a flight time of around two hours and ten minutes this morning, touching down at around 11pm local time.

Weather conditions are looking great. We have a slight breeze coming from the west but are expecting a calm flight today.

I'll be in touch a little later with some updates during the flight.

In the meantime, please sit back, relax, and enjoy your journey.

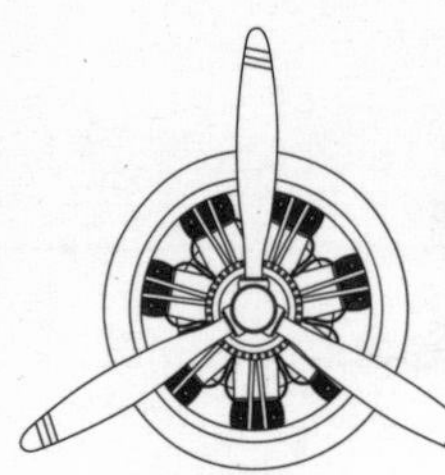

Flight Plan I

Mission 9: Memorize the counties in the order given

Briefing:

You are a pilot due to go on a training mission. Listed below are the names of several counties you must fly over, in order, as part of your test. Study the list carefully for one minute, paying close attention to the order. When you have finished, cover the list and read the following page.

Merseyside

Cheshire

Derbyshire

South Yorkshire

Nottinghamshire

Lincolnshire

Norfolk

Cambridgeshire

Rutland

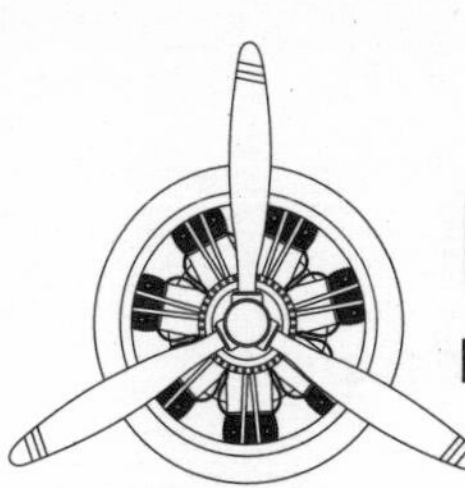

Flight Plan 2

Mission 10: Recall the counties and answer questions

Briefing:

If you have not already done so, read the instructions on the previous page first.

Now, see how many of the questions below you can answer, without checking back to the list on the previous page.

1. How many counties were on the list?

2. Which was the first county to be flown over?

3. Which county was flown over after Nottinghamshire?

4. Which county was the penultimate one to be flown over?

5. How many of the county names ended with the suffix '-shire'?

6. In what general direction were the counties to be flown over from the beginning to the end of the mission: north to south, or south to north?

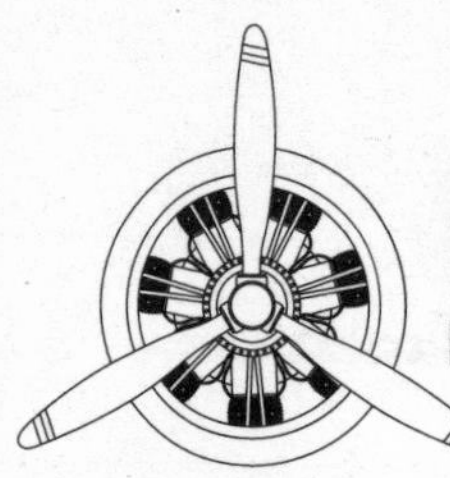

Model Memory I

Mission 11: Memorize the aircraft and their years

Briefing:

The list below contains the names of various aircraft models, alongside the year they were introduced into service in the Royal Air Force. Study the names and dates for three minutes, then cover them up and see if you can answer the questions on the opposite page.

Sopwith Camel – 1918

Supermarine Sea Otter – 1943

Westland Puma – 1971

De Havilland Tiger Moth – 1932

Eurocopter Squirrel – 1997

Avro York – 1943

Bristol Britannia – 1959

Boeing Sentry – 1991

Model Memory 2

Mission 12: Recall the aircraft and their years

Briefing:

If you have not already done so, read the instructions on the previous page first.

Now, see how many of the questions below you can answer, without checking back to the list on the previous page.

1. How many aircraft names contained animals?

2. Which two aircraft were introduced in the same year?

3. Which two English cities appeared in the aircraft names?

4. Which was the first aircraft to be introduced, according to the dates?

5. Which plane entered service in 1971?

6. Which was the fifth aircraft named in the list?

7. Which aircraft model had the shortest name (in terms of the number of letters it contained)?

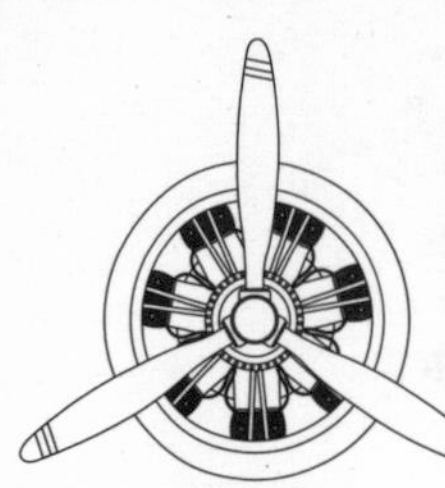

People Carrier I

Mission 13: Memorize the transport instructions

Briefing:

Examine the following transport plan carefully for three minutes, paying close attention to the sizes of groups being transported and their destinations, as well as the order of the instructions. When you have finished, cover them up and see if you can answer the questions on the opposite page.

Pick up Group A from Halifax.

Drop off six people from Group A in Washington, and take the remaining people to Lincoln.

Offload the rest of Group A (seven people) in Lincoln.

Fly to Manchester. Pick up Group B and Group C.

Drop half of Group B in Lincoln (four people).

Take all remaining passengers from Group B and Group C (fifteen people in total) to Washington.

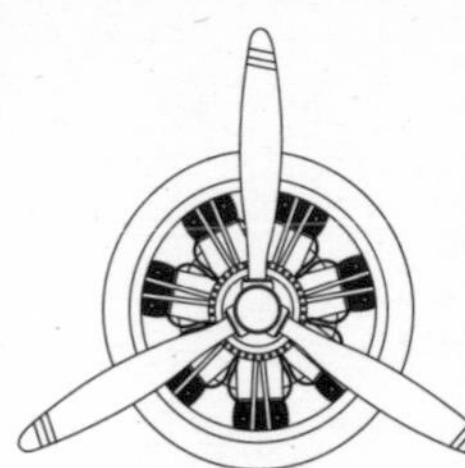

People Carrier 2

Mission 14: Recall the transport instructions

Briefing:

If you have not already done so, read the instructions on the previous page first.

Now, see how many of the questions below you can answer, without checking back to the plan on the previous page.

1. How many different cities were named in the instructions, and in what order were they visited?
2. How many people were picked up in Group B?
3. Where was the first group of people from Group A dropped off?
4. Where did Group C travel from and to?
5. How many people were in Group C?
6. Which city had the greatest number of people dropped off in it overall: Lincoln or Washington?
7. What was the total number of people picked up across all three groups?

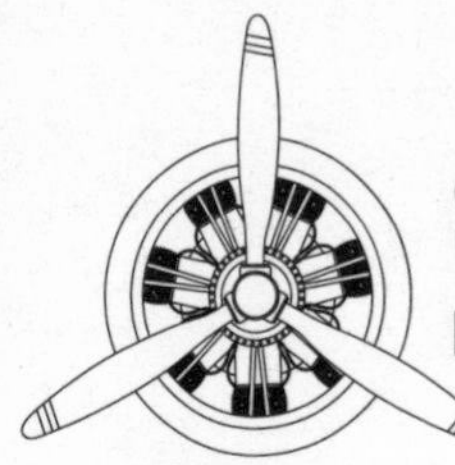

Security Details 1

Mission 15: Memorize the security codes

Briefing:

Take three minutes to memorize the following security codes, which contain fictional information required for secure access. Once time is up, cover over this page and see if you can answer the questions on the opposite page.

Network Details:
33SkyCapture

Internal Network Access Code:
649865

Your Password:
hurr1c4n31918

Your Security Key:
gyro-heli-aero

Emergency Callout:
M8A9Y8D9A8Y

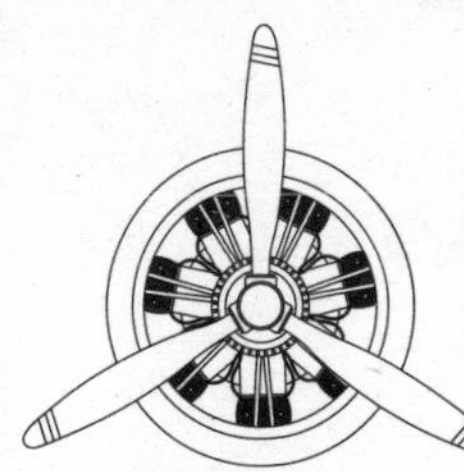

Security Details 2

Mission 16: Recall the security codes

Briefing:

If you have not already done so, read the instructions on the previous page first.

Now, see how many of the questions below you can answer, without checking back to the security details on the previous page.

1. The Internal Network Access Code is a six-digit number. What is its value?
2. Which code was the only one not to contain any numbers?
3. How many letters and digits long was the Emergency Callout code?
4. Which two-digit number formed part of the Network Details code?
5. Which was the penultimate code in the list?
6. Which model of aircraft formed part of the text of Your Password, with some letters represented by similarly shaped digits?
7. Which code contained uppercase letters, but had no lowercase letters?
8. Which code included within it the year in which the RAF was formed?

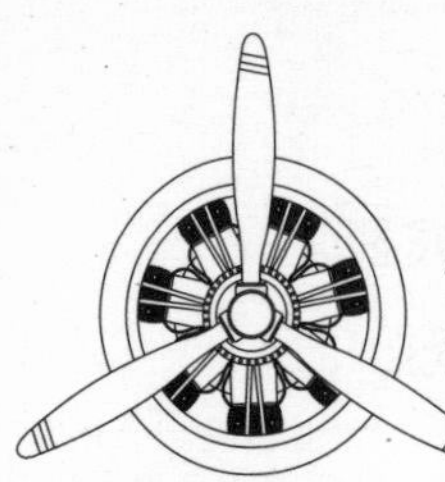

Aviation Occupations 1

Mission 17: Memorize the job titles

Briefing:

Cover the opposite page, then spend up to three minutes memorizing the following list of words. Once time is up, cover over this page instead and turn to the following page, where you'll be asked to recall it.

Air-traffic controller

Flight Attendant

Ground Crew

Sky Marshal

Fighter Pilot

Parachutist

Dispatcher

Technician

Navigator

Mechanic

Engineer

Pilot

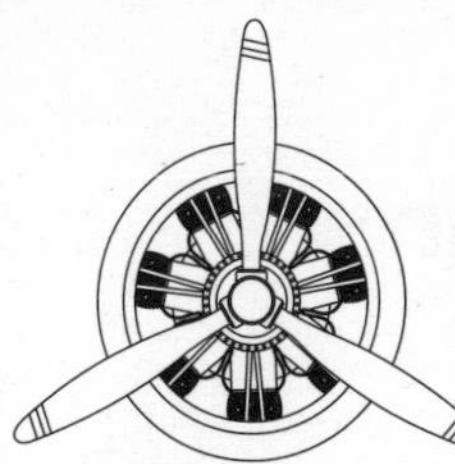

Aviation Occupations 2

Mission 18: Recall the job titles, given the first letters

Briefing:

Can you complete each of the occupations? The first letter of each is given as a memory aid.

A____________________________

D____________________________

E ____________________________

F ____________________________

F ____________________________

G ____________________________

M ____________________________

N ____________________________

P ____________________________

P ____________________________

S ____________________________

T ____________________________

RAF Ranks I

Mission 19: Memorize the listed ranks

Briefing:

First, cover the opposite page. Then spend one minute reading over the following list of twelve RAF ranks. Once time is up, cover over this page instead and turn to the following page.

Air Commodore

Air Marshal

Aircraftman

Corporal

Flight Lieutenant

Flying Officer

Group Captain

Lance Corporal

Sergeant

Squadron Leader

Warrant Officer

Wing Commander

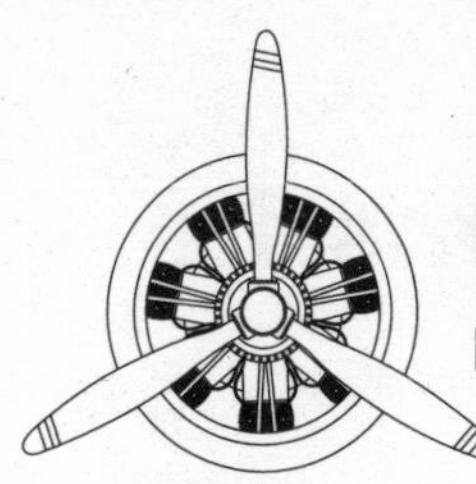

RAF Ranks 2

Mission 20: Identify the replacement ranks

Briefing:
Can you identify which of these ranks did not appear on the previous page?

Air Chief Marshal

Air Vice Marshal

Corporal

Flight Lieutenant

Flying Officer

Marshal of the Royal Air Force

Sergeant

Senior Aircraftman

RAF Master Aircrew

Chief Technician

Warrant Officer

Wing Commander

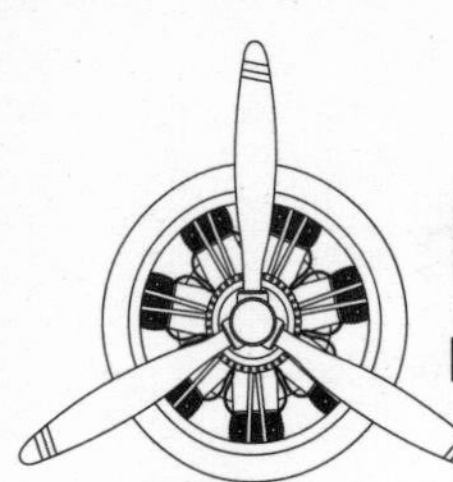

Meteorological Terms I

Mission 21: Memorize the word positions

Briefing:

First, cover the opposite page. Then spend two minutes observing the location of each of the following words. Once time is up, cover over this page instead and turn to the following page.

Humidity

Gust

Precipitation

Anticyclone

Kelvin

Squall

Monsoon

Tornado

Atmosphere

Pressure

Barometer

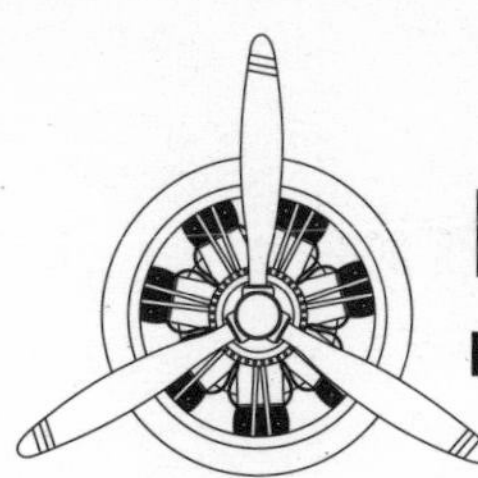

Meteorological Terms 2

Mission 22: Recall and write in the missing words

Briefing:

This copy of the previous page is missing certain words. Can you write them into the gaps provided?

Humidity

____

Precipitation

________________________ Kelvin

Squall

____

Tornado

____

____

Barometer

CHAPTER 5

KNOWLEDGE TRAINING

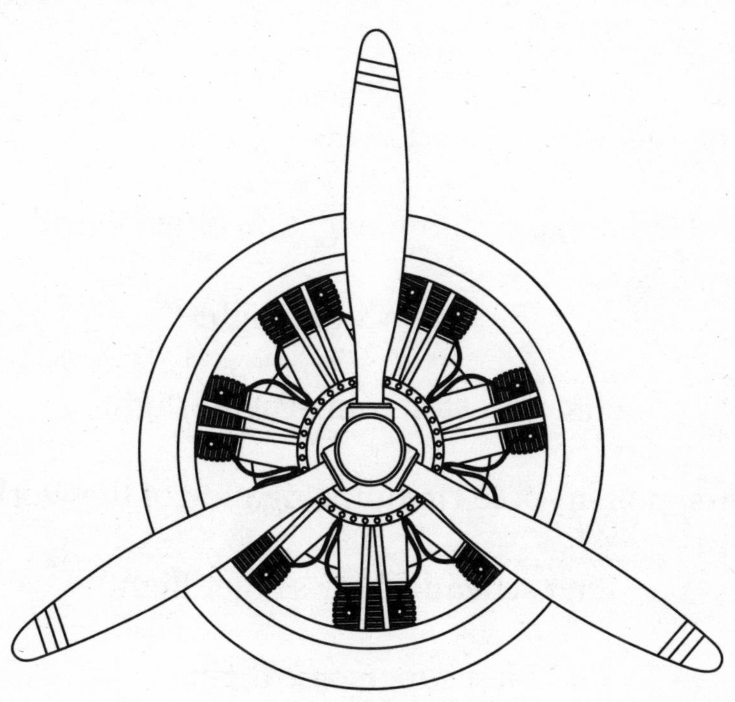

First Flights 1

Mission 1: Match each breakthrough event to its year

Briefing:

Can you match each pioneering aeronautical event to the year in which it occurred? All of the events refer to flights made with heavier-than-air aircraft.

Years

1903	1924	1932	1965
1914	1931	1947	1969

Events

First aerial circumnavigation of the world

First Concorde flight

First non-stop trans-Pacific flight

First pole-to-pole circumnavigation of the world

First scheduled passenger flight

First supersonic flight

First sustained powered flight

First transatlantic flight piloted by a woman

First Flights 2

Mission 2: Match each event to its pilot or pilots

Briefing:

Complete the mission on the opposite page first, then match each event with its corresponding pilot, or pilots, from the list below.

Pilots

Amelia Earhart

André Turcat

Chuck Yeager

Clyde Pangborn and Hugh Herndon

Fred Austin and Harrison Finch

Lowell Smith, Erik Nelson, Leslie Arnold and John Harding Jr

The Wright Brothers

Tony Jannus

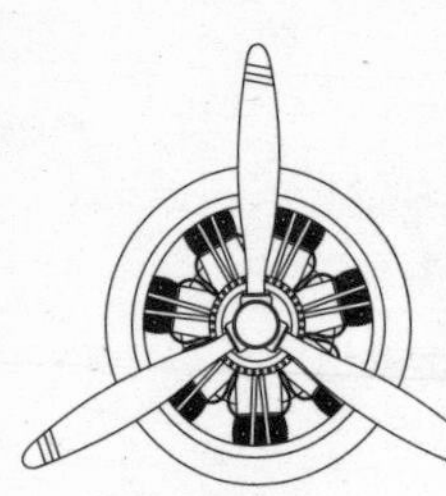

Air Force History I

Mission 3: Test your RAF and related knowledge

Briefing:

Can you answer these questions on the history of the Royal Air Force? The solutions have been provided beneath, although they are given out of order, and with the letters or numbers in each answer jumbled.

Questions

1. In what year was the RAF – the world's first independent national air force – founded?

2. In what year did the Royal Air Force Association, dedicated to the welfare of airforce personnel, first receive royal patronage?

3. The prototype of which celebrated model of aeroplane was first flown on March 5th 1936?

4. In what modern London borough can the Battle of Britain Bunker be found, from which its titular operation was controlled?

5. After more than 100 years of usage, what type of airborne vehicle was used for the final time by the RAF in 1995?

6. Who was the first woman to be awarded RAF Pilot's Wings, in 1952?

Answers

9316 FSTPIREI

9811 IHDIOLLGNN

AJNE NOEXNL IDRB LALBONO

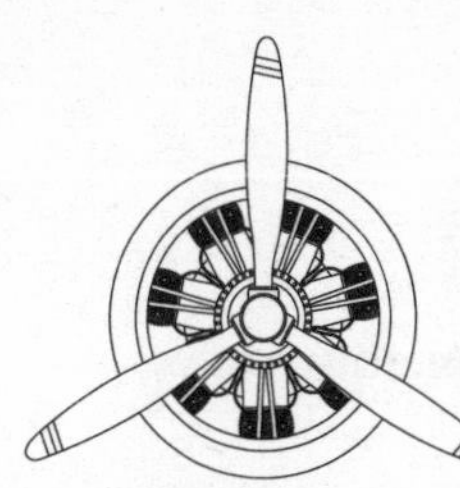

Air Force History 2

Mission 4: Further test your RAF knowledge

Briefing:

Can you answer these further questions on the history of the Royal Air Force? The solutions have been provided beneath, although they are given out of order, and with the letters in each word jumbled.

Questions

1. What name was popularly given to the RAF squadron which damaged German hydroelectric power stations during Operation Chastise?
2. By what two-word name are the Royal Air Force Aerobatic Team more commonly known?
3. In which former aerodrome is the RAF Museum London located?
4. What cereal-related code name was given to the RAF campaign in which food supplies were airdropped into Ethiopia, to help combat famine?
5. When the Supermarine Swift entered RAF service in 1954, what design feature did it introduce for the first time?
6. Who was the first RAF Chief of the Air Staff? He was known as an early advocate of strategic bombing.

Answers

AMDSSTEBRU — EOOTNRIPA ULBHSE

DHNNOE EAMRORDEO — IRS GHHU RTERAHNDC

DRE RARSWO — TWPSE ISNWG

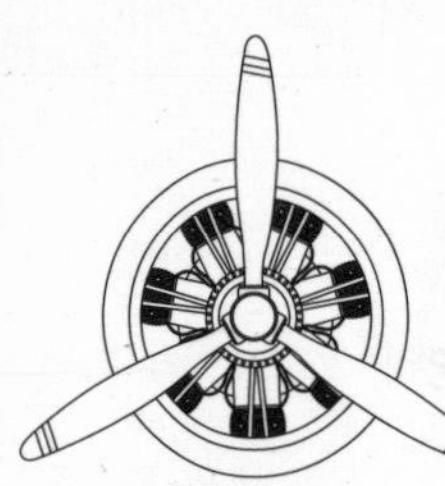

Major Airports

Mission 5: Identify the airports and the cities they serve

Briefing:

The three-letter airport codes for ten major international airports have been given below. Can you work out which city is served by each airport, and then match that city to one of the approximate locations labelled with letters on the map below? Each location is used once.

ATL	HKG
LAX	CDG
ORD	JNB
DXB	SYD
LHR	JFK

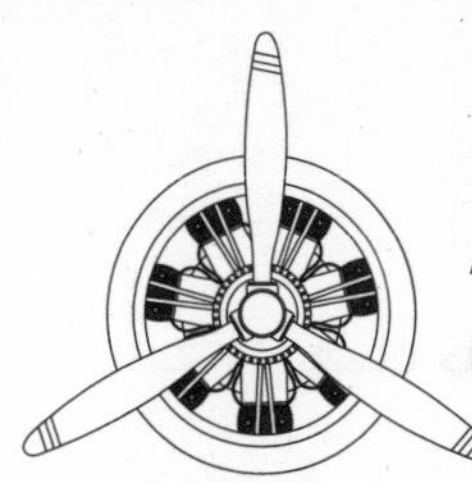

Airport Routes

Mission 6: Pair the airports to match the flights

Briefing:

Can you pair up the European airport codes below, so that each pair matches one of the labelled approximate flight paths shown below? For example, BCN and EDI would pair up to match a flight path travelling between Barcelona and Edinburgh.

AMS FRA MAD

ATH HEL NIC

BUD LGW OSL

DUB LIS WAW

B E A D F C

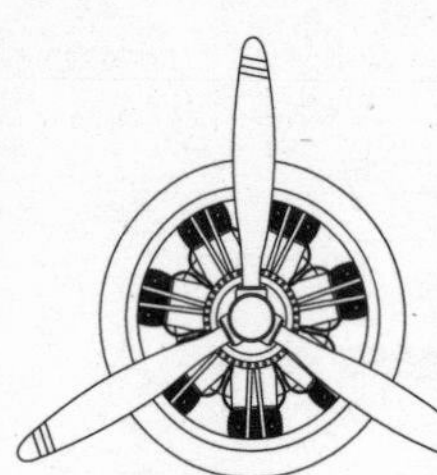

Aerobatics I

Mission 7: Complete the aerobatic links sequence

Briefing:

Can you fill in the squares with the names of five basic aerobatic manoeuvres? All letters which are shared between consecutive words have been linked. The first word has been filled in for you.

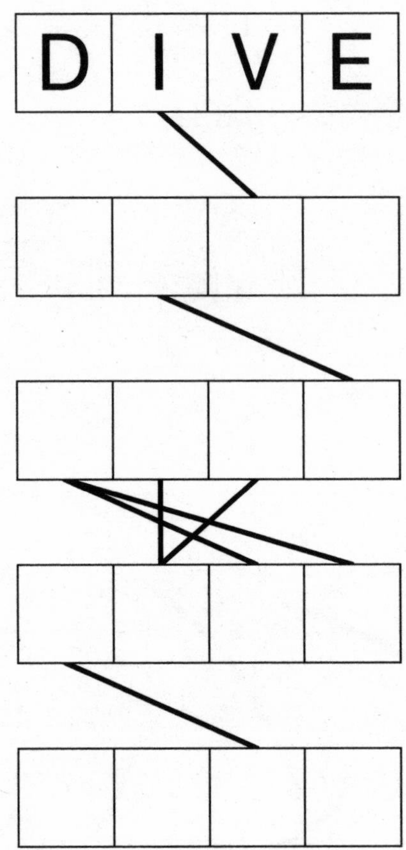

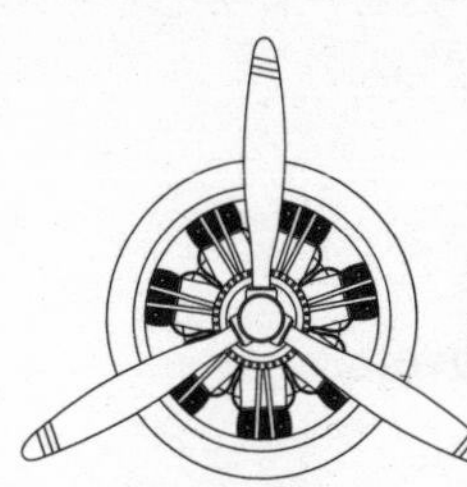

Aerobatics 2

Mission 8: Unscramble the aerobatic manoeuvres

Briefing:

Can you restore the names of five aerobatic manoeuvres which have been split into fragments, and the fragments sorted into alphabetical order? Solutions may consist of one or two words.

AF	FAL
ANE	GLE
AVA	GOV
CHE	HAMM
CUB	IGHT
EAD	LAN
ER	LIN
ERH	WIN

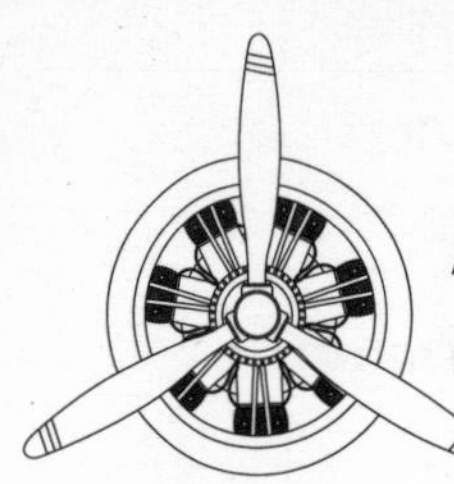

Aerobatics 3

Mission 9: Reveal the missing manoeuvre letters

Briefing:

Can you restore the names of six aerobatic manoeuvres, which have each had every other letter removed?

C_A_D_L_E

_N_L_S_ B_N_

L_Z_ E_G_T

_A_L_L_D_

Z_O_ C_I_B

_U_P_Y _U_P

Air Force Mottoes

Mission 10: Untangle the lines to reveal the mottoes

Briefing:

Can you rearrange these English translations of international air force mottoes, which have their words out of order? The nationality of each air force is given.

Brazil
country protect the that wings

Czech Republic
air is our sea the

Finland
is our power quality

Greece
always dominate heights the

Netherlands
deeds great in in numbers small

Portugal
free his of own will

United Kingdom
adversity stars the through to

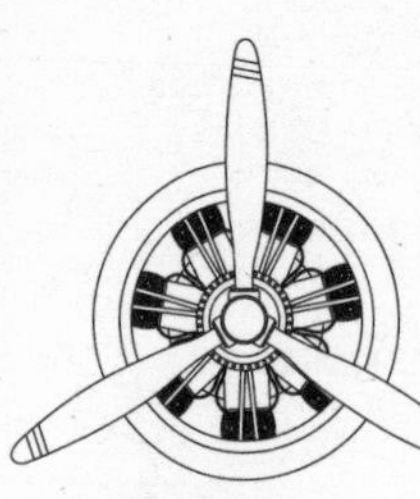

Air Force Roundels

Mission 11: Colour and identify six air force roundels

Briefing:

Colour the roundels according to the guide below to reveal six different European air force roundels. Then, can you assign each roundel to the country whose national air force uses it, choosing from the given list?

Colours: 1 = red, 2 = yellow, 3 = blue, 4 = black, 5 = white
Countries: Belgium, Finland, France, Greece, Spain, United Kingdom

A

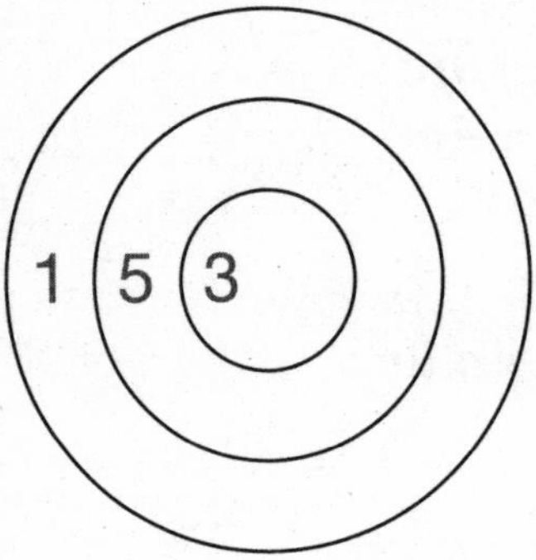

1 5 3

B

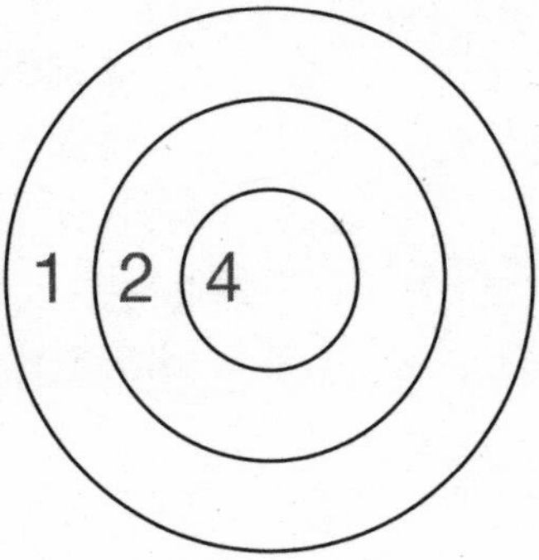

1 2 4

C

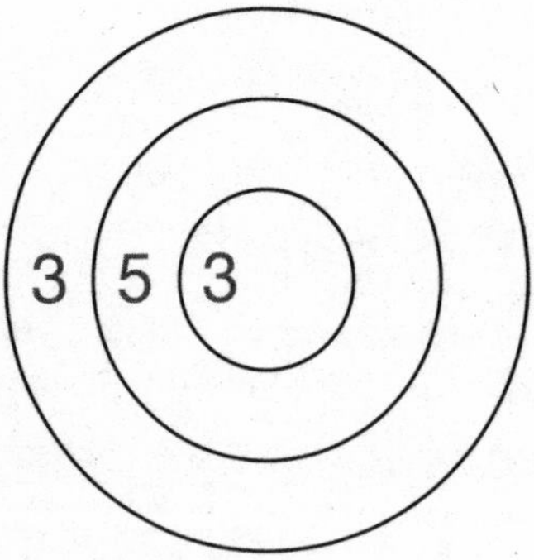

3 5 3

D

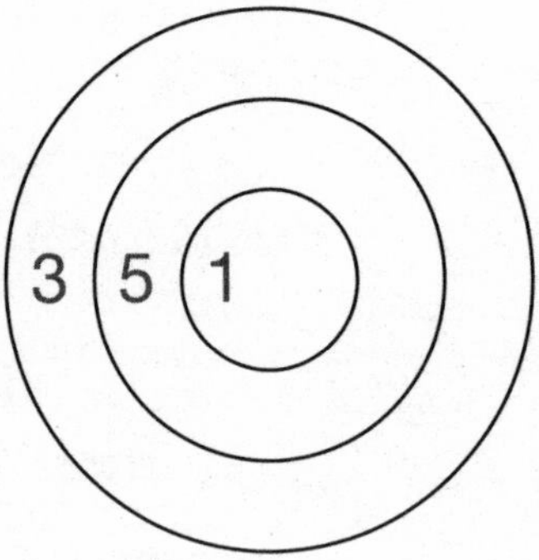

3 5 1

E

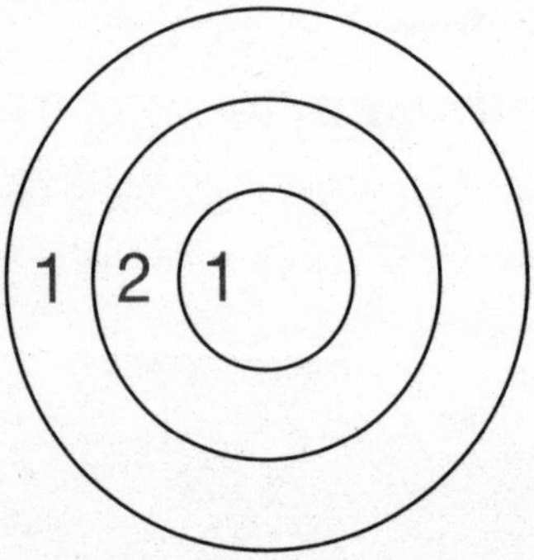

1 2 1

F

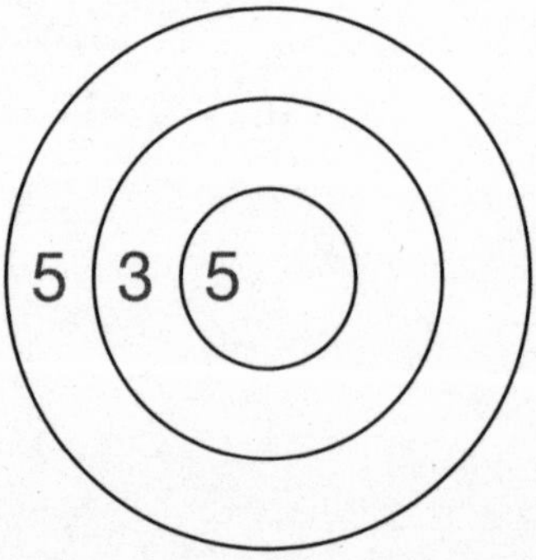

5 3 5

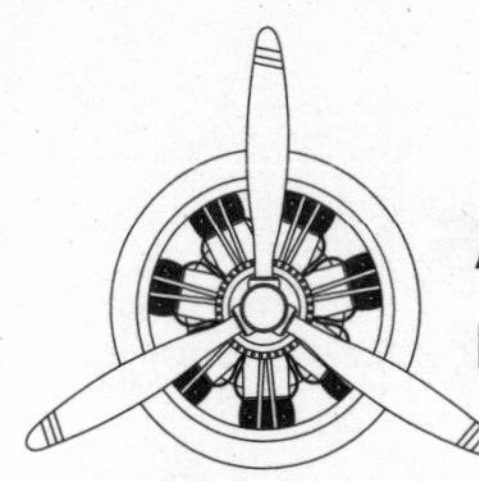

Aircraft Manufacturers

Mission 12: Solve the clues to reveal the makers

Briefing:

Can you work out the names of six aircraft manufacturers by solving the clues below? Each clue either side of the '+' solves to give one word. Combine the two in the order given to reveal the name of the manufacturer.

atmosphere + public transport vehicle

tree species + skill

just + young person

virtuous + annum

chasm + flow

excellent + maritime

Alliterative Architects

Mission 13: Match the manufacturer to each clued model

Briefing:

Pair each of the given aircraft manufacturers with a retired model of RAF plane they once made. The manufacturers are given, but the model names – all of which are a single, English word – are clued. Each model name pairs with a manufacturer whose name begins with the same letter. For example, 'violent cyclonic storm' clues 'hurricane', which would match with the manufacturer Hawker to reveal the plane: 'Hawker Hurricane'.

Avro
Blackburn
Fairey
Gloster
Handley Page
Lockheed
Miles
Percival
Sopwith
Westland

Alternative name for a large American deer

Amphibian once thought to have resistance to fire

An experienced advisor and guide

British town, site of Army Headquarters

Capital of Nova Scotia; Yorkshire town

A head of some universities and religious groups

Long armoured glove thrown to issue a challenge

It's often accompanied by thunder

Woman's name; Yorkshire town

Young deer; light brown

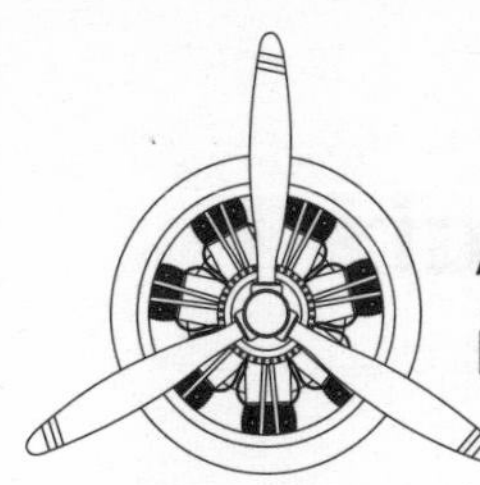

Airport-code Countries

Mission 14: Reveal hidden countries using airport codes

Briefing:

Can you work out the three-letter codes for the airports listed below, and use the solutions to reveal the names of four countries? Each set of airport codes, when correctly guessed, spells out the name of a country. A clue to the identity of each country being spelled out is also given in bold. All solutions consist of one word. For example, the airport codes for Frankfurt + Nice are FRA + NCE, clueing FRANCE.

European city-state:

Mount Cook (New Zealand) + Ascona (Switzerland)

Balkan country:

Boston (USA) + Nimba (Liberia)

Central American country:

Nicosia (Cyprus) + Acadiana Regional Airport (USA) + Guatemala City (Guatemala)

Balkan country:

Macon Downton (USA) + Edremit (Turkey) + Nimba (Liberia)

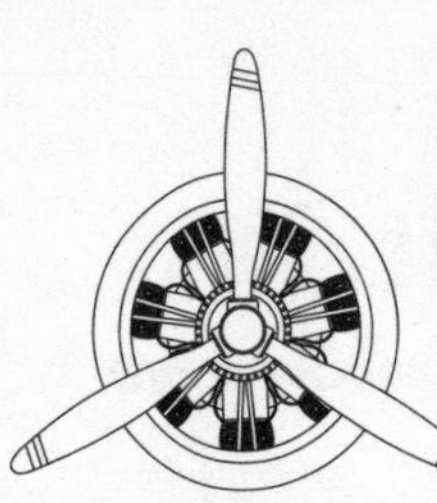

Battle of Britain Quiz 1

Mission 15: Test your knowledge

Briefing:

Can you answer these questions on the Battle of Britain? Three options to choose from are given for each answer.

1. In what year did the Battle of Britain take place?

   a. 1933
   b. 1940
   c. 1945

2. According to British historians, what was the duration of the Battle of Britain?

   a. Three and a half months
   b. Six months
   c. Nine and a half months

3. Who was the British Prime Minister during the Battle of Britain?

   a. Neville Chamberlain
   b. Winston Churchill
   c. Clement Attlee

4. What name did the Germans give to their planned invasion of Britain in World War II?

   a. Operation Sea Lion
   b. Operation Barbarossa
   c. Operation Chastise

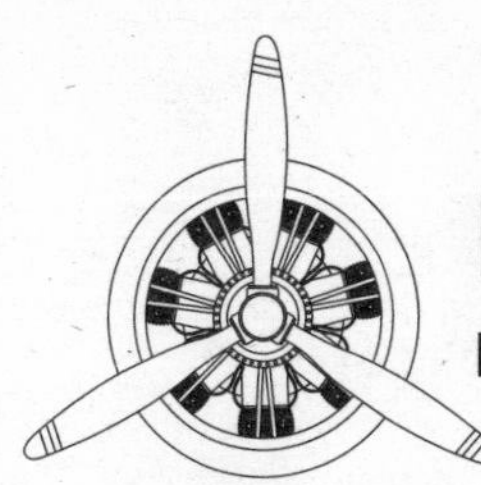

Battle of Britain Quiz 2

Mission 16: Further test your knowledge

Briefing:

Can you answer these additional questions on the Battle of Britain? Three options to choose from are given for each answer.

1. Which of these planes did *not* fly during the Battle of Britain?

a. Hawker Hurricane
b. Supermarine Spitfire
c. Panavia ('Tonka') Tornado

2. Which then-recent technological development contributed to the success of the Battle of Britain?

a. Morse Code
b. Heliograph
c. Radar

3. Which of these three quotes is attributed to Winston Churchill?

a. Never in the airfields was so much owed to so many by so few
b. Never in the field of human conflict was so much owed by so many to so few
c. Never in a time of war were so many owing so much to so few

4. Approximately how many men made up 'The Few', a name given to the men who flew in the battle?

a. 2,000
b. 3,000
c. 4,000

Airport Triples I

Mission 17: Identify each city based on its airports

Briefing:

Can you identify each of these four cities served by multiple airports? Each group contains three airport codes, all of which serve one city.

LTN
LHR
LGW

LGA
JFK
EWR

MBW
MEB
MEL

BVA
ORY
CDG

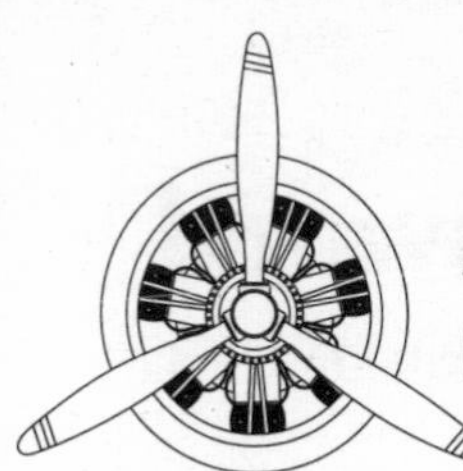

Airport Triples 2

Mission 18: Identify each city based on its airports

Briefing:

Can you identify each of these four cities served by multiple airports? Each group contains three airport codes, all of which serve one city.

LAX
SNA
LGB

SEA
LKE
BFI

ARN
BMA
NYO

GRU
VCP
CGH

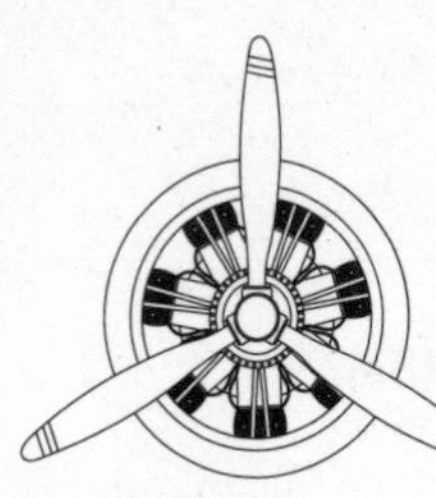

Weather-link Crossword

Mission 19: Complete the grid and find the hidden link

Briefing:

Solve the meteorological crossword below. Once complete, can you find a link between all the solutions that is *not* related to either weather or aviation?

Across

5 Swirling mass of snow (6)
7 Severe snowstorm (8)
8 Icy rain (5)
10 Large, slow moving area causing violent thunderstorms (9)
14 Temperature unit (6)
15 Rainy season in parts of Asia (7)
16 Turn to ice (6)
17 Forecast (7)

Down

1 Cloud with wispy, tufted streaks (6)
2 Sudden localized storm (6)
3 Low area of 12 down (10)
4 Fine rain (7)
6 Circular air movement (4)
9 Tropical storm (7)
11 Precipitation (8)
12 Atmospheric force (8)
13 Gentle wind (6)
15 Unpleasantly warm and humid (5)

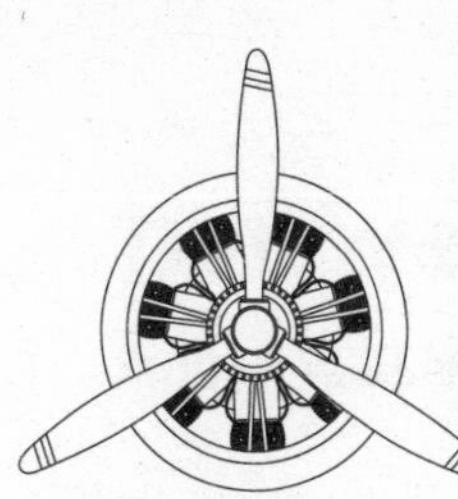

Local Winds

Mission 20: Reveal the winds and identify their areas

Briefing:

Reveal the names of five well-known local winds below, each of which has had all of its vowels removed. Once the names of the winds have been restored, can you match each wind to the area in which it can be found?

Winds

MSTRL

BRCKFLDR

SNT   N

HRMTTN

PMPR

Areas

Argentina and Uruguay

France and the Mediterranean

North-western Africa

Southern Australia

Southern California

Country Outlines 1

Mission 21: Identify the correct country for each airport

Briefing:

Can you work out which European country each of these airports can be found in, where only the three-letter airport codes have been given? A choice of two European countries is given for each airport code, and each country is represented only by its outline. Country outlines are not to scale.

BCN

A

B

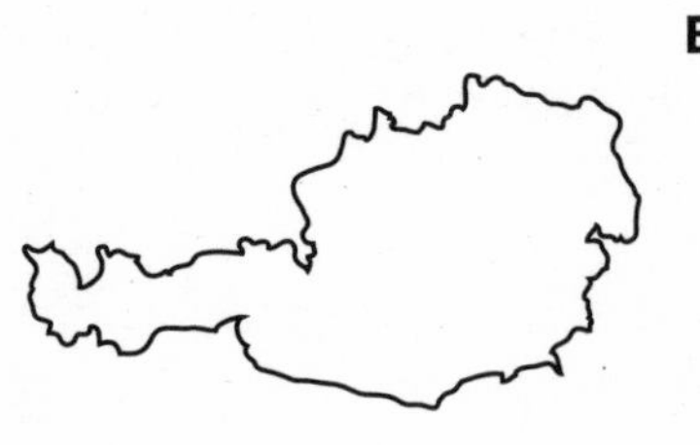

NCL

A

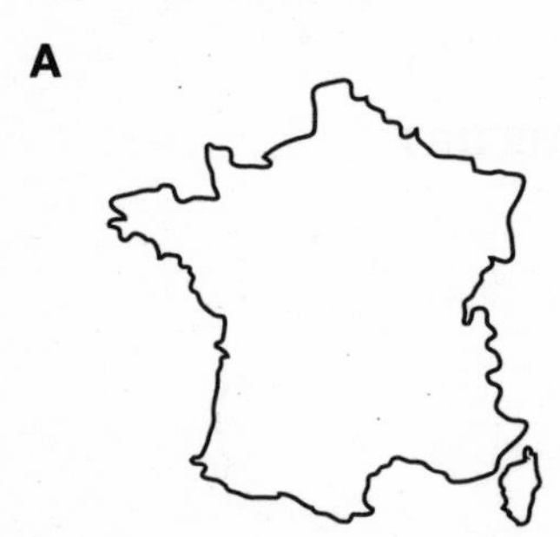

B

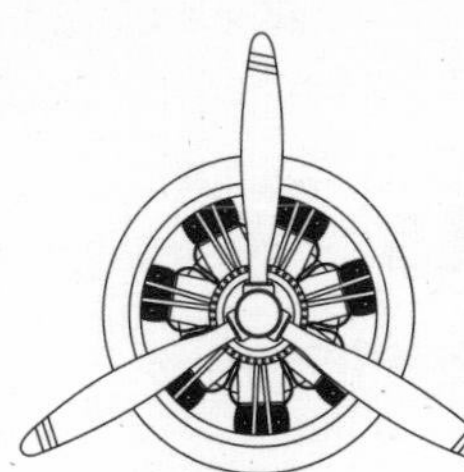

Country Outlines 2

Mission 22: Identify further countries, given airports

Briefing:

See the opposite page for instructions.

VRN

A

B

CPH

A

B

GOT

A

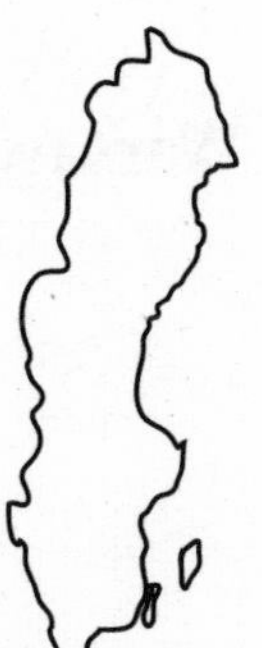

B

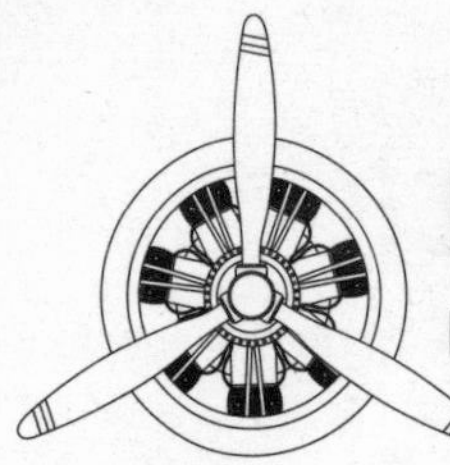

Eponymous Airports

Mission 23: Match the famous names to the airports

Briefing:

Can you match each person on the left with a city on the right, whose airport they lend their name to?

Person	City
Charles de Gaulle	Belgrade
Cristiano Ronaldo	Boston
Edward Logan	Liverpool
Frédéric Chopin	Madeira
John F. Kennedy	New Orleans
John Lennon	New York
Louis Armstrong	Paris
Nikola Tesla	Salzburg
W. A. Mozart	Warsaw

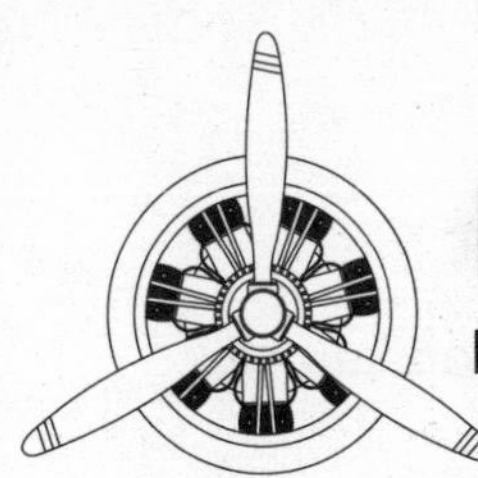

European Capital Cities

Mission 24: Reveal the names of the cities

Briefing:
Restore the names of these European capital cities, which have each had all of their vowels removed.

DNBRGH

BRN

BRTSLV

VNN

PRG

SL

THNS

NCS

Bonus Question
With the vowels removed, two of the coded cities above spell out the three-letter international code for the airport that serves them. Which two?

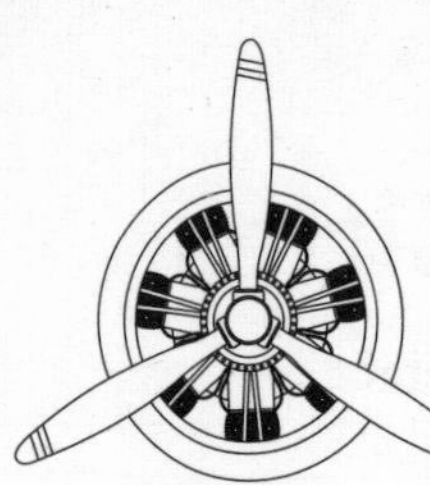

City Fragments

Mission 25: Reassemble the names of the capital cities

Briefing:

The names of six European capital cities have been broken into fragments, and the fragments have then been listed in alphabetical order. Can you restore the names to their full length and reveal the capitals?

AG	LSI
BU	MAD
COP	ME
DAP	MI
EN	NKI
ENH	NSK
EST	RID
HE	RO

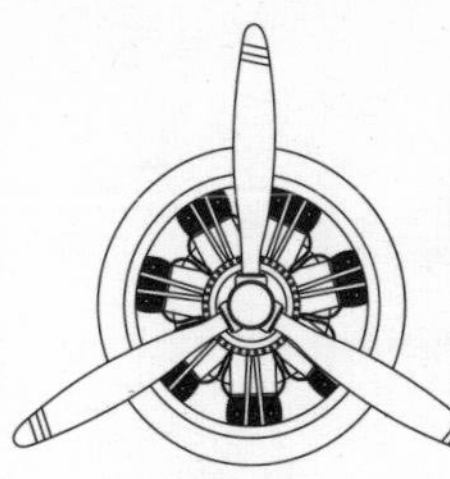

Partial Cities

Mission 26: Complete the names of the capital cities

Briefing:

Can you restore the names of six European capital cities, which have each had every other letter deleted?

B_R_I_

_U_H_R_S_

L_S_O_

_O_D_N

_E_K_A_I_

_A_S_W

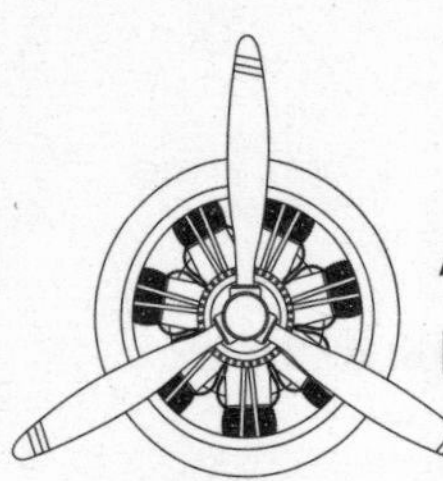

Alphabetical Anagrams

Mission 27: Unscramble the names of the capital cities

Briefing:

Can you restore the names of these five European capital cities, which have each had their letters rearranged into alphabetical order?

AGIR

AIPRS

BELRSSSU

BDILNU

AABJJLLNU

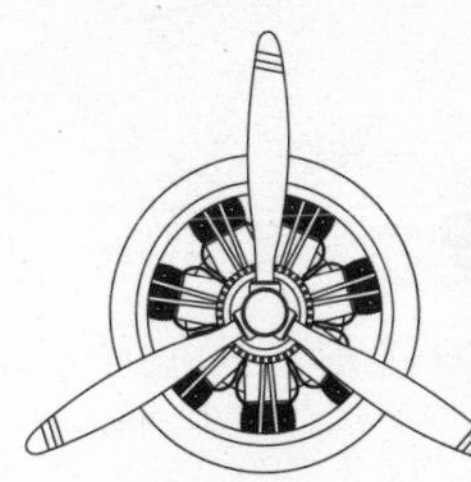

Famous Aviators

Mission 28: Complete the full names of the aviators

Briefing:

The names of some famous aviators have been mixed up on these pages. Can you match up first names and surnames to restore them?

First name	Surname
Amelia	Aldrin
Amy	Armstrong
Antoine	Bader
Buzz	Blériot
Chuck	Boeing
Douglas	de Havilland
Geoffrey	de Saint-Exupéry
Louis	Earhart
Neil	Garros
Roland	Johnson
William	Yeager

Famous Aeroplanes

Mission 29: Attach each plane to a famous fact

Briefing:
Match each aeroplane to the event or attribute it is renowned for.

Aeroplanes

Air Force One

Blériot XI

Concorde

F-117 Nighthawk

Solar Impulse 2

Spirit of St Louis

Supermarine Spitfire

Wright Flyer

Famous Facts

First aircraft built around stealth technology

First aeroplane flown across the English Channel

First solar-powered circumnavigation of the earth

First solo non-stop transatlantic flight

First heavier-than-air aircraft capable of sustained, powered flight

One of only two commercial supersonic airliners

The name for any US Air Force aeroplane carrying a US president

The only UK plane in continuous production throughout World War II

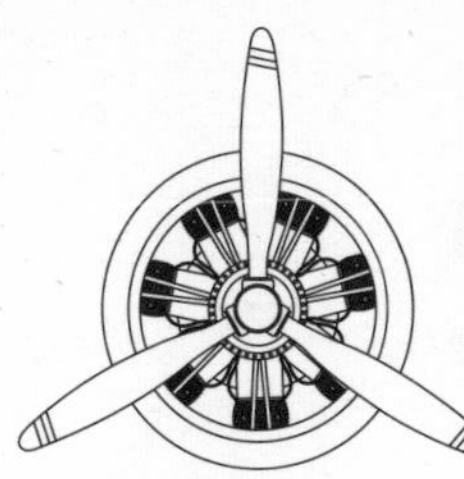

First Flights

Mission 30: Identify the country of each flag and airline

Briefing:

Match each flag-carrier airline with the outline of the national flag it flies.

Airlines

Aer Lingus	Avianca	Qantas
Air Baltic	Iberia	TAP
Atlantic Airways	Luxair	

Flags

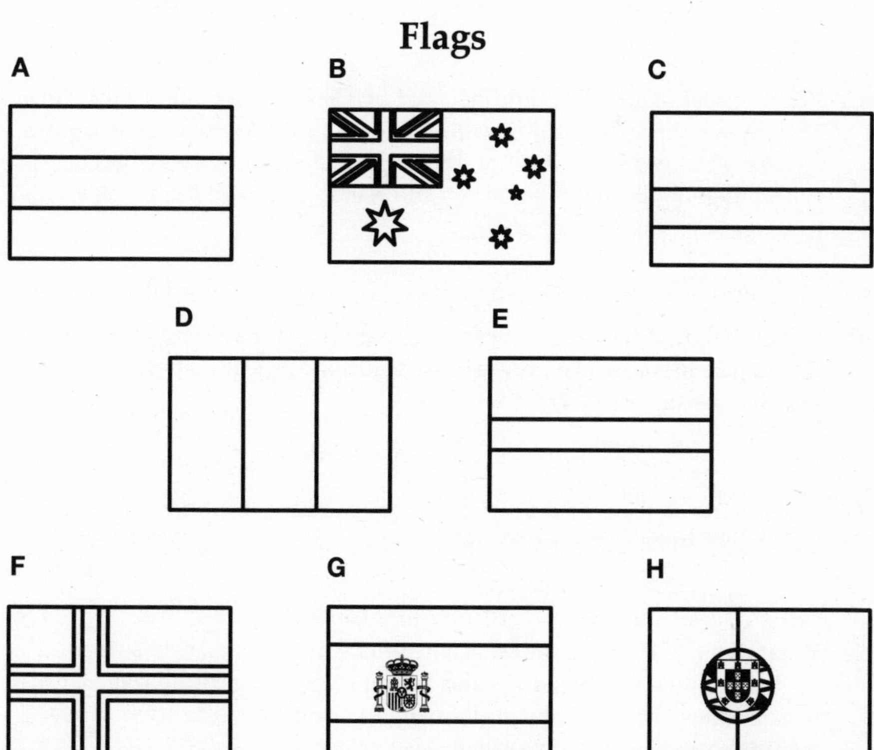

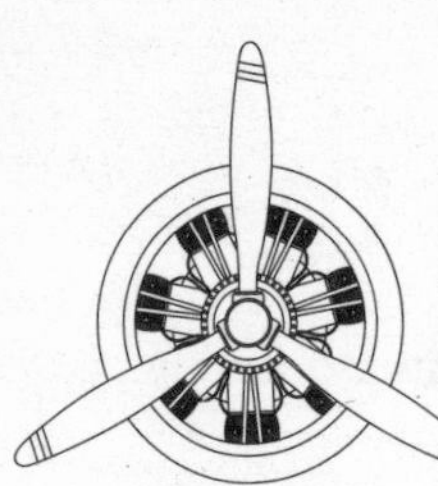

A to Z Quiz 1

Mission 31: Test your knowledge, from A to F

Briefing:

Each answer in this quiz begins with a different letter of the alphabet, as indicated by the letter given before the question. For solutions consisting of two words, or hyphenated words, only the first letter of the first word need match the given letter.

A. What is the name given to types of aircraft which can land and take off on both water and land?

B. In 1921 who became the first woman of African-American descent, and the first woman of Native American descent, to obtain a pilot's licence? The solution is her full name, of which only her first name starts with 'B'.

C. What model of aircraft manufactured by De Havilland, first flown in 1949, was redesigned and first flown again in 1953 with oval windows? Square windows – a feature on the original aircraft model – had been found to generate stress fractures and metal fatigue in the plane's fuselage, causing fatal accidents.

D. Which Italian artist and inventor created plans for a flying machine during the Renaissance period? The solution is the artist's surname, which consists of two words.

E. What is the collective name given to the rudders, fins and stabilizing devices at the tail end of a plane?

F. What name is given to the small insignia – usually a nation's flag – which appear on the wings and fins of planes to indicate their nationalities? They are generally used in addition to roundels. The solution consists of two words.

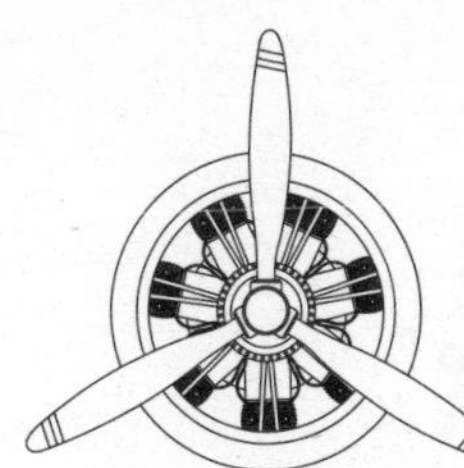

A to Z Quiz 2

Mission 32: Test your knowledge, from G to L

Briefing:

Answer these further A to Z questions. See opposite for full instructions.

G. In aviation slang, what name is given to a plane's undercarriage? The solution consists of two words.

H. What H is the air blowing directly towards the front of an aircraft, opposing the forward motion of the plane?

I. In aerobatics, what type of turn allows a pilot to change their flying direction by 180°, by climbing to a higher altitude in a half-loop, and performing a half-roll?

J. What J is a manual lever used by a pilot to control the movement and position of an aircraft?

K. What name is given to the unit of speed used in aviation, calculated as the number of nautical miles travelled per hour?

L. What is the name given to a type of aircraft which uses gases such as heated air and helium to lift it from the ground, and which includes aircraft such as blimps and hot-air balloons? The solution consists of a hyphenated word.

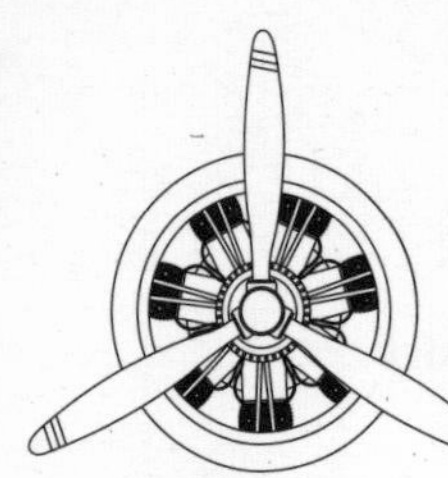

A to Z Quiz 3

Mission 33: Test your knowledge, from M to S

Briefing:

Answer these further A to Z questions. Please see page 208 for full instructions.

M. What name is given to the ratio of an aircraft's movement relative to the speed of sound?

N. What name describes a plane's rapid descent, leading from the front of the aircraft?

O. If pilots land beyond the end of a runway, what O are they said to have done?

P. What foodstuff can be found in the informal name given to an emergency landing in which the aircraft does not deploy its landing gear?

Q. What does the 'Q' stand for, in the acronymic name of Australian airline QANTAS?

R. By what informal name are overnight transatlantic flights often referred to? The solution consists of a hyphenated word.

S. What name is given to the explosive noise created by an aircraft when it reaches the speed of sound? The solution consists of two words.

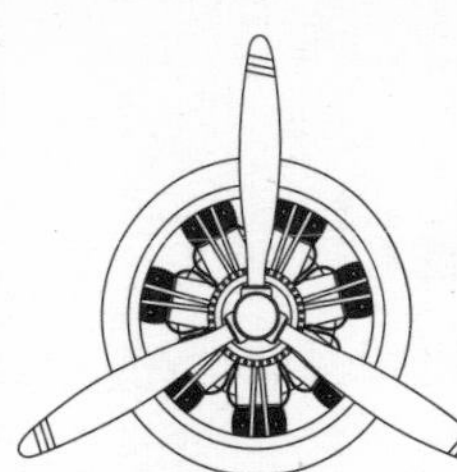

A to Z Quiz 4

Mission 34: Test your knowledge, from T to Z

Briefing:

Answer these further A to Z questions. Please see page 208 for full instructions.

T. What is the name of the forward force generated by a jet engine?

U. In airfield traffic patterning, what name is given to the flight path of an aircraft which is parallel to, and in the same direction as, the landing runway? The solution consists of two words.

V. What is the name given to plumes of condensed water which can be seen in the wake of an aircraft's path? The solution consists of two words.

W. What is the name given to a cylinder of fabric flown in airfields, and used to give an indication of weather conditions?

X. What hyphenated word is used to represent the letter 'X' in the NATO phonetic alphabet?

Y. What is the name given to the movement of an aircraft about its vertical axis?

Z. What aircraft, of the type in question L, was a rigid, navigable airship used for both civilian and military flights before the 1940s?

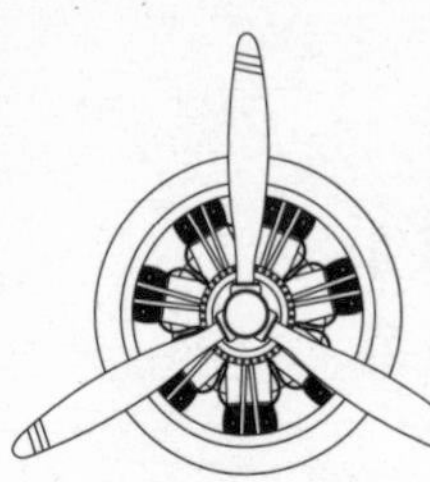

Geography and Aviation

Mission 35: Answer the questions and reveal a country

Briefing:

Can you use your general knowledge to answer the questions on international aviation below? When correctly solved, the initial letters of each solution in turn will spell out, in order, the name of a country whose flag features a botanical element.

1. Which airline is the flag carrier airline for Hong Kong? Part of its name is a historical European word for China.

2. Which city in the USA is served by the world's busiest airport, as calculated in 2019, by number of passengers?

3. Which body of water did Tryggve Gran fly over in 1914, marking the first time the crossing had been achieved in an aeroplane?

4. Which 'attentive' settlement on Ellesmere Island is both the most northerly permanently inhabited settlement in the world, and hosts the most northerly airfield in the world?

5. By which sea can the world's lowest airport be found, at a height of approximately 380m below sea level?

6. In which country can the world's most southerly commercial airport be found?

A Famous Connection

Mission 36: Reveal the famous people, and find the link

Briefing:

Reveal the names of six famous people, where every other letter has been removed from each name. Clues to the identity of each person have also been provided. Once you have uncovered each name, can you find an aviation connection which links them all?

A_E_I_O _E_P_C_I

Explorer who gives the American continents their name

_U_L_E_M_ M_R_O_I

Engineer and inventor of long-distance radio transmission

C_R_S_O_H_R _O_U_B_S

Explorer credited with 'discovering' the New World

_E_N_R_O _A _I_C_

Artist, polymath, and inventor of flying machine prototypes

_A_C_ P_L_

Explorer famous for his Silk Road travels

_A_I_E_ G_L_L_I

Scientist who discovered the first moons of Jupiter

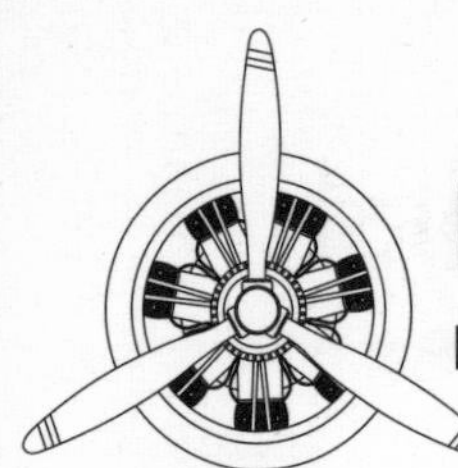

RAF Helicopters

Mission 37: Restore the consonants to reveal the aircraft

Briefing:

Can you reveal the names of five helicopters used by the RAF, each of which has had all of its consonants removed? Underlines indicate the location of each missing letter. A clue is given for each name.

_ _ I _ O O _

Strong wind, local to the Rocky Mountains

_ U _ A

Type of large cat

_ _ I _ _ I _

Mythical winged hybrid animal

_ U _ O

Roman goddess of marriage

_ U _ I _ E _

Roman king of the gods

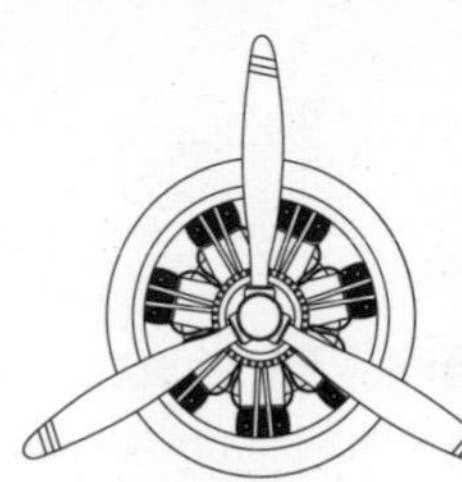

Aeroplane Crossword

Mission 38: Place twelve RAF planes into the grid

Briefing:

Fill in the crossword grid below with the names of twelve planes currently in use with the RAF. Each name is also a regular word, clued beneath.

Across

4 Private teacher (5)
6 Area cast into partial darkness (6)
7 Burrowing ground squirrel (8)
8 Book of maps (5)
10 Bolt of electrical discharge (9)
12 Medieval Scandinavian pirate (6)

Down

1 Greek hero given twelve tasks (8)
2 One on a long journey (7)
3 US state that may be either North or South (6)
5 Tropical cyclone (7)
9 Soldier on watch (8)
11 Bird of prey (4)

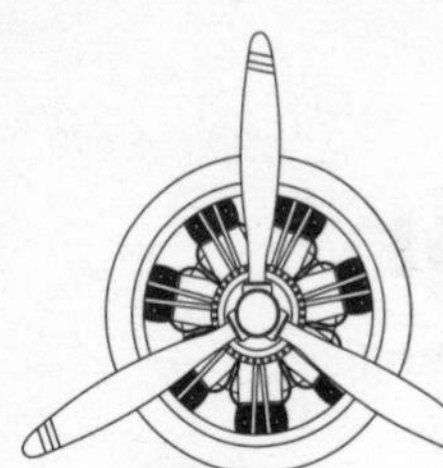

Low Visibility

Mission 39: Unscramble and identify the aircraft types

Briefing:

Can you match each of the disguised names of aircraft types below with its silhouette? Names have been jumbled and any hyphens removed, and spacing may not match that of the original word or words. Images show each type of aircraft as if viewed from above, and are not to scale.

GIG HANDLER

PILOT CHEER

GIRDLE

RED ON

JAM COMET RELIC

THE LAST

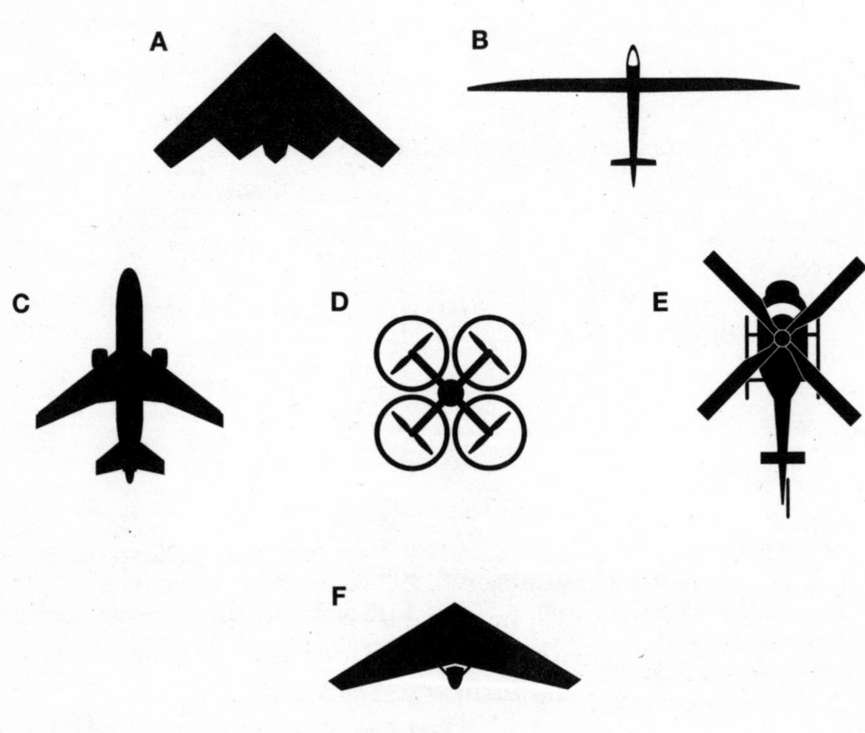

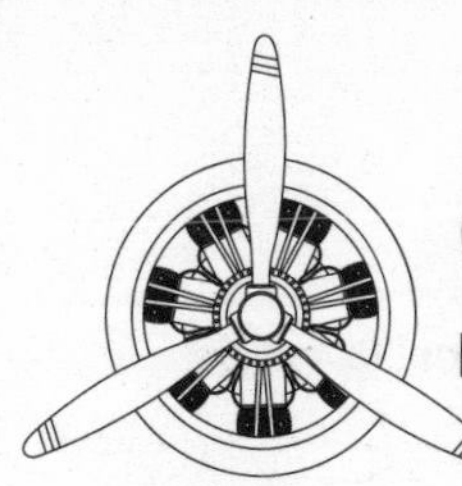

Consonantal Airlines

Mission 40: Complete each of the US airline names

Briefing:

Complete the names of the following US commercial airlines, which have each had all of their consonants removed. Underlines indicate the position of each missing letter. All the names consist of one word, with any generic words such as 'Air' or 'Airlines' having been removed. Clues for each airline have also been provided, although not in the same order as the names.

Airlines

A _ A _ _ A

A _ E _ I _ A _

_ E _ _ A

_ _ O _ _ I E _

_ A _ A I I A _

_ _ I _ I _

U _ I _ E _

Clues

A nationality
Border; it may be final?
Ghost; distilled drink
Joined together
Greek alphabet letter
Native to the most recent US state
US state

RAF Ranks

Mission 41: Reveal the ranks, then place them in order

Briefing:

Can you restore the names of these ten RAF ranks, each of which has had its letters rearranged? The spacing may not match that of the original words. Once you have restored them, can you also arrange them into order from the least to the most senior?

IF A CHARMER HAILS

I, COMRADE MOOR

HAIR ALARMS

ARCHIVAL ARMIES

FLEETING TAIL HUNT

GREY IF ON CLIFF

GAIN UP CAPTOR

COPIER OF LIFT

A SODDEN QUARREL

WORN MAGIC MEND

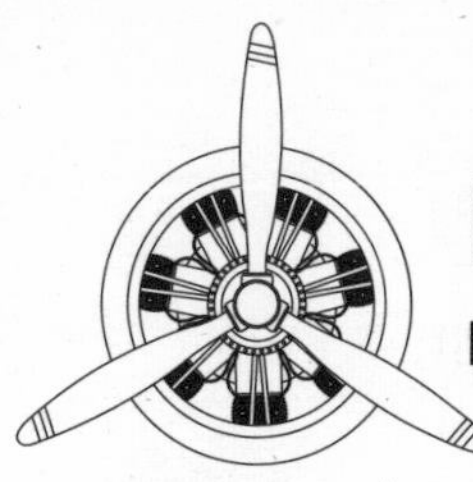

RAF Stations

Mission 42: Solve the crossword and reveal the stations

Briefing:

Solve this crossword where every entry is an RAF Station, either in the UK or abroad. Some clues have been split into two separate parts, so e.g. 'Happy + rock' might solve to GLAD and STONE, making the final entry GLADSTONE.

Across

1 Tool + Eve's counterpart (9)
7 Franklin, to friends + male child (6)
10 Glen (6)
11 Jeans brand + Chinese dynasty (7)
12 British overseas territory bordering Spain (9)
13 Soft lining + heavy weight (10)

Down

2 Excavate + near (5)
3 Climb upon + agreeable (5,8)
4 Small forest + glen (8)
5 Speaking lengthily about trivial matters (9)
6 Northumberland coastal fishing village; anagram of 'mob rule' (7)
8 Playwright George Bernard + hide underground (8)
9 Rascal + heavy weight (8)

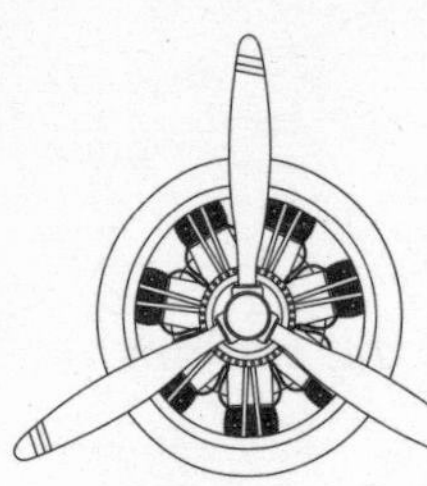

Part Assembly I

Mission 43: Identify all of the missing aeroplane parts

Briefing:

Fill each empty square below with a letter, to reveal the names of nine aeroplane parts. All squares that contain the same letters across consecutive rows are linked with straight lines. Two words are given, to get you started.

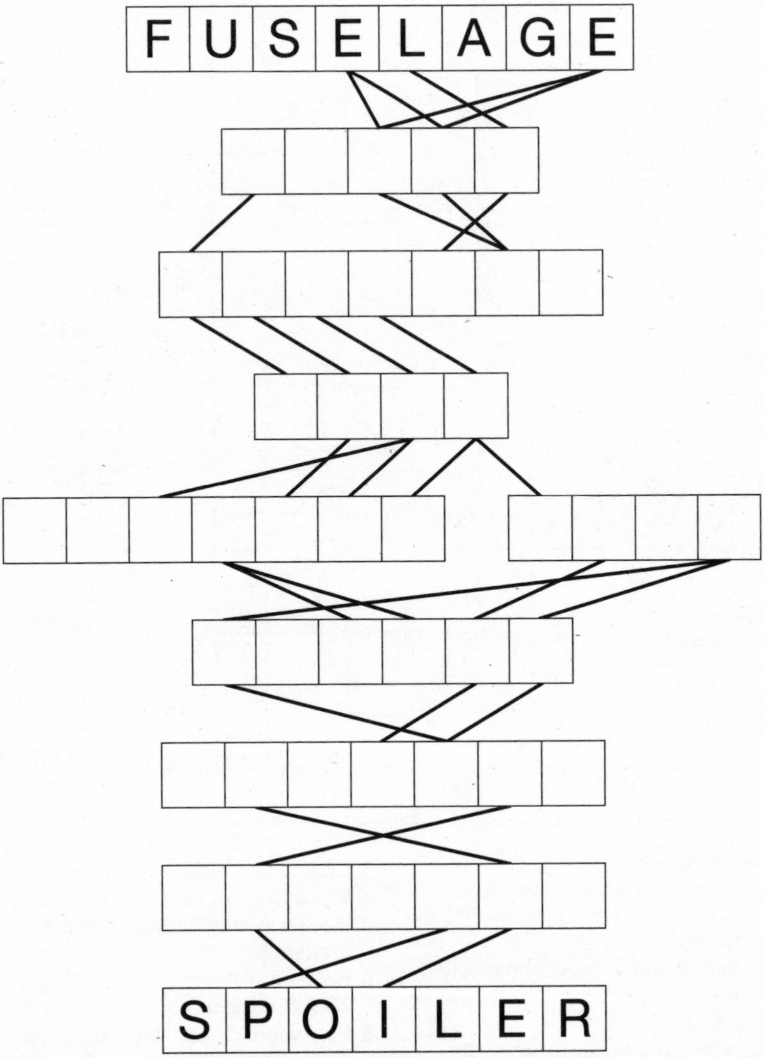

F	U	S	E	L	A	G	E

S	P	O	I	L	E	R

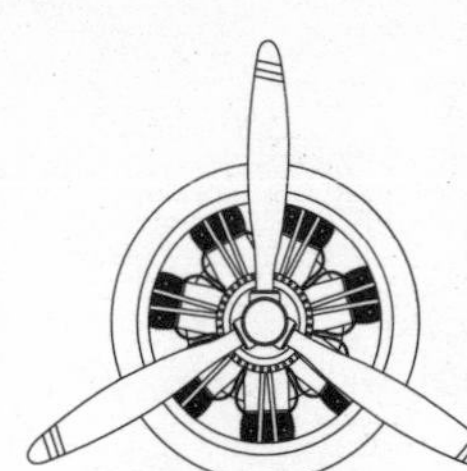

Part Assembly 2

Mission 44: Locate the aeroplane parts

Briefing:

Once you have written in the missing parts in the previous mission, can you match each part to a lettered label in the rough area of its location on the picture of an aeroplane below?

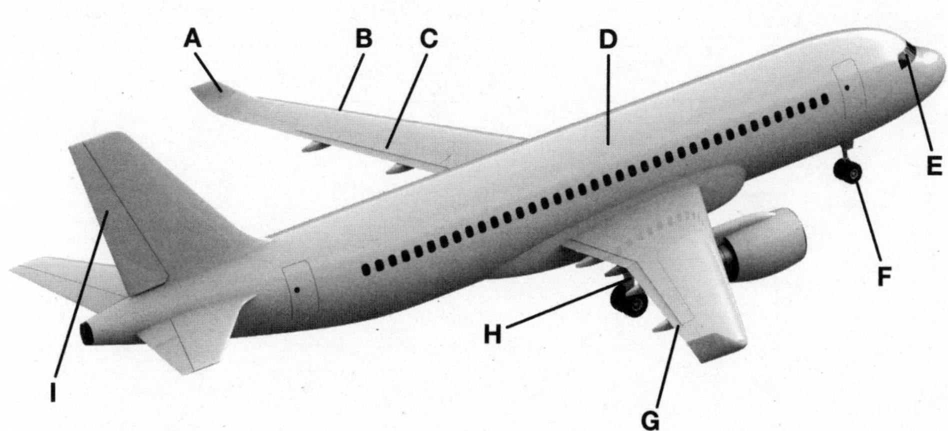

SOLUTIONS

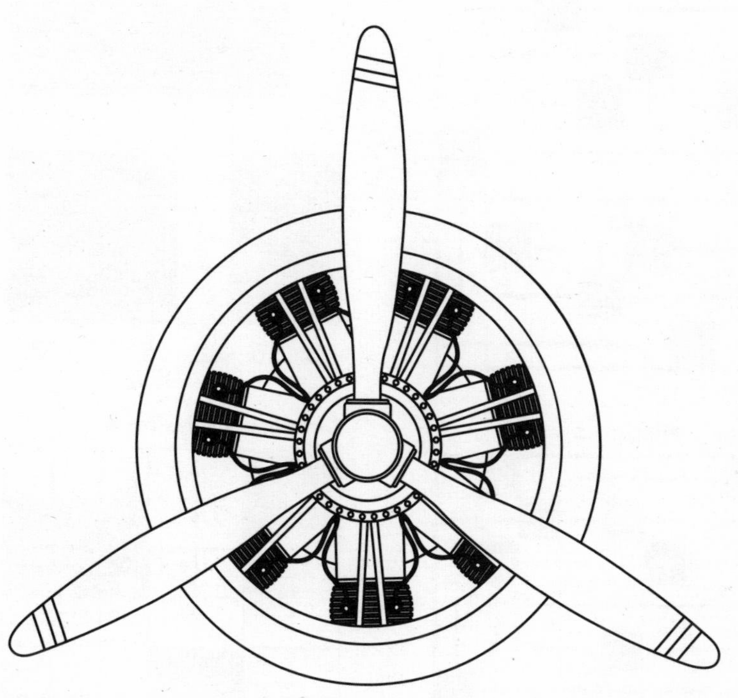

Chapter 1 Mission 1

Chapter 1 Mission 2

Chapter 1 Mission 3

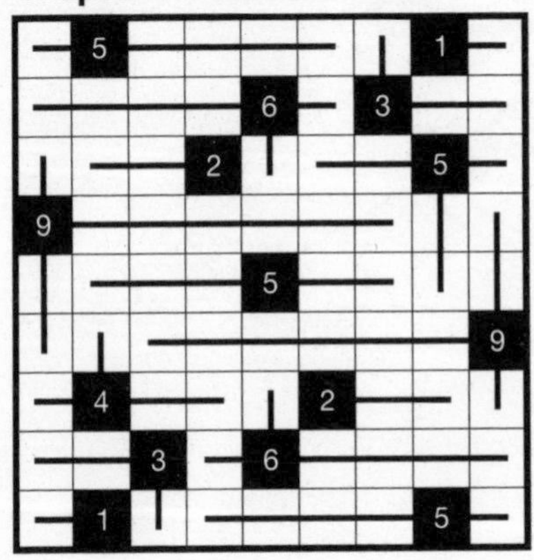

Chapter 1 Mission 4

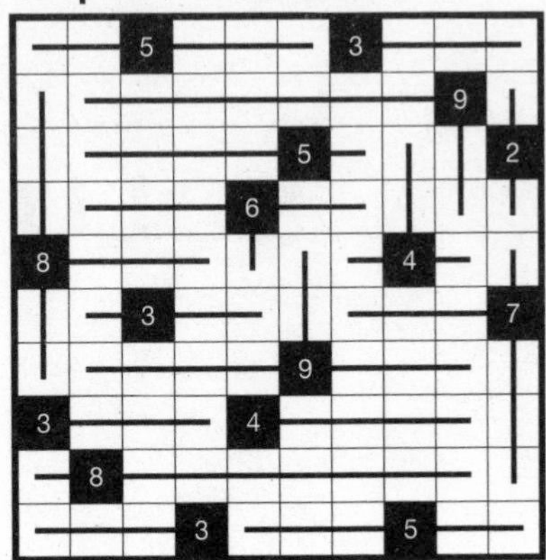

Chapter 1 Mission 5

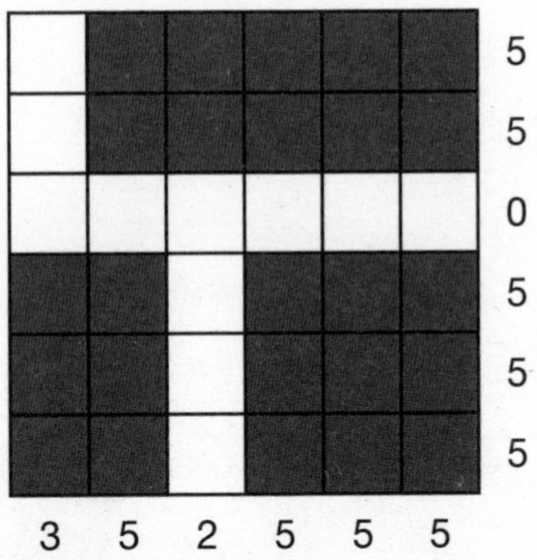

Chapter 1 Mission 6

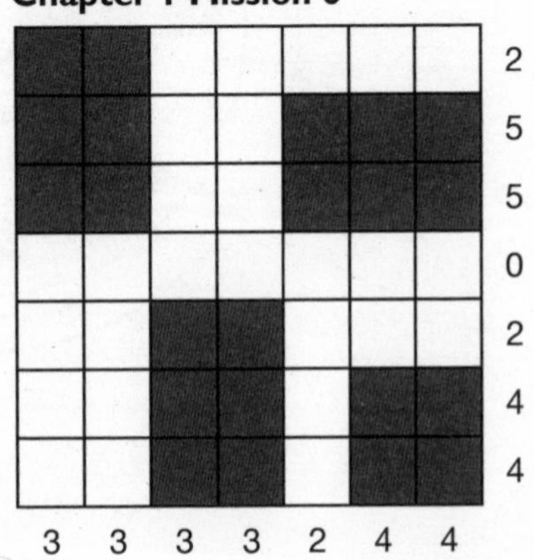

Chapter 1 Mission 7

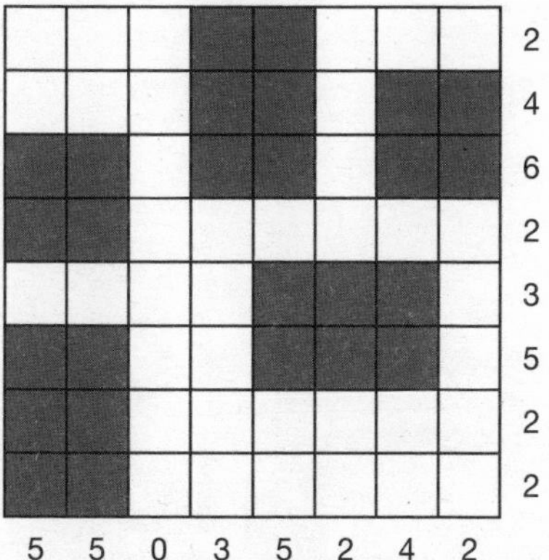

Chapter 1 Mission 10

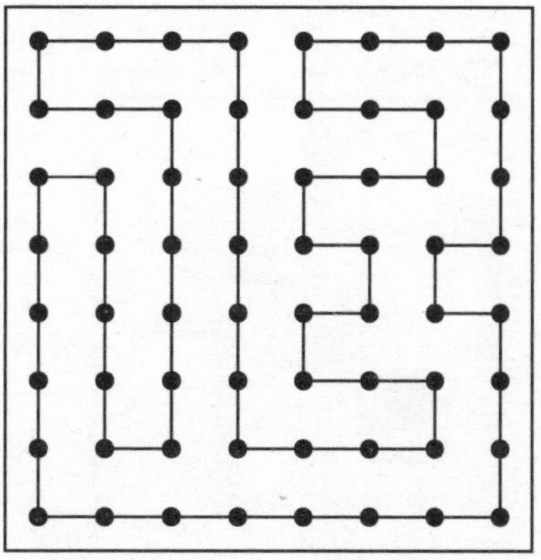

Chapter 1 Mission 8

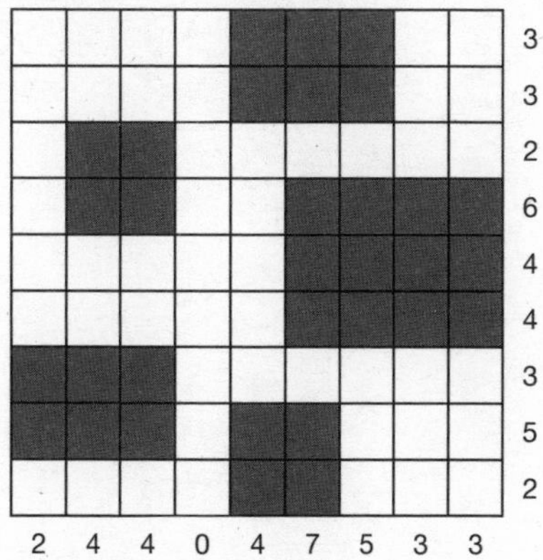

Chapter 1 Mission 11

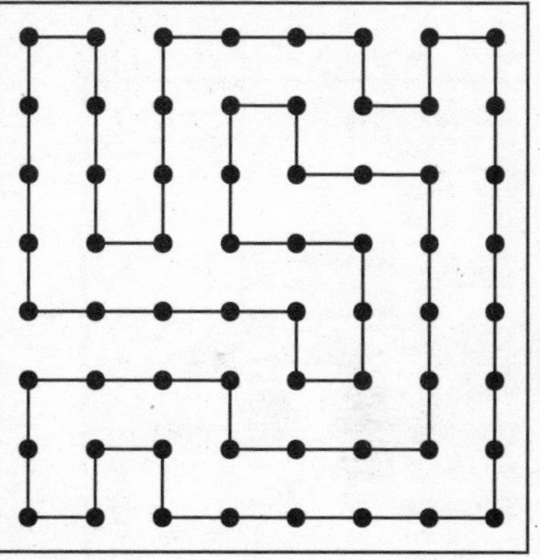

Chapter 1 Mission 9

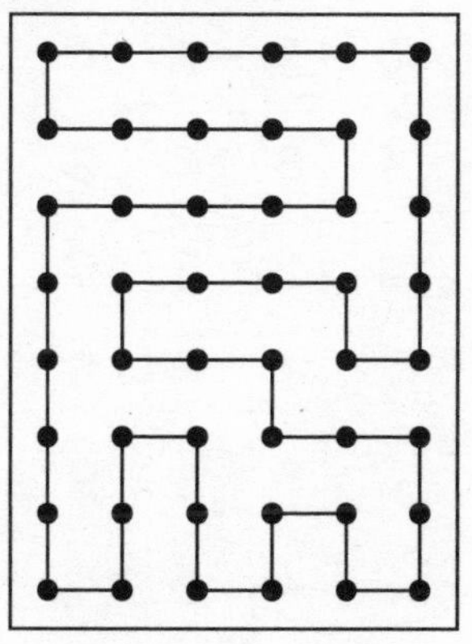

Chapter 1 Mission 12

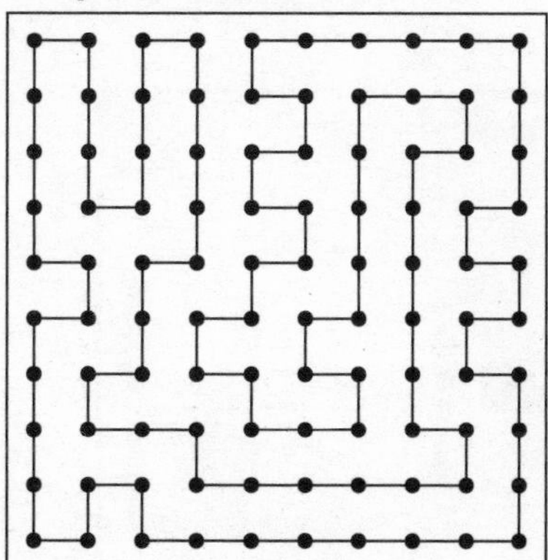

Chapter 1 Mission 13

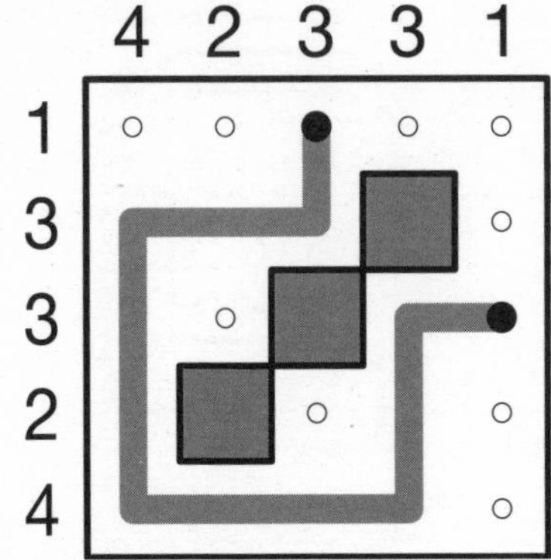

Chapter 1 Mission 16

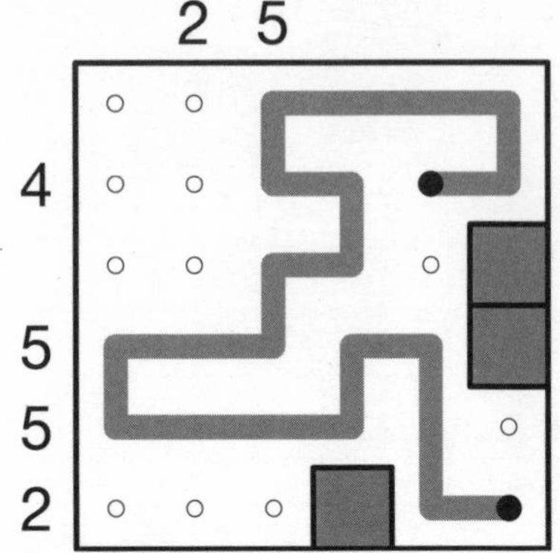

Chapter 1 Mission 14

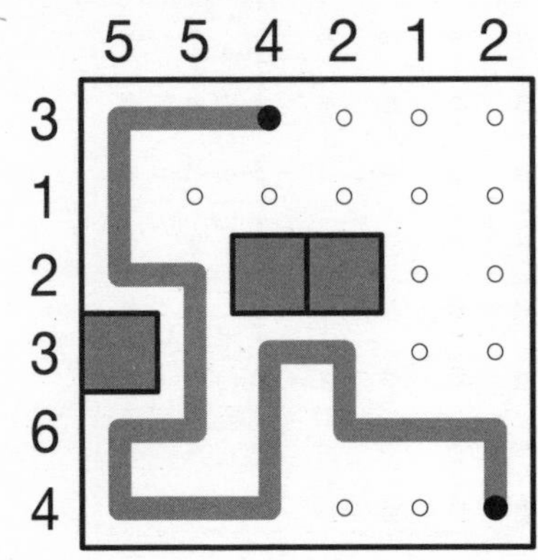

Chapter 1 Mission 17

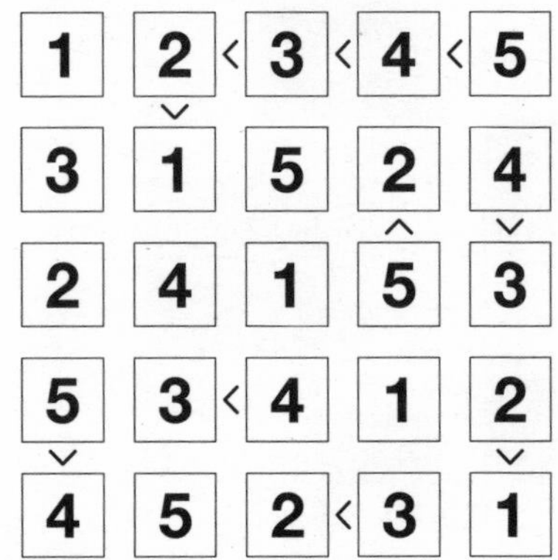

Chapter 1 Mission 15

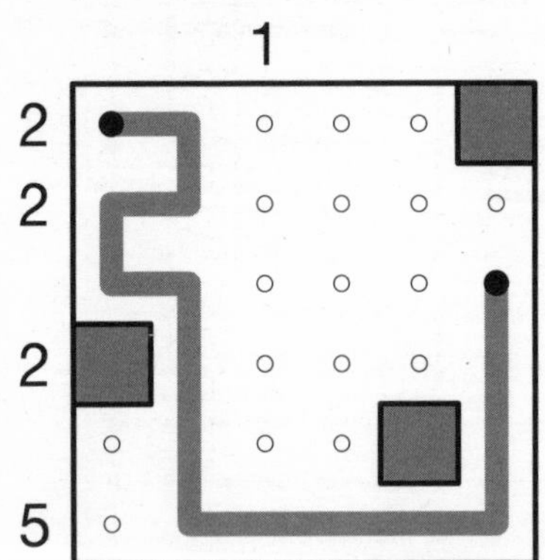

Chapter 1 Mission 18

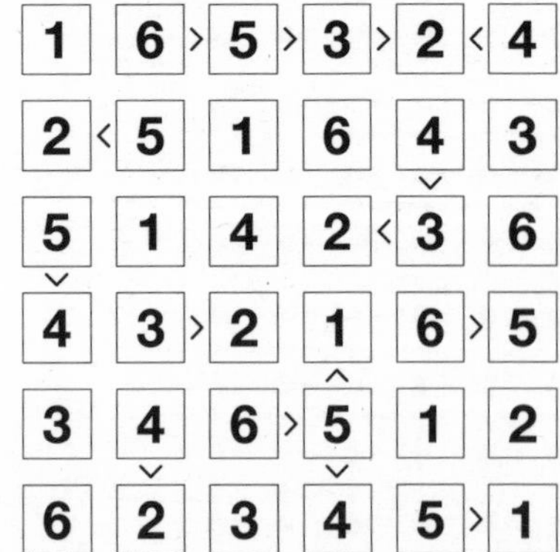

Chapter 1 Mission 19

5	1	2	7	3	6	4
1	4	5	6	7	3	2
6	7	4	3	1	2	5
7	2	3	4	5	1	6
4	3	6	5	2	7	1
3	5	1	2	6	4	7
2	6	7	1	4	5	3

Chapter 1 Mission 20

7	6	4	8	3	5	1	2
8	4	6	7	1	2	5	3
4	5	1	3	2	6	7	8
6	8	5	4	7	3	2	1
5	2	3	6	8	1	4	7
3	1	2	5	6	7	8	4
2	3	7	1	4	8	6	5
1	7	8	2	5	4	3	6

Chapter 1 Mission 21

F	E	E	B	A	D	C	F
E	D	C	B	A	F	E	E
B	D	D	A	C	F	B	B
E	A	B	C	B	D	D	F
C	C	D	E	A	C	C	A
B	A	F	F	D	E	F	A

Chapter 1 Mission 22

B	D	D	A	D	A	D	B
D	C	C	B	A	C	D	C
C	A	D	A	C	B	C	A
B	D	A	A	B	C	A	B
A	B	C	D	C	B	D	A
C	B	A	D	B	C	D	B

Chapter 1 Mission 23

B	A	E	C	A	G	B
C	D	G	F	D	C	E
A	E	E	G	F	F	A
D	F	B	C	D	B	D
G	B	G	C	B	C	A
A	E	F	G	D	E	E
B	F	A	C	G	D	F

Chapter 1 Mission 24

D	B	C	D	B	D	A	D
B	D	A	A	C	D	B	C
C	B	C	A	B	B	C	A
D	C	A	C	D	C	A	B
A	D	C	B	A	D	B	A
C	C	D	A	A	D	D	C
A	B	A	B	C	C	B	C
D	B	B	D	A	A	D	B

Chapter 1 Mission 25

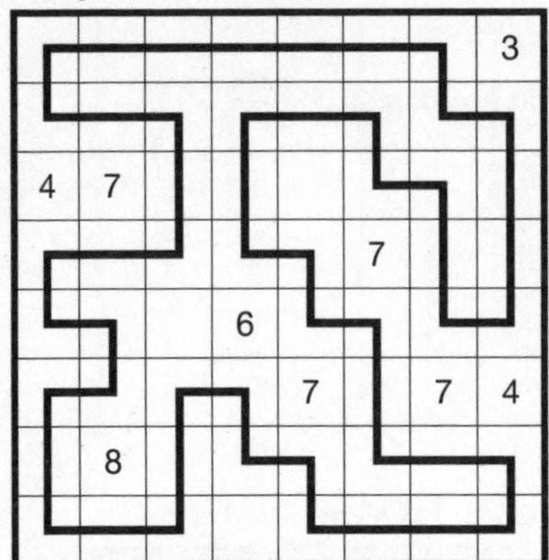

Chapter 1 Mission 28

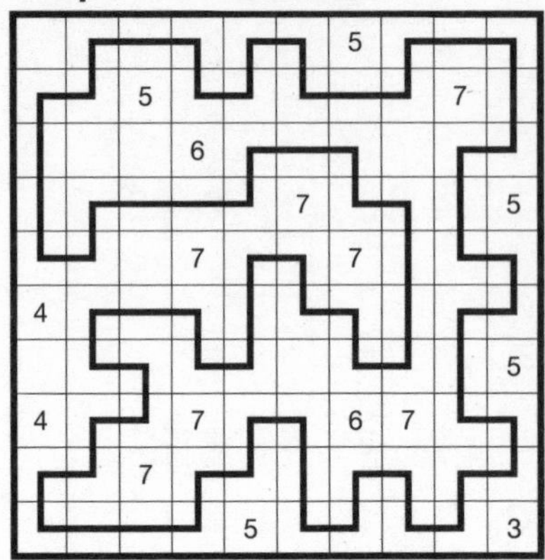

Chapter 1 Mission 26

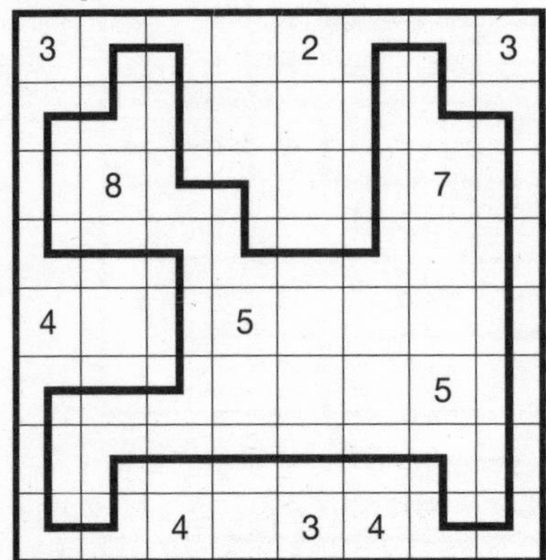

Chapter 1 Mission 29

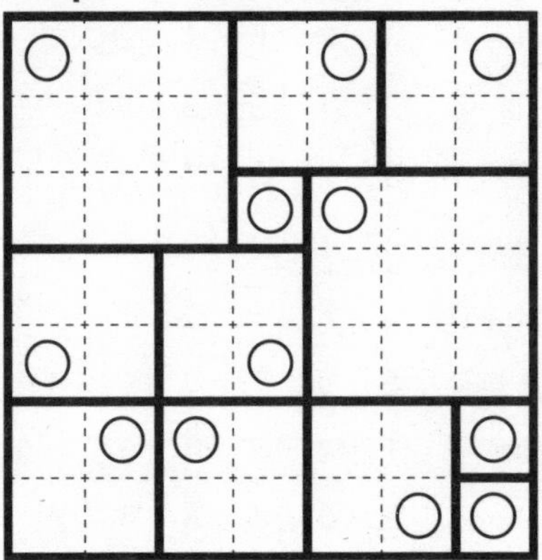

Chapter 1 Mission 27

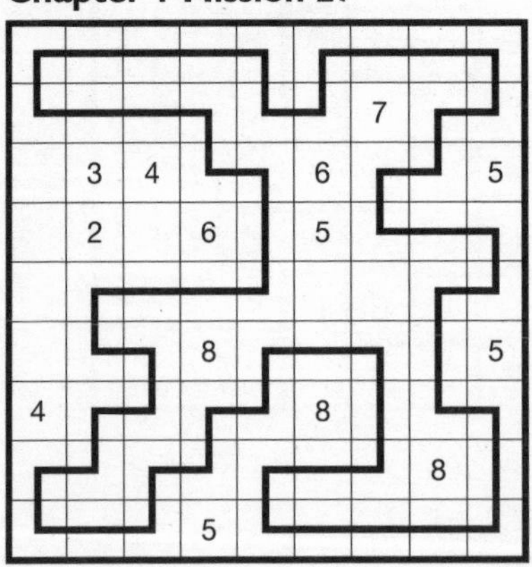

Chapter 1 Mission 30

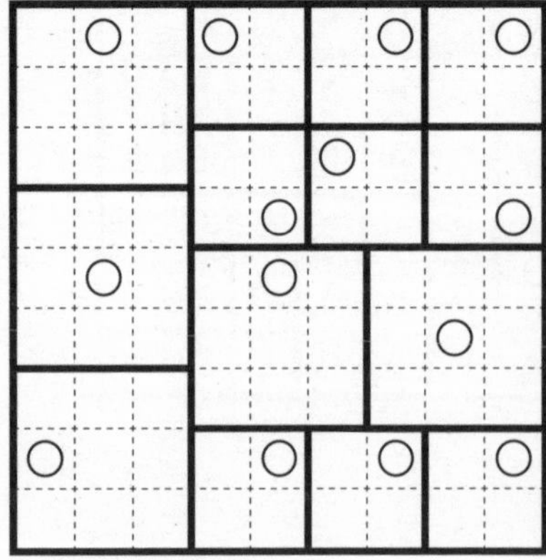

Chapter 1 Mission 31

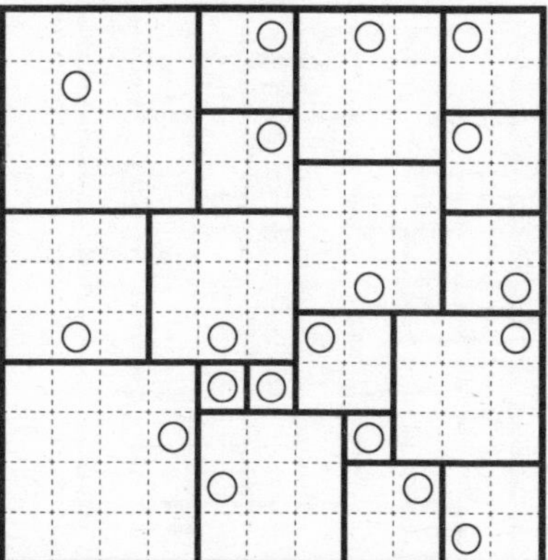

Chapter 1 Mission 32

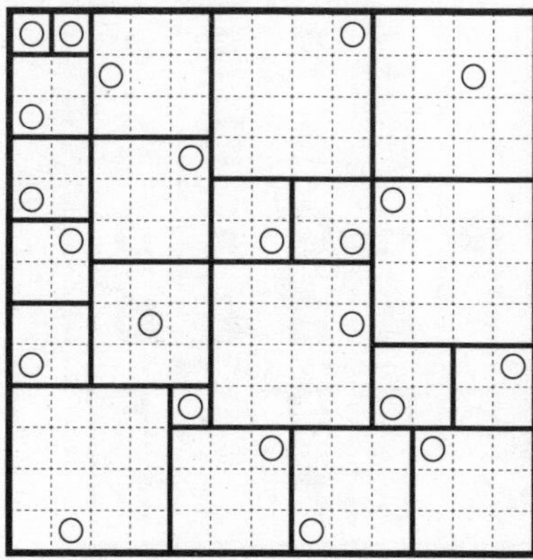

Chapter 1 Mission 33

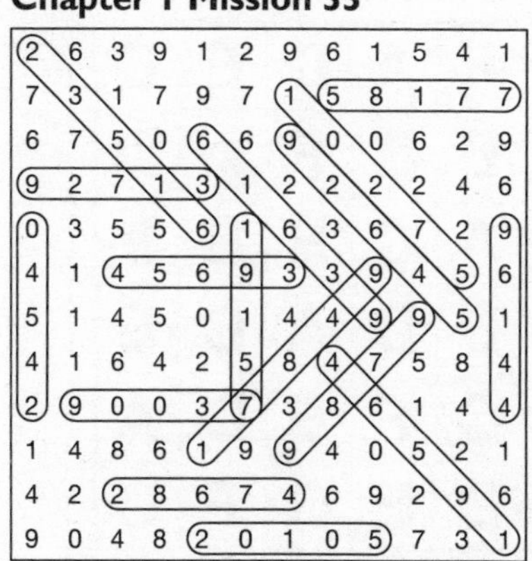

Chapter 1 Mission 34

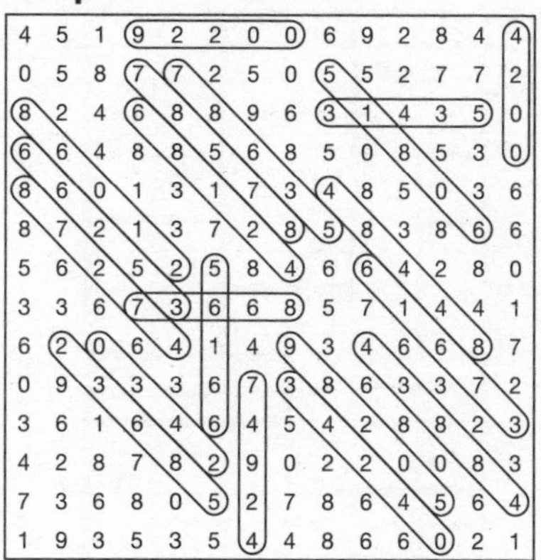

Chapter 1 Mission 35

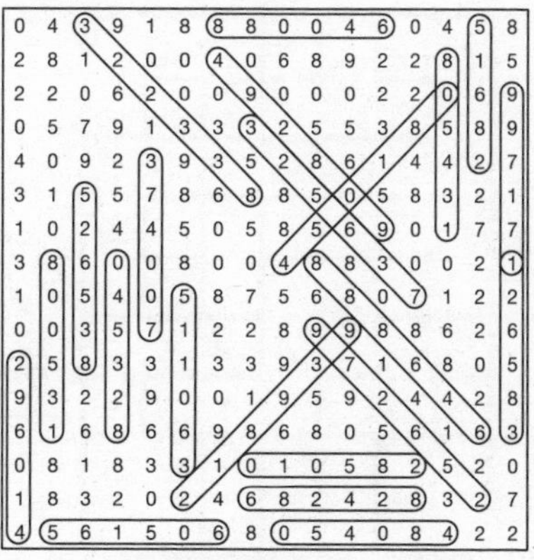

Chapter 1 Mission 36

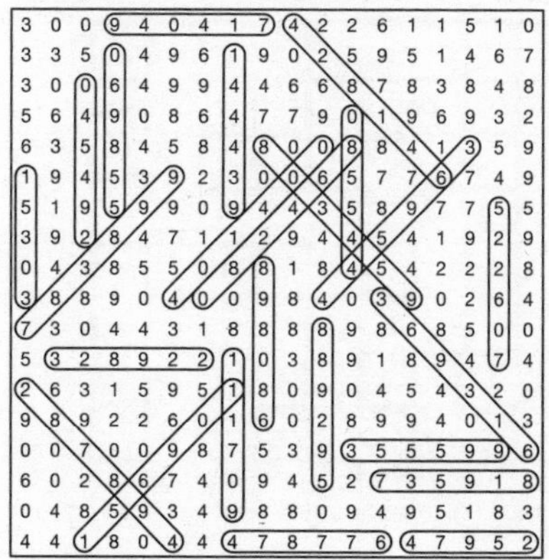

Chapter 1 Mission 37

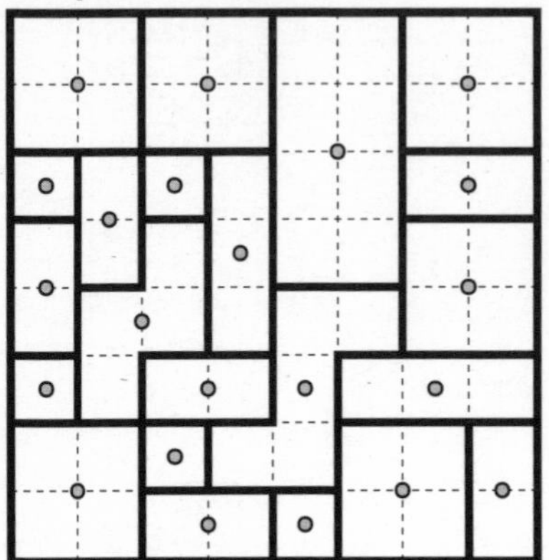

Chapter 1 Mission 38

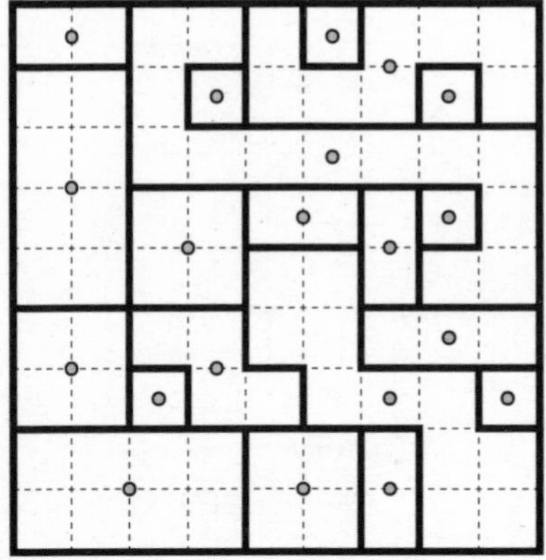

Chapter 1 Mission 39

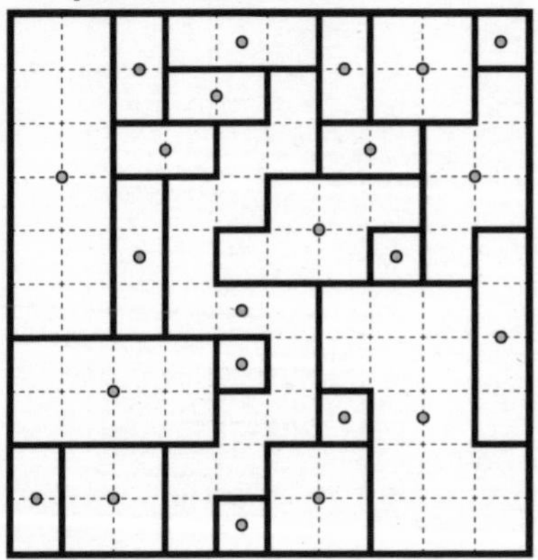

Chapter 1 Mission 40

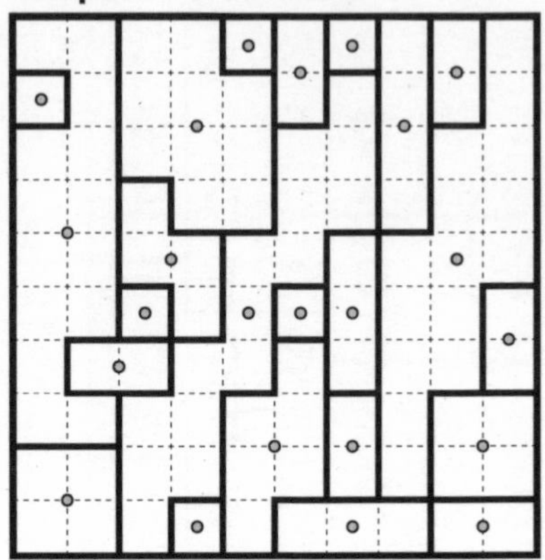

Chapter 1 Mission 41

F	C	D	E	B	A
E	B	F	A	D	C
A	D	E	C	F	B
C	F	A	B	E	D
B	E	C	D	A	F
D	A	B	F	C	E

Chapter 1 Mission 42

B	F	A	D	E	C
C	E	B	F	A	D
D	A	C	E	B	F
F	B	D	A	C	E
E	C	F	B	D	A
A	D	E	C	F	B

Chapter 1 Mission 43

E	B	F	G	D	A	C
C	D	A	B	F	E	G
A	F	G	E	C	D	B
G	C	B	D	A	F	E
F	A	E	C	B	G	D
B	G	D	A	E	C	F
D	E	C	F	G	B	A

Chapter 1 Mission 44

D	F	H	E	B	A	G	C
G	E	B	A	C	D	H	F
F	C	G	H	E	B	A	D
A	H	D	B	G	F	C	E
E	B	F	C	A	H	D	G
C	G	A	D	F	E	B	H
B	D	E	G	H	C	F	A
H	A	C	F	D	G	E	B

Chapter 1 Mission 45

2	1	2	1	1	2	3	3
1	2		2				1
2	2			3		3	3
3	1	0	2		2		
		2		1	3	1	3
0	2		0			3	2
2				1		1	2
3	1	1	2	3	2	2	2

Chapter 1 Mission 46

3	3	2	2	2	3	2	3
2			3		1		3
2		2		3	1	1	2
	2		3			3	3
3	2			2		2	
3	2	2	3		1		2
2		3		2			1
2	1	2	2	3	3	3	3

Chapter 1 Mission 47

3	3	2	3	2	2	2			
2		1		2		0	2	2	
2	3		2		0		0	3	
2			2	3		3	2		
1	1		2	3	2	2	2		3
3		3	1	2	1	1		3	2
		1	2		1	2			1
	0	1		1		2		0	1
	0	0	3		3		0		2
			3	1	2	1	2	2	1

Chapter 1 Mission 48

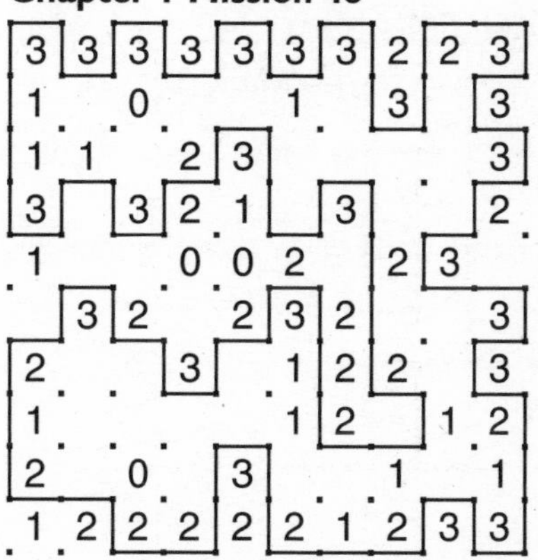

3	3	3	3	3	3	3	2	2	3
1		0			1		3		3
1	1		2	3					3
3		3	2	1		3			2
1			0	0	2		2	3	
	3	2		2	3	2			3
2			3		1	2	2		3
1					1	2		1	2
2		0		3			1		1
1	2	2	2	2	2	1	2	3	3

Chapter 2 Mission 1

In the order they appear in the list, the occupations are:

- Engineer
- Navigator
- Parachutist
- Technician
- First officer
- Second officer
- Ground crew
- Fighter pilot
- Dispatcher
- Mechanic
- Flight attendant

Chapter 2 Mission 2

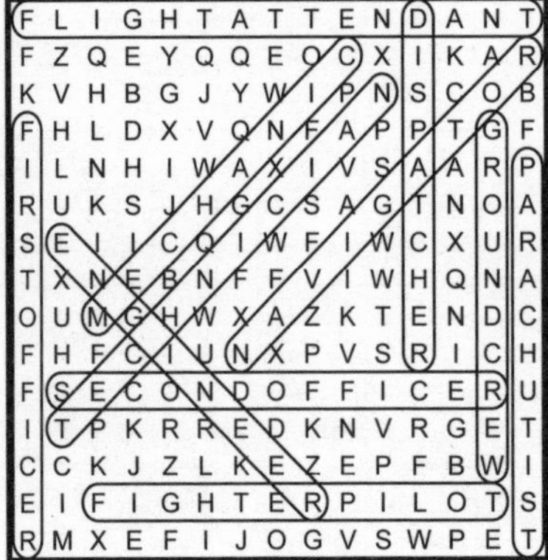

Chapter 2 Mission 3

The letters corresponding to each number are:

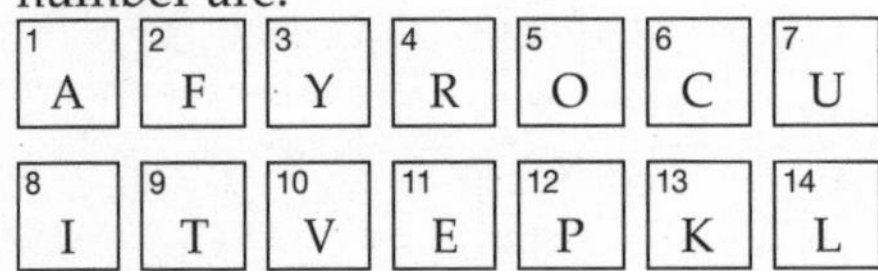

The missing terms are, respectively:

- Refuel
- Take off
- Layover
- Velocity
- Air pocket

Chapter 2 Mission 4

The decoded phrases, in order, are:

- Ahead of the curve
- Balls to the wall
- Push the envelope
- Take the flak
- Fly by the seat of your pants
- Wingman

Chapter 2 Mission 5

The decrypted quotes are as follows, with the size of shift given:

- Aviation is proof that, given the will, we have the capacity to achieve the impossible (Shift: 4)
- Aviation is the branch of engineering that is least forgiving of mistakes (Shift: 5)
- The aeroplane has unveiled for us the true face of the earth (Shift: 1)
- The air is the only place free from prejudices (Shift: 2)
- Pilots take no special joy in walking. Pilots like flying (Shift: 6)
- There's no such thing as a natural-born pilot (Shift: 3)

Chapter 2 Mission 6

The names of the speakers are given in order from top to bottom, with the size of shift and their quote:

- Neil Armstrong (Shift: 6 – Pilots take no special joy in walking. Pilots like flying)
- Eddie Rickenbacker (Shift: 4 – Aviation is proof that, given the will, we have the capacity to achieve the impossible)
- Bessie Coleman (Shift: 2 – The air is the only place free from prejudices)
- Freeman Dyson (Shift: 5 – Aviation

is the branch of engineering that is least forgiving of mistakes)

- Chuck Yeager (Shift: 3 – There's no such thing as a natural-born pilot)
- Antoine de Saint-Exupéry (Shift: 1 – The aeroplane has unveiled for us the true face of the earth)

Chapter 2 Mission 7

- Drag
- Gravity
- Yaw
- Weight
- Thrust
- Trailing Edge

Chapter 2 Mission 8

- Pitch
- Hydraulic
- Camber
- Roll
- Lift
- Turbulence

Chapter 2 Mission 9

- Cumulus
- Lenticular
- Nimbus
- Polar
- Stratiform
- Towering

Chapter 2 Mission 10

- Anvil
- Funnel
- Roll
- Rotor
- Shelf

Chapter 2 Mission 11

- Gust: Will they bring us to the entrance?
- Monsoon: We can put the autopilot system on soon.
- Snow: There's no way we'll be able to get there now.
- Sleet: We're just doing our final safety checks in the aisle; ETA into Boston is 11am local time.
- Weather: Having safely landed, I will now eat here.
- Aurora: Is it a bird? Is it a plane? Is it a flying dinosaur? Or a hang glider?.

Chapter 2 Mission 12

- Airside: I don't think I could afford the repairs I'd eventually need on that vehicle.
- Climb: You can't take more than 10 cl. I'm being serious.
- Knots: You need to speak, not shout, over the tannoy.
- Landside: There's a main meal and side dish for all First Class passengers.
- Lift: It's going to be awful if Terminal 5 is really busy.

Chapter 2 Mission 13

- Wheel: I don't know how he electrocuted himself.
- Nose: There's no service flying out to Toronto today.
- Pedal: We dropped all the way down and got a great view of the Grand Canyon.
- Elevator: Do you have a pin in your lapel? Eva tore a button off my coat and I need to disguise it.
- Yoke: Everybody ok? Everyone sitting comfortably?
- Fuselage: Make sure the catering staff use lager instead of ale in the officers' mess.

Chapter 2 Mission 14

- Ado: tornado + adoration
- Jet: inkjet + jetliner
- Pit: cockpit + pitfall
- Man: wingman + manpower
- Side: airside + sidelight
- Hammer: sledgehammer + hammerhead

Chapter 2 Mission 15

All the solutions have a meteorological connection:

- On cloud nine
- Under the weather
- Right as rain
- Storm in a teacup
- Take a rain check
- Throw caution to the wind

Chapter 2 Mission 16

Your fellow operative's surname is 'Blake'. NATO phonetic alphabet code words have been included within the message, which spell out the name of the operative. One letter has been concealed in each line of the message. In order, they are:

- Bravo – B
- Lima – L
- Alpha – A
- Kilo – K
- Echo – E

The country you will be flying over is NORWAY, which has had its letters concealed both in a similar way and also across multiple words:

- November – N
- Oscar – O: 'phot<u>os. Carr</u>y'
- Romeo – R: 'mast<u>ro (me) o</u>r'
- Whiskey – W: '<u>w; his key</u>'
- Alpha – A: 'fin<u>al pha</u>se'
- Yankee – Y

Chapter 2 Mission 17

All the solutions are parts which can be found on a helicopter:

- Blade
- Skids
- Bear paw
- Float
- Pontoon
- Rotor (sounds like 'rota')

Chapter 2 Mission 18

- Air
- Avian
- Tango
- Via
- Aviator
- Navigator

Chapter 2 Mission 19

- Ace
- Abort
- Brace
- Cairo
- Cobra
- Aerobatic

Chapter 2 Mission 20

- Alto
- Tail
- Solar
- Mistral
- Urals
- Simulator

Chapter 2 Mission 21

1. c – at an average speed of 30 kn
2. a. 200 kn
   b. 333 kn
   c. 267 kn
   d. 400 kn
3. The flight would take 7 hours,

meaning the plane would land at 4pm GMT, which is midnight in Shanghai.

Chapter 2 Mission 22

1. The Mumbai flight will arrive first, with a flight time of 6 hours and 30 minutes. The Boston flight will arrive 6 minutes later, with a flight time of 6 hours and 36 minutes.
2. 4 hours – Toronto is four hours behind GMT. The flight would have a duration of 7 hours, landing at 5pm GMT and 1pm local time in Toronto.
3. The Minsk flight will land at 4:40pm local time, and the Moscow flight will land at 6:15pm local time.

Chapter 2 Mission 23

Chapter 2 Mission 24

Chapter 2 Mission 25

Chapter 2 Mission 26

Chapter 2 Mission 27

7	8	4
6	2	5
3	1	9

Chapter 2 Mission 28

5	4	9
2	8	7
1	3	6

Chapter 2 Mission 29

8	7	6
1	2	3
9	5	4

Chapter 2 Mission 30

8	7	3
4	2	6
5	1	9

Chapter 2 Mission 31

		X	O	O	O		
	X	X	X	O	O	O	
O	O	O	X	O	X	X	X
X	X	O	X	X	X	O	X
O	O	X	O	X	O	X	O
X	X	X	O	X	X	O	X
	O	O	X	O	X	O	
		O	O	O	X		

Chapter 2 Mission 32

		X	O	O	X		
	O	X	O	O	X	X	
X	O	X	O	O	X	O	X
O	X	O	X	X	O	O	O
X	X	X	O	X	O	X	O
O	X	O	O	X	O	O	O
	O	O	X	O	X	X	
		X	X	X	O		

Chapter 2 Mission 33

			O	O	X	O			
		X	X	X	O	O	O		
	X	O	O	X	X	X	O	O	
O	X	O	X	X	O	O	X	X	X
X	O	X	O	O	X	X	O	X	X
X	O	X	O	O	X	O	X	O	O
X	X	X	O	O	X	O	X	O	X
	O	O	X	X	O	O	O	X	
		O	X	X	O	X	X		
			O	X	O	O			

Chapter 2 Mission 34

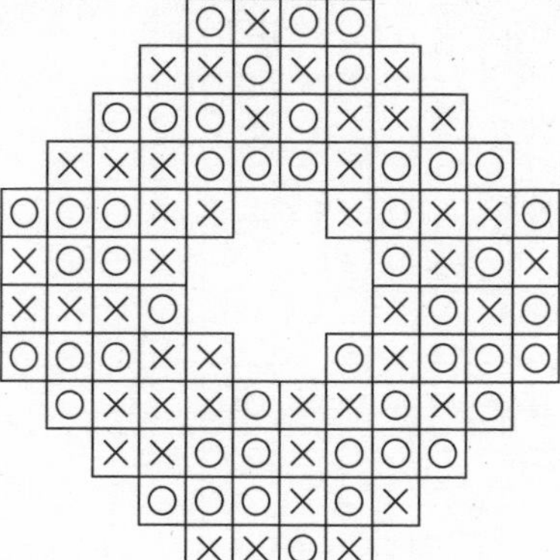

Chapter 2 Mission 37

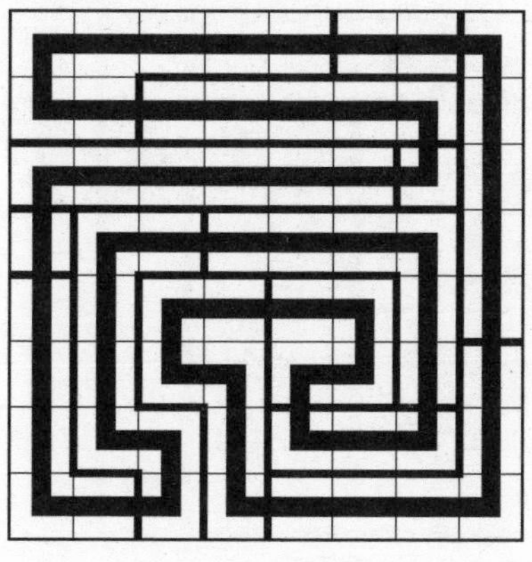

Chapter 2 Mission 35

Chapter 2 Mission 38

Chapter 2 Mission 36

Chapter 2 Mission 39

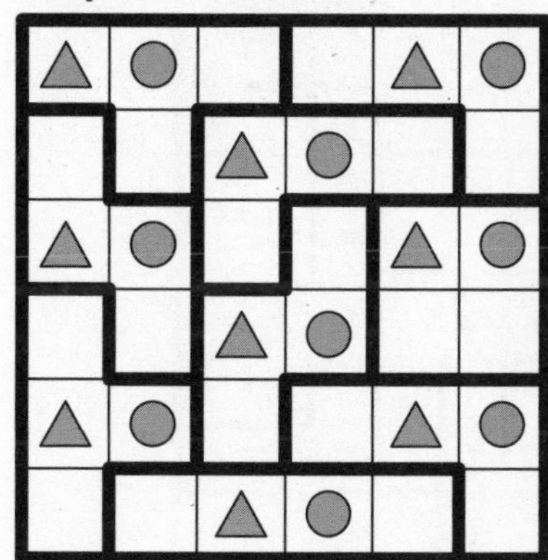

Chapter 2 Mission 40

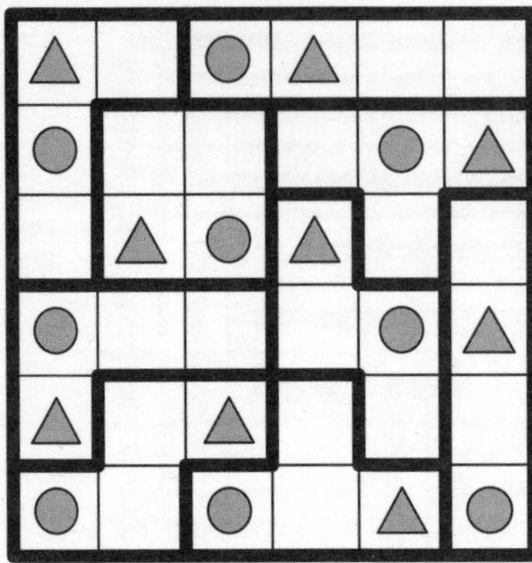

Chapter 2 Mission 41

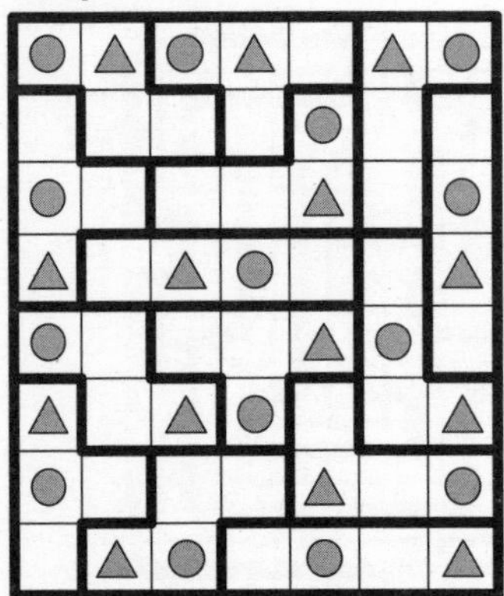

Chapter 2 Mission 42

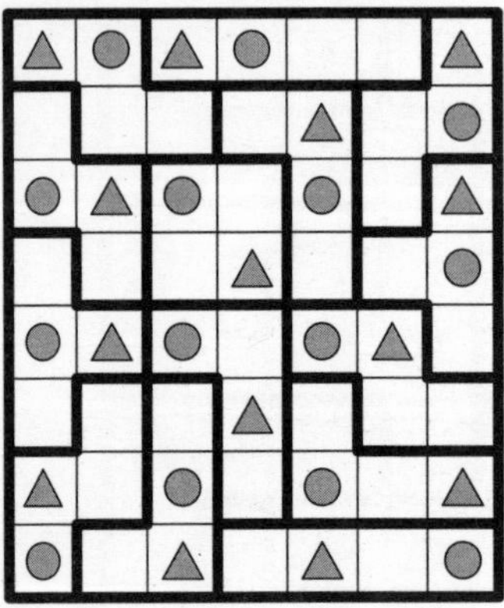

Chapter 2 Mission 43

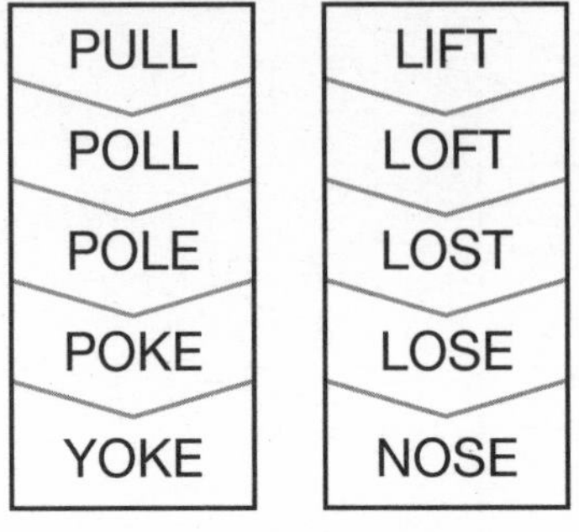

Chapter 2 Mission 44

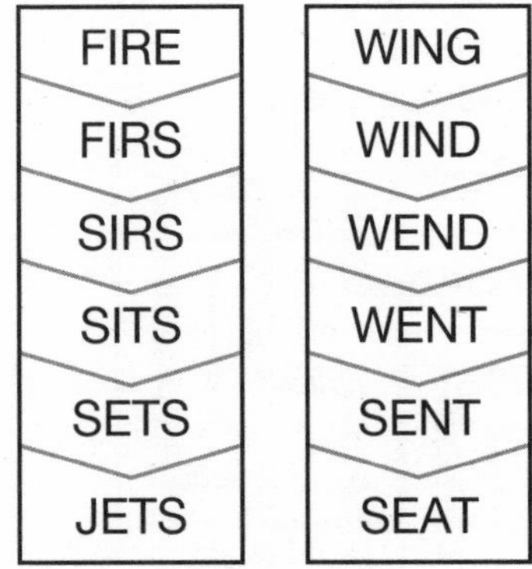

Chapter 3 Mission 1

There are 23 left turns.

Chapter 3 Mission 2

There are 29 right turns.

Chapter 3 Mission 3

There are 46 turns in total.

Chapter 3 Mission 4

5 bridges are passed under.

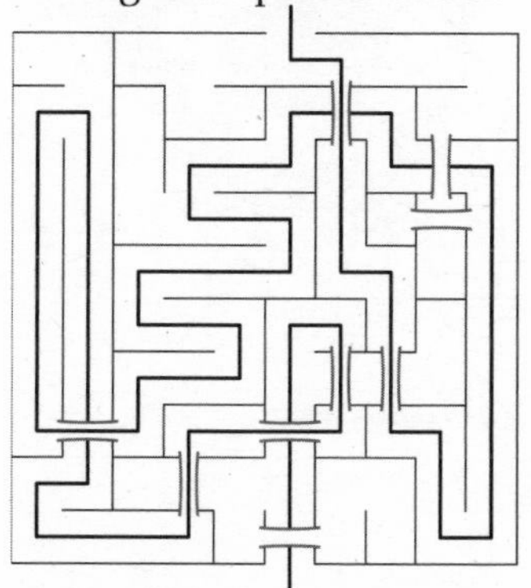

Chapter 3 Mission 5

4 bridges are passed over.

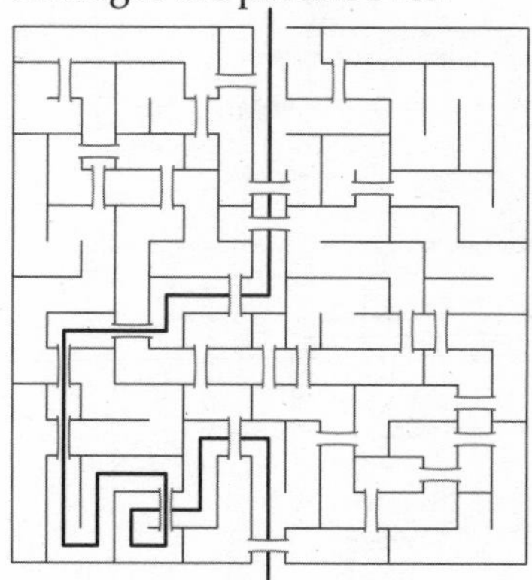

Chapter 3 Mission 6

4 bridges are crossed both over and under.

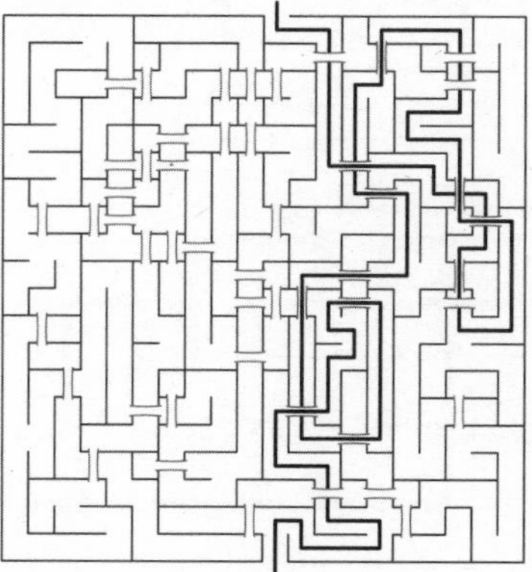

Chapter 3 Mission 7

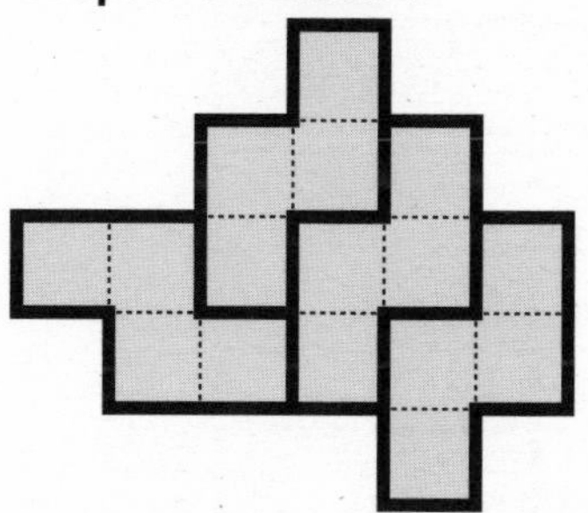

Chapter 3 Mission 8

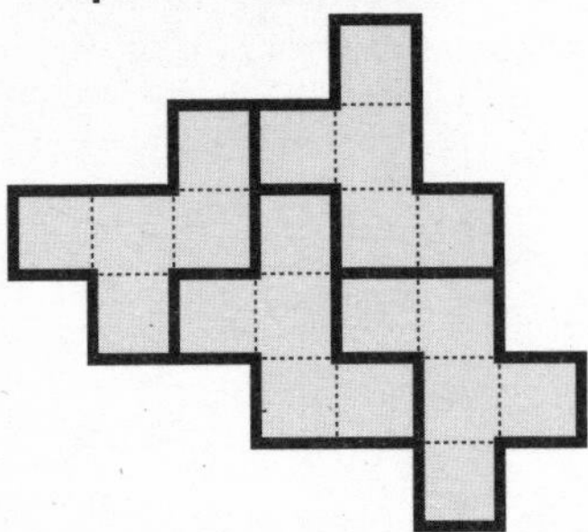

Chapter 3 Mission 9

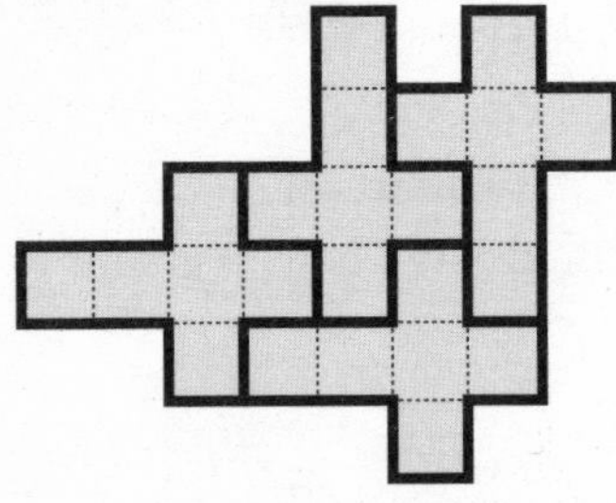

Chapter 3 Mission 10

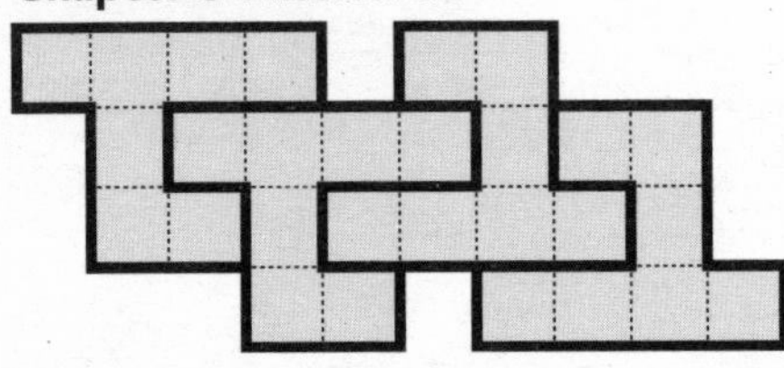

Chapter 3 Mission 11

The coded coordinates, in alphabetical order, are:
B2 B6 C3 C4 C5 D3 D5 E3 E4 E5 F2 F6
The resulting image shows a drone:

Chapter 3 Mission 12

The coordinates, in numerical order, are as follows:
2D, 2E, 2F, 2G
3C, 3G
4B, 4D, 4E, 4G
5A, 5C, 5D, 5E, 5G
6A, 6C, 6D, 6F
7A, 7E
8A, 8B, 8C, 8D

The resulting image is a roundel:

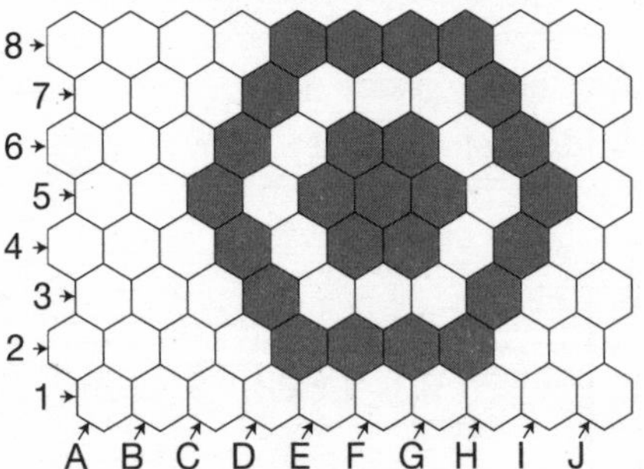

Chapter 3 Mission 13

C:

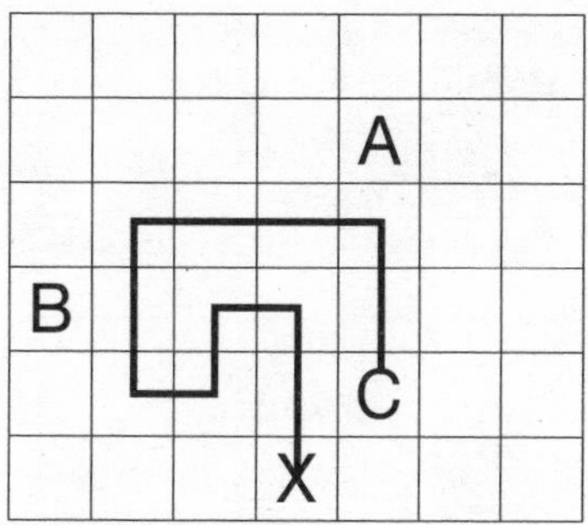

Chapter 3 Mission 14

C:

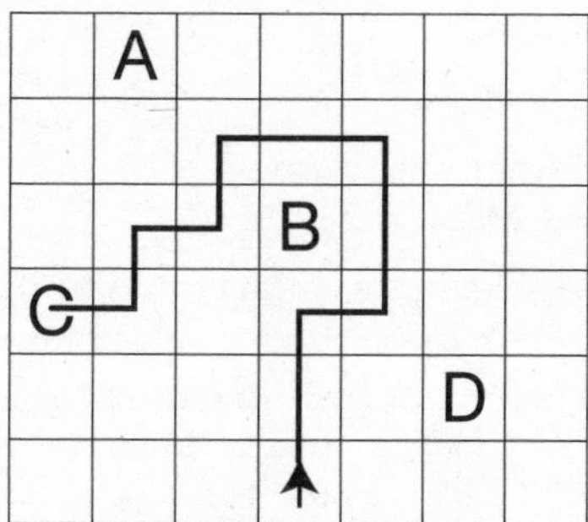

Chapter 3 Mission 15

Flight path B:

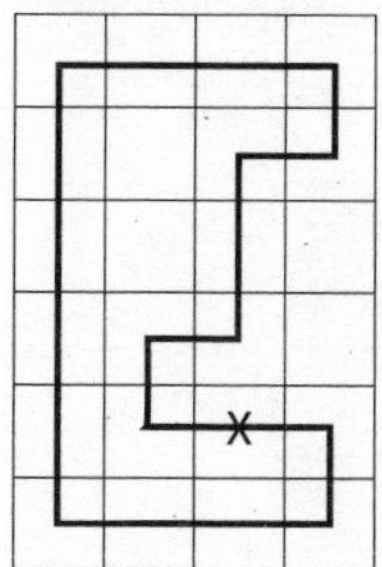

Chapter 3 Mission 16

Flight Path C is the only one which does not fly through a blocked square:

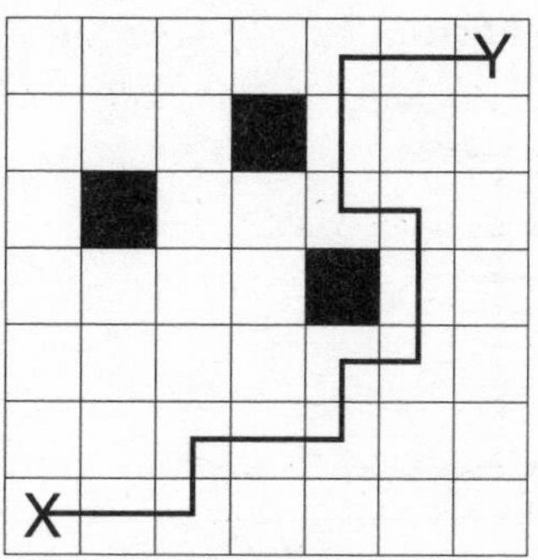

Chapter 3 Mission 17

In the instructions, 'THRUST' means move forward, 'FALL' means move downward, and 'LIFT' means move upward. The aircraft will therefore end up at point C:

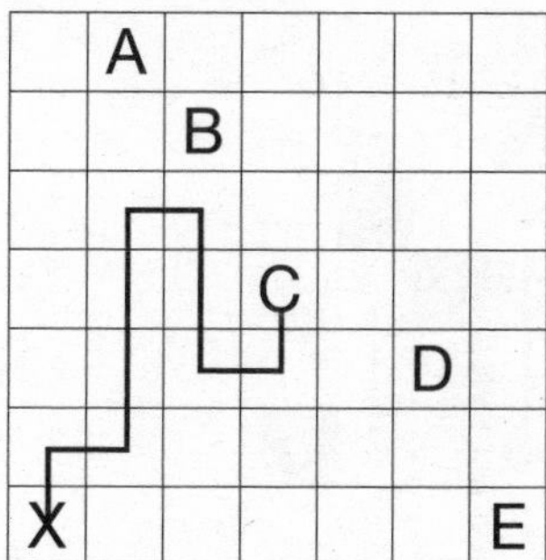

Chapter 3 Mission 18

The shape is an arrow:

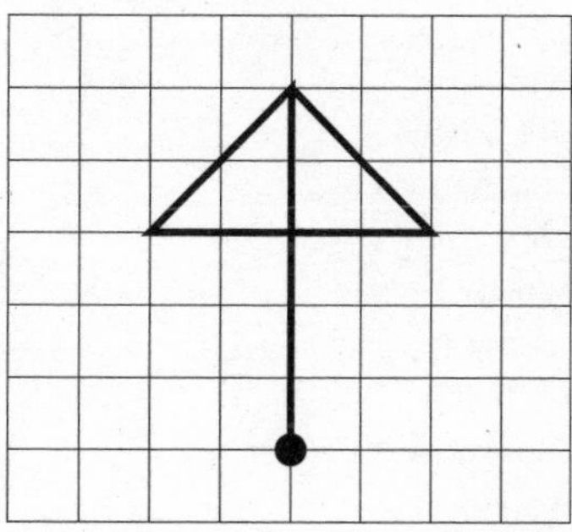

Chapter 3 Mission 19

The shape is a jewel:

Chapter 3 Mission 20

Flight Path B is the only one which does not fly through a blocked square:

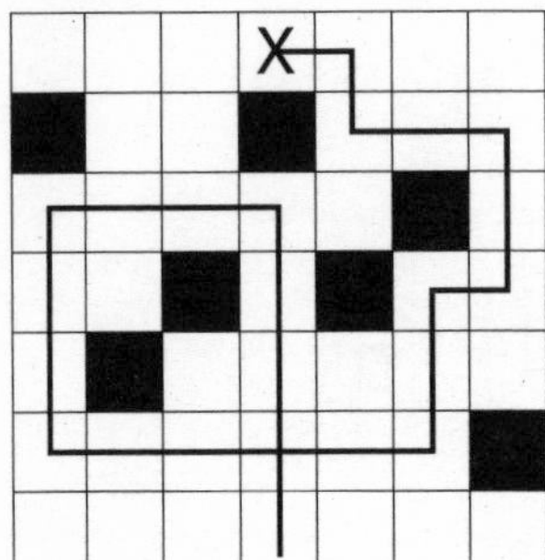

Chapter 3 Mission 21

The airport codes correspond to the following cities:

- SEA Seattle
- LAS Las Vegas
- LAX Los Angeles
- DEN Denver
- MSP Minneapolis
- DTW Detroit
- BOS Boston
- BNA Nashville
- IAH Houston
- MSY New Orleans
- MIA Miami
- ORD Chicago

So the answers to the questions are:

1. a. Houston to Los Angeles
2. a. Detroit to Seattle
3. b. Chicago to Miami
4. Mike – the letter spelled out is 'M':

Chapter 3 Mission 22

There are 35 cubes in total (4 on the top level, 5 on the second level, 12 on the third level and 14 on the bottom level).

Chapter 3 Mission 23

There are 26 cubes in total (2 on the top level, 5 on the second level, 7 on the third level and 12 on the bottom level).

Chapter 3 Mission 24

There are 53 cubes in total (5 on the top level, 13 on the second level, 14 on the third level and 21 on the bottom level).

Chapter 3 Mission 25

There are 58 cubes in total (2 on the top level, 7 on the second level, 11 on the third level, 16 on the fourth level and 22 on the bottom level).

Chapter 3 Mission 26

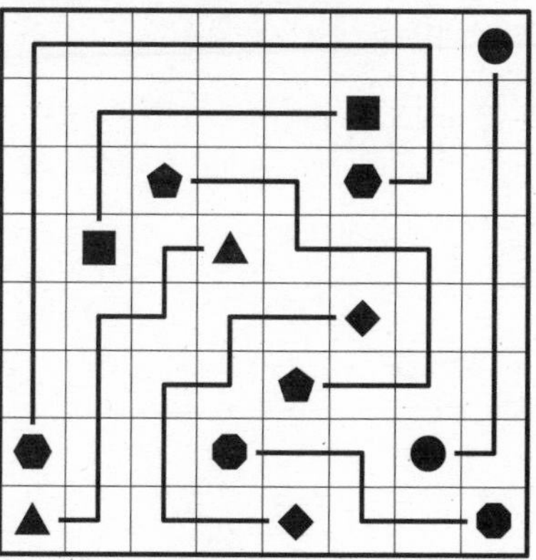

Chapter 3 Mission 29

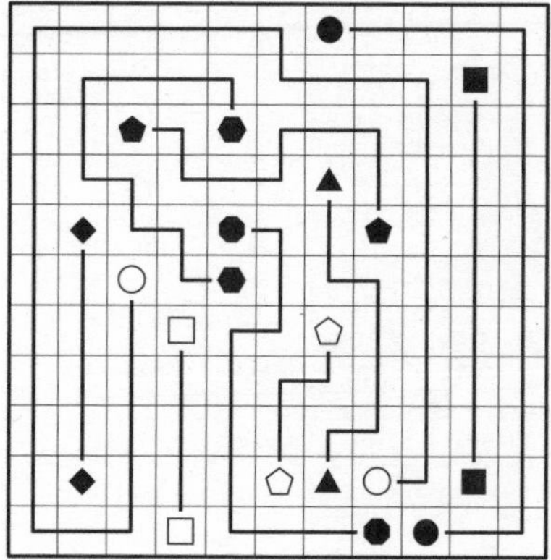

Chapter 3 Mission 27

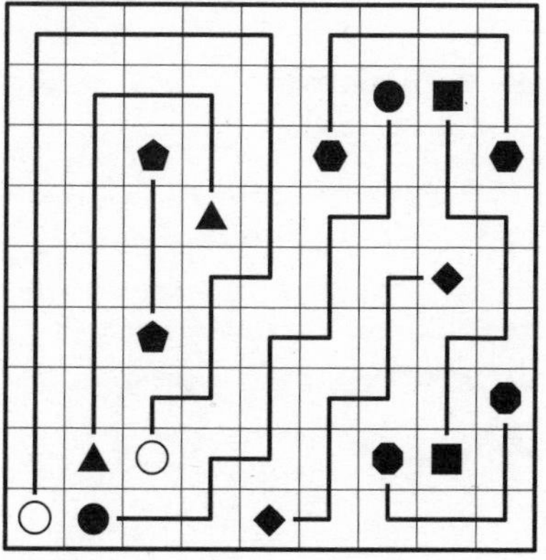

Chapter 3 Mission 28

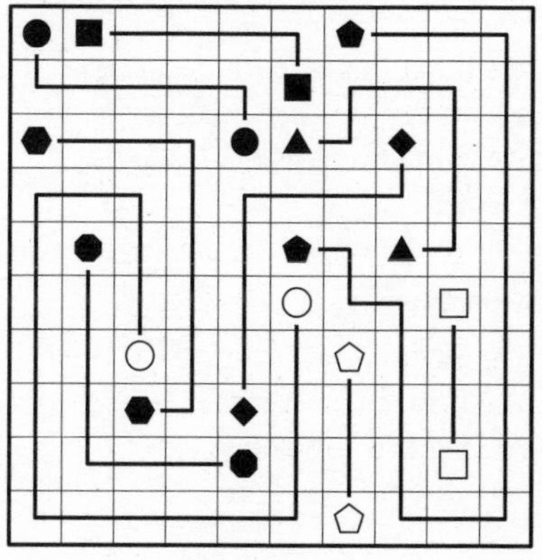

Chapter 3 Mission 30

The cities named on the note correspond to the following airport codes from the grid:

- Bergen: BGO
- Copenhagen: CPH
- Geneva: GVA
- Malaga: AGP
- Manchester: MAN
- Riga: RIX
- Warsaw: WAW
- Zurich: ZRH

When shaded in, the solution spells out the letter 'S', indicating that the pilot will be flying with the 'Sierra' group, since sierra is the NATO codeword for 'S':

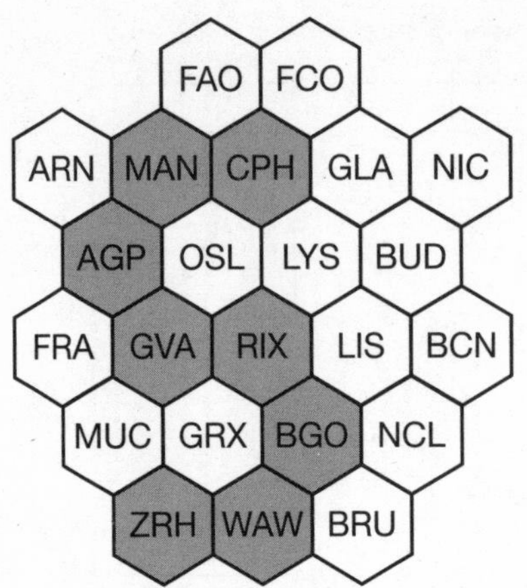

Chapter 3 Mission 31

Helicopter D:

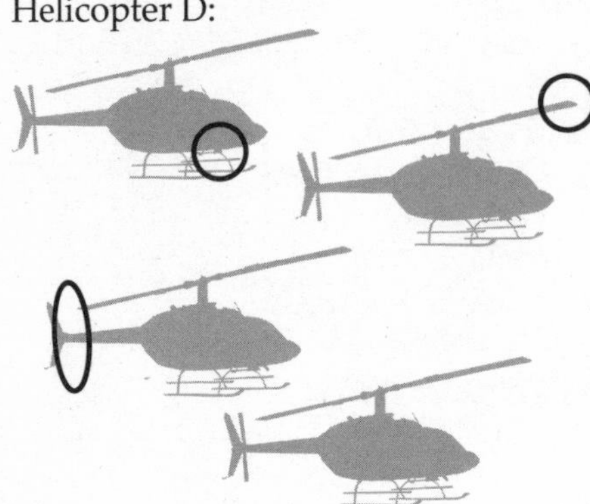

Chapter 3 Mission 32

A: Cyprus
B: Republic of Ireland
C: Germany
D: Austria
E: Portugal
F: France

Chapter 3 Mission 33

Propellers B and C:

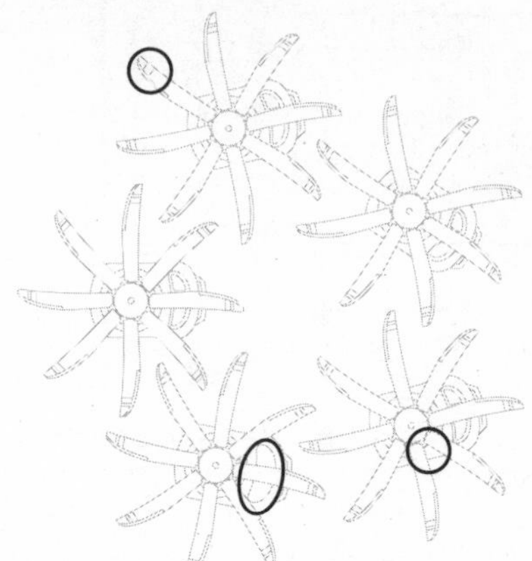

Chapter 3 Mission 34

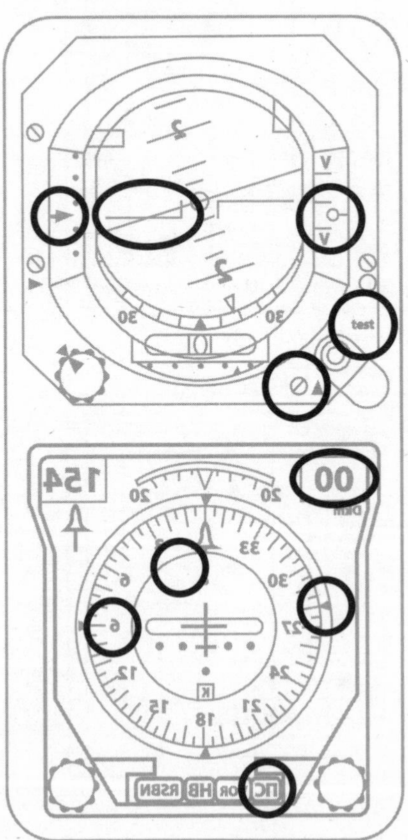

Chapter 3 Mission 35

E: A has a face that does not appear on the cube net; B has an incorrect righthand face; C has an incorrect front face; D has its front and side faces swapped

Chapter 3 Mission 36

A: B has a face that does not appear on the cube net; C has its front and side faces swapped; D has an incorrect top face; E has its front and top faces swapped

Chapter 3 Mission 37

A: B has its front and side faces swapped; C has an incorrect front face; D has its top face rotated incorrectly; E has its top and side faces swapped

Chapter 3 Mission 38

D: A has its front and top faces swapped; B has its top face rotated incorrectly; C has an incorrect side face; E has its front and top faces swapped

Chapter 3 Mission 39

A

Chapter 3 Mission 40

B

Chapter 3 Mission 41

D

Chapter 3 Mission 42

D

Chapter 4 Missions 1 + 2

The changed images are:

Chapter 4 Missions 3 + 4

The missing images are:

- The aeroplane taking off over an item of luggage
- The plane taking off over a runway
- The GATE sign
- The arrow pointing through an airport scanner
- The clock hanging from a bar

Chapter 4 Missions 5 + 6

The swapped images are:

Chapter 4 Missions 7 + 8

The differences are:

Good morning, ladies and gentlemen. This is your pilot speaking.

We would like to welcome you on board this Boeing 757 flight to Barcelona. We are expecting a flight time of around two hours and ten minutes this morning, touching down at around 11pm local time.

Weather conditions are looking great. We have a slight breeze coming from the west but are expecting a calm flight today.

[The cabin crew will be performing their final safety checks in a moment, so I'll leave them to it but] I'll be in touch a little later with some updates during the flight.

In the meantime, please sit back, relax, and enjoy your journey.

Chapter 4 Missions 9 + 10

1. Nine
2. Merseyside
3. Lincolnshire
4. Cambridgeshire
5. Six
6. North to south

Chapter 4 Missions 11 + 12

1. Five (the first five listed: camel, sea otter, puma, tiger moth and squirrel)
2. Supermarine Sea Otter and Avro York
3. Bristol and York
4. Sopwith Camel, in 1918
5. Westland Puma
6. Eurocopter Squirrel
7. Avro York

Chapter 4 Missions 13 + 14

1. Four: Halifax, Washington, Lincoln and Manchester
2. Eight: four people was given as 'half' of Group B
3. Washington
4. From Manchester to Washington
5. Eleven: fifteen people were dropped off in Washington, which included half of Group B (four people)
6. Washington: Lincoln had eleven, and Washington had twenty-one
7. Thirty-two

Chapter 4 Missions 15 + 16

1. 649865
2. Your Security Key
3. Eleven (six letters and five digits)
4. 33
5. Your Security Key: gyro-heli-aero
6. Hurricane – the letters 'i', 'a' and 'e' were replaced with 1, 4, and 3, respectively
7. Emergency Callout: M8A9Y8D9A8Y
8. Your Password: the year was 1918

Chapter 4 Missions 17 + 18

The occupations are as listed in mission 17.

Chapter 4 Missions 19 + 20

The replacement ranks are:

- Air Chief Marshal
- Air Vice Marshal
- Marshal of the Royal Air Force
- Senior Aircraftman
- RAF Master Aircrew
- Chief Technician

Chapter 4 Missions 21 + 22

The missing words, from top to bottom are:

- Gust
- Anticyclone
- Monsoon
- Atmosphere
- Pressure

Chapter 5 Mission 1

- 1903: First sustained powered flight
- 1914: First scheduled passenger flight
- 1924: First aerial circumnavigation of the world
- 1931: First non-stop trans-Pacific flight
- 1932: First transatlantic flight piloted by a woman
- 1947: First supersonic flight
- 1965: First pole-to-pole circumnavigation of the world
- 1969: First Concorde flight

Chapter 5 Mission 2

In chronological order of their achievement, the pilots are:

- The Wright Brothers (First sustained powered flight)
- Tony Jannus (First scheduled passenger flight)
- Lowell Smith, Erik Nelson, Leslie Arnold and John Harding Jr (First aerial circumnavigation of the world)
- Clyde Pangborn, Hugh Herndon (First non-stop trans-Pacific flight)
- Amelia Earhart (First transatlantic flight piloted by a woman)
- Chuck Yeager (First supersonic flight)
- Fred Austin, Harrison Finch (First pole-to-pole circumnavigation)
- André Turcat (First Concorde flight)

Chapter 5 Mission 3

1. 1918 (9811)
2. 1936 (9316)
3. Spitfire (FSTPIREI)
4. Hillingdon (IHDIOLLGNN)
5. Balloon (LALBONO)
6. Jean Lennox Bird (AJNE NOEXNL IDRB)

Chapter 5 Mission 4

1. Dambusters (AMDSSTEBRU)
2. Red Arrows (DRE RARSWO)
3. Hendon Aerodrome (DHNNOE EAMRORDEO)
4. Operation Bushel (EOOTNRIPA ULBHSE)
5. Swept Wings (TWPSE ISNWG)
6. Sir Hugh Trenchard (IRS GHHU RTERAHNDC)

Chapter 5 Mission 5

A. LAX – Los Angeles
B. ORD – Chicago
C. ATL – Atlanta
D. JFK – New York City
E. LHR – London
F. CDG – Paris
G. JNB – Johannesburg
H. DXB – Dubai
I. HKG – Hong Kong
J. SYD – Sydney

Chapter 5 Mission 6

The pairs, in order of the labelled flight paths, are:

A. LGW and LIS (London and Lisbon)
B. DUB and OSL (Dublin and Oslo)
C. ATH and MAD (Athens and Madrid)
D. AMS and BUD (Amsterdam and Budapest)
E. FRA and HEL (Frankfurt and Helsinki)
F. NIC and WAW (Nicosia and Warsaw)

Chapter 5 Mission 7

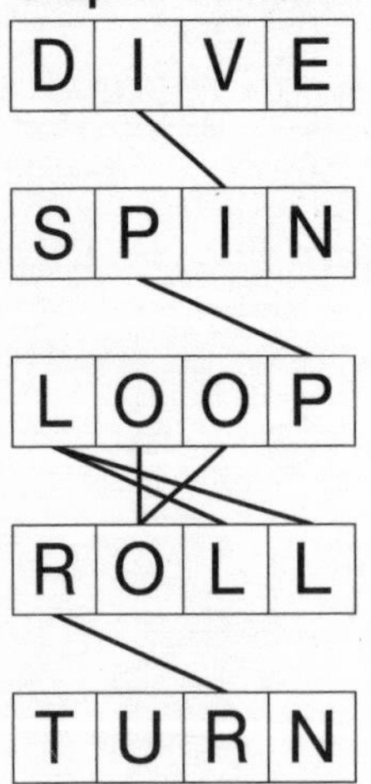

Chapter 5 Mission 8

The manoeuvres, in alphabetical order, are:

- Avalanche
- Cuban eight
- Falling leaf
- Hammerhead
- Wingover

Chapter 5 Mission 9

- Chandelle
- English bunt
- Lazy eight
- Tailslide
- Zoom climb
- Humpty bump

Chapter 5 Mission 10

- Brazil: 'Wings that protect the country'
- Czech Republic: 'The air is our sea'
- Finland: 'Quality is our power'
- Greece: 'Always dominate the heights'
- Netherlands: 'Small in numbers, great in deeds'
- Portugal: 'Of his own free will'
- United Kingdom: 'Through adversity to the stars'

Chapter 5 Mission 11

A. France
B. Belgium
C. Greece
D. United Kingdom
E. Spain
F. Finland

Chapter 5 Mission 12

- Airbus
- Beechcraft

- Fairchild
- Goodyear
- Gulfstream
- Supermarine

Chapter 5 Mission 13

In alphabetical order of manufacturer, the models are:

- Avro Andover (British town, site of Army Headquarters)
- Blackburn Beverley (Woman's name; Yorkshire town)
- Fairey Fawn (Young deer; light brown)
- Gloster Gauntlet (Long armoured glove thrown to issue a challenge)
- Handley Page Halifax (Capital of Nova Scotia; Yorkshire town)
- Lockheed Lightning (It's often accompanied by thunder)
- Miles Mentor (An experienced advisor and guide)
- Percival Provost (A head of some universities and religious groups)
- Sopwith Salamander (Amphibian once thought to have resistance to fire)
- Westland Wapiti (Alternative name for a large American deer)

Chapter 5 Mission 14

- MON + ACO = Monaco
- BOS + NIA = Bosnia
- NIC + ARA + GUA = Nicaragua
- MAC + EDO + NIA = Macedonia

Chapter 5 Mission 15

1. b: 1940
2. a: Three and a half months
3. b: Winston Churchill
4. a: Operation Sea Lion

Chapter 5 Mission 16

1. c: Panavia ('Tonka') Tornado
2. c: Radar
3. b: Never in the field of human conflict was so much owed by so many to so few
4. b: 3,000

Chapter 5 Mission 17

- London
- New York City
- Melbourne
- Paris

Chapter 5 Mission 18

- Los Angeles
- Seattle
- Stockholm
- São Paulo

Chapter 5 Mission 19

All of the solutions contain one set of double letters:

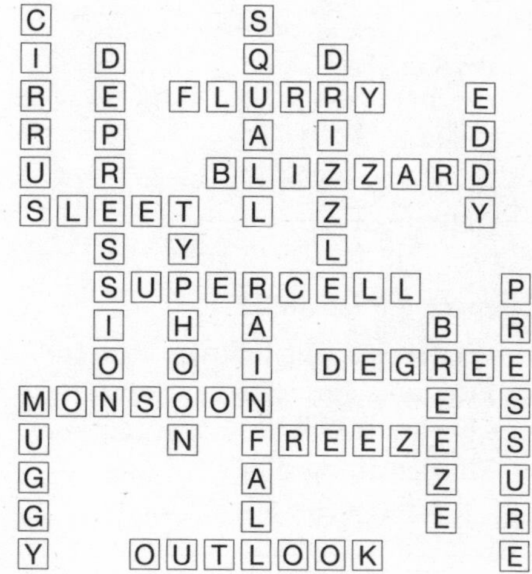

Chapter 5 Mission 20

The named winds are, in order:

- Mistral
- Brickfielder
- Santa Ana
- Harmattan
- Pampero

The areas they can be found are as follows:

- Argentina and Uruguay: Pampero
- France and the Mediterranean: Mistral
- North-western Africa: Harmattan
- Southern Australia: Brickfielder
- Southern California: Santa Ana

Chapter 5 Mission 21

- A: BCN is the airport code for Barcelona, Spain
- B: NCL is the airport code for Newcastle, UK

Chapter 5 Mission 22

- B: VRN is the airport code for Verona, Italy
- A: CPH is the airport code for Copenhagen, Denmark
- A: GOT is the airport code for Gothenburg, Sweden

Chapter 5 Mission 23

The matches are as follows, with full airport names given in brackets:

- Charles de Gaulle – Paris (Paris Charles de Gaulle)
- Cristiano Ronaldo – Madeira (Cristiano Ronaldo Madeira International Airport)
- Edward Logan – Boston (Logan International Airport)
- Frédéric Chopin – Warsaw (Warsaw Chopin Airport)
- John F. Kennedy – New York (John F. Kennedy International Airport)
- John Lennon – Liverpool (Liverpool John Lennon Airport)
- Louis Armstrong – New Orleans (Louis Armstrong New Orleans International Airport)
- Nikola Tesla – Belgrade (Belgrade Nikola Tesla Airport)
- W. A. Mozart – Salzburg (Salzburg Airport W. A. Mozart)

Chapter 5 Mission 24

- Edinburgh
- Bern
- Bratislava
- Vienna
- Prague
- Oslo
- Athens
- Nicosia

Bonus question: Prague (PRG) and Bern (BRN)

Chapter 5 Mission 25

In alphabetical order, the full city names are:

- Budapest
- Copenhagen
- Helsinki
- Madrid
- Minsk
- Rome

Chapter 5 Mission 26

- Berlin
- Bucharest
- Lisbon
- London
- Reykjavik
- Warsaw

Chapter 5 Mission 27

- Riga
- Paris
- Brussels
- Dublin
- Ljubljana

Chapter 5 Mission 28

In alphabetical order of first name, the full names are:

- Amelia Earhart
- Amy Johnson
- Antoine de Saint-Exupéry
- Buzz Aldrin
- Chuck Yeager
- Douglas Bader
- Geoffrey de Havilland
- Louis Blériot
- Neil Armstrong
- Roland Garros
- William Boeing

Chapter 5 Mission 29

- Air Force One: The name for any US Air Force aeroplane carrying a US president
- Blériot XI: First aeroplane flight across the English Channel
- Concorde: One of only two commercial supersonic airliners
- F-117 Nighthawk: First aircraft built around stealth technology
- Solar Impulse 2: First solar-powered circumnavigation of the earth
- Spirit of St Louis: First solo non-stop transatlantic flight
- Supermarine Spitfire: The only UK plane in continuous production throughout World War II
- Wright Flyer: First successful heaver-than-air aircraft capable of sustained, powered flight

Chapter 5 Mission 30

A. Luxembourg: Luxair
B. Australia: Qantas
C. Colombia: Avianca
D. Republic of Ireland: Aer Lingus
E. Latvia: Air Baltic
F. Faroe Islands: Atlantic Airways
G. Spain: Iberia
H. Portugal: TAP

Chapter 5 Mission 31

A. Amphibious
B. Bessie Coleman
C. Comet
D. da Vinci
E. Empennage
F. Fin flashes

Chapter 5 Mission 32

G. Greasy side
H. Headwind
I. Immelmann
J. Joystick
K. Knot
L. Lighter-than-air (or LTA)

Chapter 5 Mission 33

M. Mach (number)
N. Nosedive
O. Overshot
P. Pancake (as in 'pancake landing')
Q. Queensland
R. Red-eye
S. Sonic boom

Chapter 5 Mission 34

T. Thrust
U. Upwind leg
V. Vapour trails
W. Windsock
X. X-ray
Y. Yaw
Z. Zeppelin

Chapter 5 Mission 35

The country spelled out is CANADA, whose national flag features a maple leaf:

1. Cathay Pacific
2. Atlanta
3. North Sea
4. Alert
5. Dead Sea
6. Argentina (the airport is Ushuaia, in Tierra del Fuego)

Chapter 5 Mission 36

In the order they appear, the names are:

- Amerigo Vespucci
- Guglielmo Marconi
- Christopher Columbus
- Leonardo Da Vinci
- Marco Polo
- Galileo Galilei

All of the men have an Italian airport named after them:

- Amerigo Vespucci Airport, Florence
- Bologna Guglielmo Marconi Airport, Bologna
- Genoa Cristoforo Colombo Airport, Genoa (named after Christopher Columbus)
- Leonardo da Vinci–Fiumicino Airport, Rome
- Venice Marco Polo Airport, Venice
- Galileo Galilei Airport, Pisa

Chapter 5 Mission 37

- Chinook
- Puma
- Griffin
- Juno
- Jupiter

Chapter 5 Mission 38

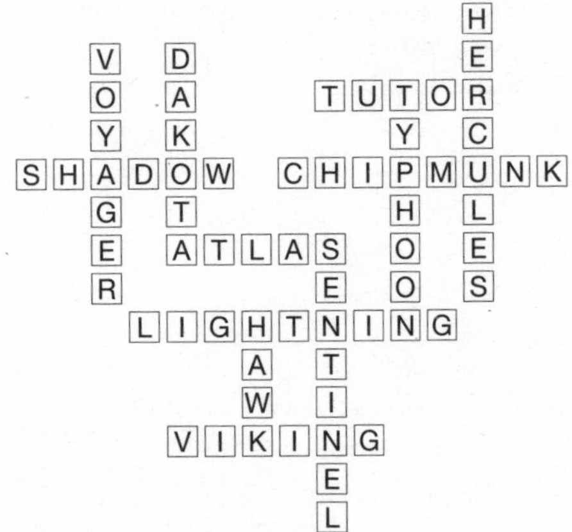

Chapter 5 Mission 39

A. Stealth (THE LAST)
B. Glider (GIRDLE)
C. Commercial Jet (JAM COMET RELIC)
D. Drone (RED ON)
E. Helicopter (PILOT CHEER)
F. Hang-glider (GIG HANDLER)

Chapter 5 Mission 40

The airlines, in the order they appear in the list, are:

- Alaska (US state)
- American (A nationality)
- Delta (Greek alphabet letter)
- Frontier (Border; it may be final?)
- Hawaiian (Native to the most recent state)
- Spirit (Ghost; distilled drink)
- United (Joined together)

Chapter 5 Mission 41

In the order they appear, the restored ranks are below. Numbers in brackets indicate the level of rank, with 1 being the least senior and 10 being the most senior.

- Air Chief Marshal (10)
- Air Commodore (7)
- Air Marshal (9)
- Air Vice Marshal (8)
- Flight Lieutenant (3)
- Flying Officer (2)
- Group Captain (6)
- Pilot Officer (1)
- Squadron Leader (4)
- Wing Commander (5)

Chapter 5 Mission 42

Solutions created by combining words are as follows:

Across

1. SPADE + ADAM
7. BEN + SON
11. LEE + MING
13. WADDING + TON

Down

2. DIG + BY
3. MOUNT + PLEASANT
4. WOOD + VALE
8. SHAW + BURY
9. SCAMP + TON

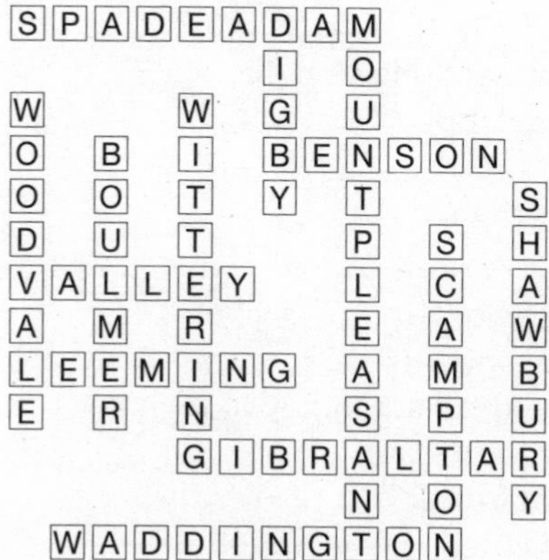

Chapter 5 Mission 43

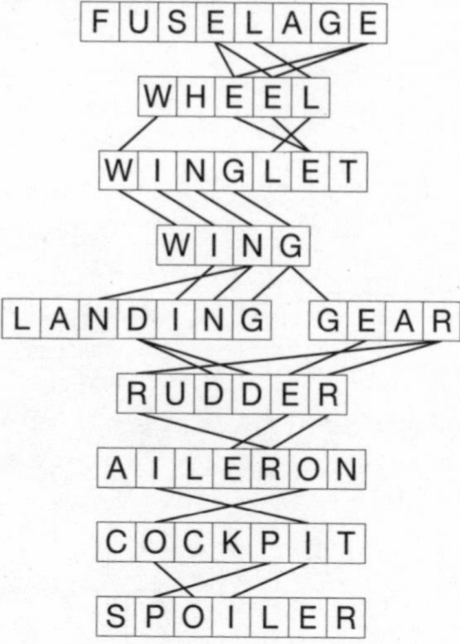

Chapter 5 Mission 44

A. Winglet
B. Wing
C. Spoiler
D. Fuselage
E. Cockpit
F. Wheel
G. Aileron
H. Landing Gear
I. Rudder

Image Credits

10-223 (propeller image), 141, 244 shaineast/Shutterstock.com; 129, 242 (top-right) moonday studio/Shutterstock.com; 139, 244 (left) khoroshailo dmitrii/Shutterstock.com; 140, 198-199 martin951/Shutterstock.com; 142-143, 244 (bottom-right) NikKulch/Shutterstock.com; 154-155, 245 (top-right) Aha-Soft/Shutterstock.com; 156-157 phipatbig/Shutterstock.com; 158-159, 245 (bottom-right) mayrum/Shutterstock.com; 182-183 Pyty/Shutterstock.com; 207 Puwadol Jaturawutthichai/Shutterstock.com; 216 CharacterFamily/Shutterstock.com; 221 Holy Polygon/Shutterstock.com

The Mammoth Book of New Sudoku

From the same author,
Dr Gareth Moore

An Encylopedia of Sudoku

A comprehensive collection featuring every significant variant ever created

Over **25** major Sudoku types

Nearly **150** different variants

Almost **500** puzzles, all created especially for this book, including Jigsaw Sudoku, Killer Sudoku and multi-grid Samurai Sudoku

No other collection of Sudoku comes close – this is without doubt the most definitive volume of Sudoku variants ever compiled, with full instructions and solutions included throughout.

Visit www.littlebrown.co.uk for more information